TRANSDISCIPLINARY RESEARCH, SUSTAINABILITY, AND SOCIAL TRANSFORMATION

This book addresses the gap in the existing literature on the governance of transdisciplinary research partnerships in transformational sustainability research by exploring the governance of knowledge co-production in coupled socio-ecological system dynamics.

Multiple social and ecological crises raise new cross-sectoral research questions that call for an evolution in contemporary science in the direction of society-wide knowledge co-production on sustainability transformations of interdependent social and ecological systems. This book proposes a new approach to this based on enabling capacities for collaboration among scientific researchers and societal actors with diverse values, perspectives, and research interests. By drawing upon the thriving literature on the conditions for community and multistakeholder-driven collective action, the analysis sheds new light on the governance arrangements for organizing so-called transdisciplinary research partnerships for sustainability. This book identifies robust conditions that lead to effective collaborative research with societal actors and digs deeper into capacity building for partnership research through fostering social learning on sustainability values among research partners and organizing training and knowledge exchange at institutions of higher education.

The book proposes solutions for addressing collective action challenges in transdisciplinary partnerships in an accessible and broadly interdisciplinary manner to a large audience of sustainability scholars and practitioners. It will be of interest to students and researchers in the fields of sustainable development, social ecological transitions, and science policy, while also being a useful resource for engineers, QSE managers, and policymakers.

Tom Dedeurwaerdere is Professor of the Theory of Governance and Philosophy of Science at the Université catholique de Louvain (UCLouvain), Louvain-la-Neuve, Belgium. He has extensively published in scholarly journals on the organization of scientific research commons and collective action for sustainability transformations. His previous books include *Social Innovation in the Service of Social and Ecological Transformation: The Rise of the Enabling State* (with Olivier de Schutter, 2022), *Governing Digitally Integrated Genetic Resources, Data, and Literature: Global Intellectual Property Strategies for a Redesigned Microbial Research Commons* (with Jerome H. Reichman and Paul F. Uhlir, 2016) and *Sustainability Science for Strong Sustainability* (2014).

Routledge Studies in Sustainability

For more information on this series, please visit: www.routledge.com/Routledge-Studies-in-Sustainability/book-series/RSSTY

TRANSDISCIPLINARY RESEARCH, SUSTAINABILITY, AND SOCIAL TRANSFORMATION

Governance and Knowledge Co-Production

Tom Dedeurwaerdere

Designed cover image: © Getty Images

First published 2024
by Routledge
4 Park Square, Milton Park, Abingdon, Oxon OX14 4RN

and by Routledge
605 Third Avenue, New York, NY 10158

Routledge is an imprint of the Taylor & Francis Group, an informa business

© 2024 Tom Dedeurwaerdere

British Library Cataloguing-in-Publication Data
A catalogue record for this book is available from the British Library

Library of Congress Cataloging-in-Publication Data
Names: Dedeurwaerdere, Tom, author.
Title: Transdisciplinary research, sustainability, and social transformation : governance and knowledge co-production / Tom Dedeurwaerdere.
Description: Abingdon, Oxon ; New York, NY : Routledge, 2024. | Includes bibliographical references and index.
Identifiers: LCCN 2023036189 (print) | LCCN 2023036190 (ebook) | ISBN 9781032624273 (hardback) | ISBN 9781032624242 (paperback) | ISBN 9781032624297 (ebook)
Subjects: LCSH: Social change. | Social action. | Community development. | Political participation.
Classification: LCC HM831 .D43 2023 (print) | LCC HM831 (ebook) | DDC 303.44—dc23/eng/20230901
LC record available at https://lccn.loc.gov/2023036189
LC ebook record available at https://lccn.loc.gov/2023036190

ISBN: 978-1-032-62427-3 (hbk)
ISBN: 978-1-032-62424-2 (pbk)
ISBN: 978-1-032-62429-7 (ebk)

DOI: 10.4324/9781032624297

To Brice, Mathilde and Samuel,
for their love and inspiration,
may they see the timely advance of
pathways to just and sustainable futures

CONTENTS

FIGURES

TABLES

ACKNOWLEDGMENTS

The project for this book began as a side activity of a starting grant of the European Research Council (ERC) in 2013. With a group of research fellows, we started to reflect on the integration of knowledge from academic research with knowledge from societal actors involved in real-world sustainability transformations. The journal publication from this side activity, with Florin Popa and Mathieu Guillermin, sparked the interest of many societal actors and colleagues at the university and led us into a much deeper investigation into the broad field of transdisciplinary sustainability research, which is the topic of this book.

Since then, I have had the pleasure of discussing these issues with the large community of scholars and societal actors who have made seminal contributions over the last three decades in trying to understand the many challenges to overcome in the building of research partnerships for transformational sustainability research.

The debts incurred in writing this book therefore started to accumulate well before the actual writing. A major impetus for the work is the personal experience of facing knowledge co-production challenges in large-scale fundamental research programs based on partnerships between researchers and societal actors. This personal experience—and the possibility for trial and error learning in this relatively young field—would not have been possible without being part of the research environment at the Centre for Philosophy of Law, Université catholique de Louvain. I take this opportunity to thank the co-directors of the Centre, Jacques Lenoble—now emeritus—and Marc Maesschalck, for their confidence and pathbreaking work in understanding the conditions of critical and transformational partnership-based research. Two prominent scholars of the digital knowledge commons, Jerome

Reichman and Paul Uhlir, directly participated in several of these collaborative research projects. Their insights and their important role in connecting high-profile research on global knowledge commons to the international negotiations around the implementation of the Access and Benefit Sharing provisions of the Convention on Biological Diversity was enormously helpful in the present endeavor. I also had the incredible chance to co-direct many of the research projects on social innovation for social and ecological transition with my colleague at the Centre for Philosophy of Law, Olivier De Schutter. I would like to thank him for this long-standing collaboration and the fruitful exchanges that contributed to many of the ideas on knowledge co-production with societal actors developed in this book.

Further, being hosted, in 2018 and 2019, by many colleagues during my "video interviews" trip on transdisciplinary research throughout Europe was a life-changing experience, which provided many of the examples discussed and analyzed in the book (videos available at www.lptransition.be/td). A warm thanks for the many stimulating discussions, during these project visits, on innovative approaches to implementing transdisciplinarity partnership research in practice: Michael Stauffacher and Chistian Pohl at the ETH Zürich, Switzerland; Adrian Ely at the University of Sussex, United Kingdom; Ariane König at the University of Luxembourg, Luxembourg; Derk Loorbach at the University of Rotterdam, the Netherlands; Anna Kramers at the KTH, Sweden; Uwe Schneidewind at the Wuppertal Institute for Climate, Environment and Energy, Germany; Simon De Muynck at the Centre d'écologie urbaine, Belgium; Sandra Lavorel at the University of Grenoble, France; Mathieu Berger at the UCLouvain, Belgium; Pierre Stassart at the Université de Liège, Belgium; Fabienne Barataud at INRAE-Mirecourt, France; and all the other colleagues I met during these research visits.

The various versions of the manuscript benefited greatly from many discussions and comments, which made for an improved manuscript. In particular, I gratefully acknowledge the feedback on earlier drafts and the assistance with cross-checking the case studies on transdisciplinary research described in the book by many fellow researchers: Agathe Osinski, Selim Louafi, Michael Madison, Laurent Hazard, Gill Ainsworth, Brendan Coolsaet, Bianca Vienni Baptista, Stéphane Ginestet, Merritt Polk, Flurina Schneider, Audrey Podann, Suzanne Smit Luyt, and Joseph Maxwell. My gratitude is also due to Caroline Van Schendel for her help with editing the manuscript.

I certainly forgot some of the colleagues and fellow travelers on the journey who contributed to the book; let me thank them here. Finally, many gaps and mistakes might remain, in spite of all this support, and I take full responsibility for these. And, of course, I want to thank my family, Brice, Mathilde, Samuel, and Anne-Sophie, who made it all so much more meaningful and enjoyable.

INTRODUCTION

The current crisis of the resource-intensive development model has had a major impact on how human societies envision sustainable and global futures. In particular, the convergence of multiple social and ecological crises in the first decades of the new millennium raises new challenges that necessitate an evolution in our modes of living, a deepening of democratic decision-making processes, and society-wide knowledge mobilization to foster long-term social and ecological sustainability. In this context, citizens, entrepreneurs, and public officials place great hope in collaborative research and innovation to improve our comprehension of scientifically credible and socially desirable sustainability transformations.

Much transformative research has addressed specific sustainability issues and proposed solutions for specific actors. However, many of the problems we face today defy settlement because they are characterized by very heterogeneous and boundless problem features (Polk, 2014). For this reason, they are often referred to as "wicked" (Rittel and Webber, 1973). They involve multiple and often strongly contested societal values, are causally complex, and engage actors from multiple sectors and societal spheres of activity (Harris et al., 2010; Polk, 2015).

These different features of wicked problems suggest that the traditional division of labor between scientific and societal actors' expertise in societal responses to the crisis is insufficient to address complex sustainability problems (Haasnoot et al., 2013). In particular, wicked-problem situations have led to a set of research questions on sustainability challenges that cannot be addressed through conventional multidisciplinary and academic expert-led-only approaches.

DOI: 10.4324/9781032624297-1

A study directed by the Organization for Economic Cooperation and Development (OECD) on "Addressing Societal Challenges" (OECD, 2020) stated that engaging societal actors across the boundaries of science and practice will be crucial to addressing urgent social and ecological challenges. As highlighted in the report, the impacts of global warming, biodiversity loss, natural disasters, economic migration, and health pandemics are manifested at multiple scales and require both technological and social innovations" (ibid, p. 9). To achieve such innovations, "different scientific disciplines, including natural and social sciences and humanities need to work together and fully engage other public and private sector actors, including policymakers" (ibid).

In response to these new societal demands for collaborative research and social innovation, scientific researchers and societal actors have initiated different forms of knowledge co-production and partnerships for interdisciplinary socio-ecological research in all fields of sustainability, in both basic and applied research. However, less effort has been made to understand the institutional conditions for moving beyond the myriad of these incipient and piecemeal efforts toward a more systematic reform of social practices and institutional rules within the modern science fabric. Nevertheless, to address the scale and urgency of contemporary socio-ecological challenges, researchers, societal actors, and science officials underline the need for such systematic reform.

Therefore, the discussion in this book proposes taking a fresh look at the collective action challenges involved in building large-scale boundary-crossing interdisciplinary research collaborations among researchers and societal actors—including citizens, members of associations, teachers, entrepreneurs, public officials, and policymakers. These collaborative research practices are described in scholarly literature under the umbrella of "transdisciplinary research." Indeed, transdisciplinary research has been promoted as a novel approach to produce societally relevant, value-laden, and scientifically robust knowledge on sustainability transformations that transcends established boundaries among scientific disciplines and between science and society.

The objective of the investigation of transdisciplinary research in this book is to identify the appropriate mix of governance mechanisms for organizing knowledge co-production processes that contribute to the generation of actionable knowledge outputs in real-world sustainability transformations. Two core lessons emerged from our inquiry into the governance challenges. First, to generate actionable knowledge outputs, researchers and societal actors must look beyond knowledge integration and actively co-design research questions, frameworks, and approaches. Second, to build capacities for research co-design in transdisciplinary research, funders and research managers must build a flexible, polycentric institutional organizational environment for boundary-crossing knowledge exchange, the acquisition of competencies for knowledge co-production beyond academia, and transdisciplinary team formation.

By addressing the issue of governance of knowledge co-production in transformational sustainability research through the lens of the theory of collective action, our analysis intends to add value to the existing literature both theoretically and practically. First, at the level of tools for theoretical analysis, this book presents an innovative framework for successfully navigating collective action challenges in boundary-crossing collaborations, based on insights from the literature on the governance of knowledge commons. This framework is introduced by discussing various types of collective action failures encountered in building partnerships between scientific researchers and societal actors involved in value-laden and multifaceted sustainability transformations. To highlight the significance of institutional rules for knowledge co-production in overcoming these collective action failures, the framework is applied to various institutional rules for organizing research co-design, social learning on sustainability values, and the institutional enabling of boundary-crossing collaboration.

Second, to examine the practical implementation challenges of these collective action arrangements, this study adopts a bottom-up empirical approach. Through a comparative assessment of the process design of transdisciplinary research in a sample of 44 projects, we analyze the conditions for the successful co-production of usable knowledge on value-laden socio-ecological transformations. This sample is constructed through a "most different" case study selection, with the view to encompassing a broad diversity of research traditions ranging from technological and biophysical research to socioeconomic and sociocultural research approaches. This comparative assessment aims to identify robust combinations of conditions that lead to effective collaborative research with societal actors. Subsequently, the analysis delves deeper into capacity building for partnership research through fostering social learning about sustainability values among research partners and organizing transdisciplinary training and knowledge exchanges at higher education institutions.

To present the findings of the analysis, various governance mechanisms are illustrated with a wealth of in-depth case studies from various thematic areas of sustainability transformations. The overall aim is to present collective action challenges in transdisciplinary research in an accessible and broadly interdisciplinary manner to a large audience of sustainability scholars and practitioners. Indeed, writing this book would not have been possible without the intensive experimentation and collective learning on transdisciplinary research by a growing community of societal actors and scholars from all scientific disciplines and professional backgrounds over the last three decades. The upscaling of transdisciplinary research on society-wide sustainability transformations is therefore likely to benefit from the mutual learning that occurs between researchers and societal actors across all these disciplinary backgrounds and across different types of science and society interfaces. This book also aims to invite its readers to embark on that mutual learning journey with transdisciplinary scholars and practitioners.

References

Haasnoot, M., Kwakkel, J. H., Walker, W. E. and ter Maat, J. (2013). Dynamic adaptive policy pathways: A method for crafting robust decisions for a deeply uncertain world. *Global Environmental Change*, 23(2), 485–498.

Harris, J., Brown, V. A. and Russell, J. (Eds.). (2010). *Tackling wicked problems: Through the transdisciplinary imagination*. Thames: Taylor and Francis.

OECD. (2020). *Addressing societal challenges using transdisciplinary research*. OECD Science, Technology and Industry Policy Papers 88, OECD Publishing, Paris.

Polk, M. (2014). Achieving the promise of transdisciplinarity: A critical exploration of the relationship between transdisciplinary research and societal problem solving. *Sustainability Science*, 9, 439–451.

Polk, M. (2015). Transdisciplinary co-production: Designing and testing a transdisciplinary research framework for societal problem solving. *Futures*, 65, 110–122.

Rittel, H. W. and Webber, M. M. (1973). Dilemmas in a general theory of planning. *Policy Sciences*, 4(2), 155–169.

1

TRANSDISCIPLINARY RESEARCH PARTNERSHIPS FOR ENVIRONMENTAL JUSTICE AND CITIZENSHIP WITHIN PLANETARY BOUNDARIES

The increase in human knowledge and advances in technological innovation, along with the expansion of globally integrated economic activities, have allowed advanced industrial societies to evolve into mass consumption societies during the second half of the 20th century (Matsuyama, 2002). This transformation, especially strong during the so-called golden 1960s, yielded considerable growth in material well-being and was accompanied by improved social welfare provisions in many countries worldwide. In the following decades, emerging and developing economies adopted many features of this development model (Stearns, 2006).

This model is now in crisis. As extensively documented by researchers and international organizations, the current path of resource-intensive growth is rapidly exhausting non-renewable resources and already disrupting global life-supporting processes on the planet, such as the global carbon cycle or the ecosystems serving as habitats for many endangered species (Rockström et al., 2009). Further, the current development model raises important global and local social equity issues as the average per capita resource use of the people living in the advanced economies cannot be generalized to the entire world population without further aggravating the ecological crisis (Chancel and Piketty, 2015). Moreover, multi-scale and multi-sectoral sustainability problems raise new governance challenges that call for new forms of multi-stakeholder collective action at local, regional, and global scales (Jordan et al., 2015; Dorsch and Flachsland, 2017).

Some interdependencies in *socio-ecological systems*[*1] are not new features of human societies. Historical agro-pastoral land use practices directly impacted many of the ecosystems we know today. Further, natural resources have been exploited on a large scale by all major empires (Costanza et al.,

DOI: 10.4324/9781032624297-2

2007). However, the current planetary challenges seem to dwarf these historical examples of socio-ecological interdependencies by the scale of the impacts, the speed of the process, the scope of the potential risks, and the diversity of stakeholders involved and impacted from various sectors of human activity (Aarts and Drenthen, 2020). Moreover, the current interaction path between the natural dynamics of planetary ecosystems and the dynamics of social systems has produced irreversible exhaustion of natural resources and living organisms and a lock-in of socio-ecological systems in development paths that further promote the overexploitation of the stock of exhaustible nature resources (Norgaard, 1984).

Although necessary in the short term, piecemeal adaptations to address the undesirable consequences of the development model are likely to be insufficient to address the large-scale and society-wide interdependencies between social and ecological systems. As shown in many models of resource use, if human beings wish to live within safe planetary boundaries now and for future generations, human societies must transform society-wide systems of production and consumption, including the fields of energy, housing, mobility, and agrifood production, among others (Falk et al., 2020).

In response to this challenge of society-wide sustainability transformations, researchers, social movements, social entrepreneurs, and policymakers have developed a broad array of new approaches to human progress and well-being around an alternative narrative of living within planetary boundaries, ecological justice, and environmental citizenship (Petit et al., 2022). These three societal value frameworks aim to address *social and ecological sustainability** challenges in a just and socially legitimate manner.

First, the mobilization around planetary boundaries acknowledges the need for urgent action to maintain the functioning of basic life-supporting systems and processes on Earth (Gunderson and Holling, 2002; Folke et al., 2002; Rockström et al., 2009; du Plessis, 2012). This call for action is motivated by the awareness of potential risks generated by major system instabilities and the wish to preserve the diversity of human and non-human life forms and social practices that co-evolved with and depended on the planetary processes (Larrère, 1997, pp. 83–84).

Second, the overall objective of environmental justice regards the need to address the specific social justice issues that arise in interdependent socio-ecological systems (Larrère and Larrère, 2014, p. 320). Indeed, the growth in intensity and scale of socio-ecological interactions has important consequences for social justice and equity. The emergence of new ecological and technological risks induces distributional issues between those who endure the consequences of these risks and those who are not impacted or who can pay for adaptation measures. Such distributional issues also involve the question of who benefits from the new opportunities created by sustainability transformations. In short, societies face an array of choices to make between various sustainability transformation pathways to overcome the current crises, with different costs and benefits for different social groups (UN, 2019).

More generally, environmental justice scholars highlight three important justice-related concerns for sustainability transformations (Fraser, 2009; Schlosberg, 2013; Schlosberg et al., 2019; Coolsaet, 2016, 2020). They are often labeled in shorthand as the three concerns of "distribution, process, and recognition." They relate to individual distributive concerns based on the criteria of socioeconomic justice (distribution), concerns over the fairness of the process of collective decision-making (process), and recognition of the contribution of all concerned sociocultural groups to the process of change (recognition). Further, environmental justice scholars also highlight power issues as an important cross-cutting category (Schlosberg, 2013). As will be seen in the case studies on sustainability research, addressing power asymmetries in knowledge co-production processes is crucial to promoting just sustainability solutions and the effective involvement of disenfranchised social groups in knowledge production on desirable and feasible sustainability transformations.

Third, promoting environmental citizenship addresses innovations toward forms of collaborative governance and collective decision-making that are needed to advance the objectives of sustainable development within Earth's planetary boundaries and in accordance with environmental justice (Dobson, 2007). Indeed, the current crisis involves a broad area of collective goods, such as human life-supporting climate, air quality, biodiversity, or sustainable management of plant and crop diseases, that require collective action beyond the conventional nation-state, involving societal actors at various scales and from highly diverse sectors of activity.

This third core value framework partially overlaps with the second, as it underlines the importance of building capacities for meaningful participation of all parties beyond merely formal process guarantees for inclusive governance of all parties in societal transformations (Arnstein, 1969). However, the framework of environmental citizenship emphasizes the role of participation beyond situations of environmental injustice and stresses the importance of new forms of participation by citizens and stakeholders in all forms of public and private collective action that are required to address the current sustainability crises in an effective manner (De Schutter and Dedeurwaerdere, 2022).

As this short overview shows, the current crisis of the resource-intensive growth model has major impacts on the relationship between the evolution of human societies and the various ecological and natural resource systems on Earth. The unprecedented scope of social and ecological interdependencies, if left on an unsustainable trajectory, can have disastrous consequences for the future survival of humankind on Earth. In response, societal actors and policymakers actively elaborate new value frameworks to envision a sustainable and socially just future within planetary boundaries, which, however, remain under intense social debate.

In this context, there is an urgent need to provide scientifically credible and socially legitimate perspectives on the feasible and desirable sustainability transformations required to address the crisis (UN, 2019). As will be argued in this introductory chapter, conventional specialized disciplinary science and expert-led advice are largely insufficient in providing the body of usable knowledge—applied and basic—needed to accelerate the incipient societal transformations toward a sustainable evolution of natural and social systems. Indeed, the achievement of sustainable human development objectives in interdependent social and ecological systems requires new modes of knowledge generation. These new modes must cross the boundaries of various disciplines to produce an improved understanding of the complex social and ecological interdependencies. Moreover, they must involve the concerned societal actors and researchers in mutual learning on the overall sustainability values that can guide human action in various specific societal transformation pathways.

1.1 Organizing research on integrated social and ecological systems

Over the last three decades, science policy officials and sustainability researchers have developed major new modalities for organizing scientific research (Kates, 2011). These new modes of knowledge mobilization aim to overcome the failures of conventional disciplinary research for addressing cross-sectoral and value-laden sustainability issues. Two major features characterize this emerging landscape of scientific research in support of sustainability research: (1) an *integrated** interdisciplinary approach encompassing social and ecological system dimensions and (2) a partnership approach based on *knowledge co-production** and *social learning** among scientific researchers and societal actors. The end goal of this combination of interdisciplinary and partnership approaches is the production of knowledge on specific sustainability transformations that is scientifically credible, socially legitimate, and socially relevant.

First, as per many scholars, the mere aggregation of specialized disciplinary expertise is insufficient to provide usable knowledge on sustainability transformations (Fernandes and Philippi, 2017). However, such interdisciplinary approaches do not constitute a new kind of "interdisciplinary discipline." Rather, integrated interdisciplinary approaches to interdependent social and ecological systems require combining perspectives that mobilize radically heterogeneous epistemological, conceptual, and empirical perspectives (Norgaard, 1989; Goddard et al., 2019). Therefore, for each specific transformation pathway, researchers must actively collaborate to integrate heterogeneous perspectives into common research frameworks (Ostrom, 2007).

Second, the analysis of the integrated socio-ecological systems cannot be separated from the value-related discussions on the core sustainability values regarding environmental sustainability, justice, and citizenship (Brandt et al., 2013; Dedeurwaerdere, 2014). Indeed, in interdependent social and ecological system dynamics, the analysis of the biophysical, socioeconomic, and sociocultural levers of societal transformations cannot be conducted independently of a discussion on value-related considerations, which co-define the basic orientations of the sustainability transformations of these systems. One set of examples that will be further illustrated in this book relates to the research on the thresholds for sustainable resource use. Defining such thresholds involves biophysical analysis, socioeconomic considerations, and value-related positions in environmental or social ethics. For instance, how much territory do we reserve for pristine nature, which plays an important role in rare species protection? How much territory do we dedicate to carbon capture in forests or wetlands relative to other possible land use purposes? Further, how do we consider the diverse societal actors' perspectives on social justice when analyzing various sustainable practices of natural resource use with different distributional impacts?

In practice, the discussions on the overall orientation of sustainability transformations involve a set of heterogeneous societal values or societal values that remain under intense debate. Therefore, reliable scientific knowledge production on the transformation pathways depends on involving societal actors in clarifying the various values at stake in framing a specific field of sustainability transformations.

The transgression of the conventional boundaries of academic disciplinary and interdisciplinary science—by integrating knowledge from societal actors in the research process—has three important purposes in the context of sustainability research (see Pohl et al., 2021). First, this collaboration with societal actors aims to construct a more integrative and complete approach to sustainability transformations by integrating empirical and analytic knowledge from scientific research with experiential knowledge on specific feasible and desirable pathways from societal actors. Second, the partnership with societal actors has a transformational purpose by producing usable knowledge directly related to the social possibilities of change in specific interdependent social and ecological systems. Third, the partnership also has a critical dimension. Indeed, whenever societal or scientific debates over sustainability value are fraught with distorted communication processes, given rent-seeking or power imbalances, a critical approach is needed to deconstruct dominant structures of knowledge that perpetuate unsustainable development paths. This critical aspect of the knowledge integration from societal actors calls for appropriate governance mechanisms for the collaborative practice within the research partnerships, which is at the heart of the analysis of sustainability research in this book.

As will be illustrated through the various case studies, to improve our understanding of feasible and desirable possibilities of change, societal actors and scientists embarked on innovative boundary-crossing research endeavors that combined interdisciplinary knowledge integration and collaborative research partnerships. Over the last three decades at least, these approaches have been designated more generally under the umbrella of *transdisciplinary sustainability research** (Hirsch Hadorn et al., 2008). The latter designates basic and applied sustainability research practices based on knowledge co-production among researchers from various scientific disciplines (for the interdisciplinary analysis of interdependent socio-ecological systems) and knowledge co-production among scientific researchers and societal actors (the partnership research aspect).

In this context, some transdisciplinary research approaches may give the impression that the mobilization of societal actors for improved contextual information gathering is sufficient to induce the effective production of usable knowledge on sustainability transformations. However, as discussed at length in this book, such a focus on knowledge integration, although an important aspect, is insufficient to successfully organize transdisciplinary research. The organization of knowledge co-production in transdisciplinary research requires dedicated governance mechanisms to overcome a set of hurdles that can hamper collaboration among research partners. Major potential hurdles to be discussed include the lack of involvement in co-constructing common frameworks and the failures in mutual learning on socially legitimate and relevant sustainability values. To introduce these issues, this chapter further presents the sustainability problems that motivate transdisciplinary sustainability research, introduces the key components of the transdisciplinary research process, and gives a short overview of the various book chapters.

1.2 The promises of transdisciplinary sustainability research

Throughout human history, science has played a key role in fostering progress in human well-being. One paradigmatic case is the contribution of theoretical knowledge in mathematics, physics, and biology to improvements in many areas of human activity, to cite just one well-known field of research with large-scale impacts. For instance, ancient knowledge of mathematics and physics played a key role in developing public infrastructure to channel drinking water into cities and organize complex irrigation systems in ancient civilizations from China and India to the Middle East and Europe (Swetz, 1979; Koutsoyiannis and Angelakis, 2003). In the 19th century, the control of many infectious diseases became possible with the pioneering work of Robert Koch and Louis Pasteur on the microbial theory of disease (Satcher, 1995). In the 1970s, the Consultative Group on International Agricultural Research set up a scientific crop breeding program in collaboration with research centers throughout the world, which majorly contributed to reducing global hunger through the huge increase in crop yields of cereals such as rice, wheat, and maize (Byerlee and Dubin, 2009).

Scholars document similar broad impacts of science on progress in human well-being throughout history, ranging from the biophysical sciences to the social sciences and humanities (Mokyr, 2011). In the process, the field of science evolved from operating within small networks of well-connected individuals to large-scale collective endeavors (Ravetz, 2006). Especially after the Second World War, public sector science underwent a rapid transformation, evolving toward so-called big science, organized around large-scale research consortia that address various societal missions through publicly funded research (Nelson, 1993; Stokes, 1997; Mazzucato, 2018).

The reform of the science fabric by setting up large-scale expert-driven research consortia by national and international governments, however, falls short of addressing the knowledge needs for cross-sectoral and multistakeholder sustainability issues. Indeed, except for specific research niches, postwar innovations in multi-disciplinary and interdisciplinary research consortia remain characterized by functional autonomy from society, are led by independent scientists, and are largely self-governing in their scientific priorities, their procedures for information gathering, and the quality assurance of the produced knowledge (Kitcher, 2011). Even though science policy increasingly requires democratic accountability and proof of the societal relevance of functionally autonomous, so-called ivory-tower science, overall, the strict division of labor between scientific expertise and societal actors' knowledge remains strong. In particular, the design of the scientific methods, the framing of the research approaches, and the organization of research processes remain outside of the remit of collaboration with societal actors (ibid).

Among the noted large-scale science efforts is the Intergovernmental Panel on Climate Change (IPCC). This Panel organizes the writing of a report in intervals of approximately six years with a community of over 700 scientists (for the 2021–2023 sixth assessment report) to deliver state-of-the-art knowledge on climate change to policymakers. Despite being an authoritative and essential resource for decision-making on climate change, IPCC reports remain largely insufficient to guide specific societal transformations to address climate change. The latter is mainly because of the strong focus on the biophysical basis and impacts of climate change in the report (Bjurström and Polk, 2011). Indeed, rather than investigating in depth the various interdependencies between biophysical, socioeconomic, and sociocultural drives for reaching effective climate change adaptation and mitigation, the main purpose of the report is to map the biophysical trends and discuss the policy targets for mitigation and adaptation action. Nevertheless, without integrated knowledge on specific feasible, socially relevant, and legitimate sustainability transformation pathways, such multi-disciplinary expert reports are unlikely to provide the necessary guidance to address the current social and ecological crises.

As noted, the emergence of new cross-sectoral research questions on sustainability transformations of interdependent social and ecological systems calls for the next stage in the contemporary science evolution in the direction of transdisciplinary knowledge co-production. Relative to functionally autonomous "ivory-tower" science, transdisciplinary research involves societal actors in research partnerships with scientific researchers in a much more encompassing way.

Scholars have provided a more specific definition of the key components of transdisciplinary research projects. While multi-disciplinarity has been described as the mere juxtaposition of disciplinary perspectives, transdisciplinarity goes a step further (Hirsch Hadorn et al., 2008), in particular by

1 integrating information from different disciplines and types of knowledge (from scientific researchers and societal actors) to address a common specific problem and research question through a jointly constructed framework and
2 organizing a partnership between researchers and societal actors for co-managing the knowledge integration process and organizing social learning on the diversity of societal values

In short, transdisciplinary research is based on interdisciplinary knowledge integration and organizing knowledge co-production partnerships between researchers and societal actors, as illustrated in Figure 1.1.

Over the last decades, to navigate this emerging landscape of multi-disciplinary, interdisciplinary, and transdisciplinary research approaches, national and international research agencies have organized various international meetings with science and stakeholder communities. First, as per a state-of-the-art report based on a workshop organized by the United States National Academies of Sciences, interdisciplinarity is a research, education, and problem-solving mode that integrates methods, tools, concepts, and theories from one or more disciplines to address common problems (National Academy of Sciences, 2005, p. 306). According to the report, the concept of interdisciplinary research emerged in the early 20th century in response to the need to address complex problems or develop comprehensive general views of a problem area. As underlined by Klein (2010), the scope varies from narrow interdisciplinarity, involving disciplines with compatible methods and epistemologies (e.g., physics and molecular biology), to broad interdisciplinarity that bridges disparate approaches (e.g., combining sociocultural history of land use practices and biophysical analysis of ecosystem functions).

This form of broad interdisciplinarity is most relevant (Pohl et al., 2021) to understanding society-wide sustainability transformations. Indeed,

Interdisciplinarity
- Crosses disciplinary boundaries
- Common goal setting
- Integration of disciplines
- Development of integrated knowledge and theory

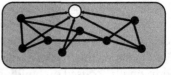

● Disciplinary research participants
○ Goal of research project

Transdisicplinarity
- Crosses disciplinary and academic/non-academic boundaries
- Common goal setting
- Integration of disciplines and non-academic participants
- Development of integrated knowledge and theory among science and society

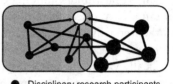

● Disciplinary research participants
⬤ Non-academic research participants
○ Goal of research project

FIGURE 1.1 Comparison of key features of interdisciplinary and transdisciplinary research

Figure by the author, based on an adaptation of the ideas developed in Tress et al. (2005).

sustainability transformations require bridging disparate sources of knowledge on social and ecological system dynamics to cross boundaries between various sectoral and often disconnected decision-making processes in public and private organizations, which often address distinct aspects of social and biophysical systems. This requirement to develop broad interdisciplinarity research practices is strongly underlined in the first generation of transdisciplinary research in the 1970s by scholars such as Jean Piaget, Leo Apostel, and Erich Jantsch, who focused on the elaboration of overarching syntheses in specific domains of reality (Hirsch Hadorn et al., 2008; Klein, 2010).

The second generation of transdisciplinary research moved the analysis of socio-ecological systems beyond the walls of conventional academic and expert-led interdisciplinary science by involving societal actors and citizens in knowledge mobilization and social learning on society-wide sustainability transformations (Hirsch Hadorn et al., 2008). A major historical landmark event showcasing, for the first time, the broad international uptake of this move toward partnership-based research approaches to sustainability issues was the *International Transdisciplinary Conference* in 2000, organized in Zürich by the Priority Program Environment of the Swiss Academy of Sciences. This conference gathered over 700 participants from 57 nations to discuss their success and challenges in conducting transdisciplinary research. Although this research field is broad and shaped by various lines of thinking and heterogeneous approaches to research, participants widely shared the concern for transcending disciplinary paradigms and various types of knowledge to address real-world sustainability problems (ibid, p. 29).

In general, this second generation of transdisciplinary research practices additionally focused on building partnerships with societal actors to consider the diversity of legitimate value perspectives on sustainability transformations in the design of the research process. Indeed, the goal of reaching a socially robust understanding of sustainability transformations requires that sustainability researchers move from a general interdisciplinary analysis of all theoretically possible socio-ecological dynamics to an analysis of specific socio-ecological transformation pathways that are socially desirable and scientifically valid. The latter implies the identification of the problems that are considered most relevant by concerned societal actors and the matching of the research framework to real-world social possibilities of change. Hence, research partners must co-construct the research design in a way all partners consider relevant and socially legitimate.

Accordingly, per the study directed by the Organisation for Economic Cooperation and Development (OECD) on "Addressing Societal Challenges" (OECD, 2020)—referred to in the introduction—transdisciplinarity is defined as "the integration of academic researchers from unrelated disciplines and non-academic participants in creating new knowledge and theory to achieve a common goal, involving the creation of new knowledge and theory." According to the study, drawing upon the breadth of scientific and non-scientific knowledge domains, such as local and traditional knowledge, practitioners' know-how, and cultural norms and values, knowledge co-production aims to supplement and transform scientific insights. Thus, it offers a way to address issues involving diverse societal values being debated. Further, expanding on existing scientific evidence and organizing social learning processes can generate more innovative solutions and holistic understanding (ibid, p. 9).

Given the importance of the disciplinary organization of research in many research institutions and universities, science policy officials and research evaluators may face considerable challenges in situating transdisciplinary research in the current institutional landscape. In this context, it is important to highlight some possible misunderstandings. First, some scholars might tend to equate transdisciplinary research with more applied research. Nevertheless, the difference between transdisciplinary research and disciplinary research is not situated in the production of more direct, applicable research results relative to more theoretical and basic approaches to reality. On the contrary, transdisciplinary and disciplinary research share basic and applied research strands (Mittelstrass, 2018, p. 72). Regarding transdisciplinary research for sustainability, practices may range from applied knowledge co-production within an action research setting to more basic strands of strategic research, foresight studies, or general theoretical syntheses of complex socio-ecological interdependencies that cannot be apprehended through disciplinary or multi-disciplinary approaches.

Furthermore, not all situations justify investment in transdisciplinary research. The choice of multi-disciplinary, interdisciplinary, or transdisciplinary research hinges on the type and representation of the research problem the research partners aim to address (Hirsch Hadorn et al., 2006, pp. 123–124). The latter can be illustrated schematically through the case of sustainability problems regarding water management in a river basin, as in Table 1.1. Water management might concern local and isolated problem features or more encompassing, interdependent socio-ecological problem features. For instance, the inhabitants and users of a river basin may focus on a set of well-defined problems, such as building a bridge over the river or solving a pollution problem caused by a local actor. Alternatively, they may be concerned with water management problems in so-called river basin contracts for addressing various interrelated social demands around biodiversity protection, recreation, and industrial use of water (Huitema and Meijerink, 2014). Such different problem situations have implications for organizing multi-disciplinary, interdisciplinary, or transdisciplinary research. Indeed, it may be that the involved partners prioritize solving some technical problems related to a well-identified local problem. In such a case, they likely opt for conducting disciplinary or multi-disciplinary research. Conversely, the focus may be on the problems generated by the dynamics of interdependencies and value-laden controversies in the river basin contract, which are more adequately addressed through modes of transdisciplinary research.

TABLE 1.1 Illustration of sustainability research topics addressing situations with different degrees of socio-ecological interdependency and heterogeneity of societal value perspectives

Research questions related to river basin management	Rather homogeneous societal value perspective	Heterogeneous societal value perspectives
Various rather independent social and ecological dynamics	Research question on the architecture of a pedestrian bridge to cross the river	Solving a contentious local river pollution issue affecting diverse actors
Strongly interdependent social and ecological dynamics	Research on the adaptation of legal frameworks to new threats to valuable biodiversity in the river basin	Research on balancing objectives of recreational use, industry development, and biodiversity in the river basin

In this context, Spangenberg (2011) suggests the distinction between science for incremental sustainability change (technical and disciplinary) and science of system-wide sustainability transformations (interdisciplinary and transdisciplinary). Regarding "science for incremental sustainability change," scientific research aims to bridge technical knowledge gaps that must be addressed to solve problems within a given sustainability transformation pathway. For such purposes, disciplinary knowledge and methods are well adapted to provide in-depth knowledge of a system component from a highly specialized perspective on sub-system features. In contrast, regarding the "science of system-wide sustainability transformations," the research process is designed to understand the overall dynamics of interaction between the social and ecological system features in given sustainability transformations. The latter is the specific object of analysis of transdisciplinary sustainability science, as illustrated in the lower right box of Table 1.2. Both interdisciplinary analyses of coupled socio-ecological systems and partnerships for knowledge co-production between societal actors and researchers are involved in this undertaking.

In general, transdisciplinary sustainability research aims to produce better knowledge and a better general understanding of sustainability problems characterized by strong system interdependencies and diverse societal values that play a role at multiple scales of socio-ecological interactions. As is the case with all scientific research, such knowledge will be provisional and subject to further refinement. Nevertheless, as the many case studies in this book show, integrating processes of transdisciplinary knowledge co-production in sustainability research is a key requirement to advance the undertaking of scientifically credible and socially robust knowledge production on multiscale and multistakeholder sustainability challenges.

1.3 Addressing governance challenges in partnerships between scientific researchers and societal actors

Scholarly discussions on transdisciplinary research have produced a wealth of research on approaches to knowledge integration among researchers from various disciplines and societal actors (Hirsch Hadorn et al., 2008; Bergmann et al., 2012). Subsequently, with the proliferation of researcher and social-actor partnerships in transdisciplinary sustainability research, scholars furnished insights into various aspects of knowledge co-production and social learning. However, except for some notable exceptions (e.g., Pohl et al., 2021), few systematic studies probe the overall institutional design of knowledge co-production in transdisciplinary research.

What is often implicit in this scant regard for governance issues of knowledge co-production is the assumption that the conventional disciplinary mechanisms of journal-based peer review, community building through scientific

TABLE 1.2 Categories of sustainability problems typically addressed through disciplinary, multi-disciplinary, and transdisciplinary research

Application domains of sustainability science	Rather homogeneous societal value perspective	Heterogeneous societal value perspectives
Various rather independent social and ecological dynamics	• Analyze components of social and ecological systems and their interactions • Well-identified research problems and purposes Typically addressed through disciplinary (one main system component) or multi-disciplinary research (parallel or sequential analysis of components)	• Analyze components of social and ecological systems and their interactions • Multiple diverging perspectives on the research problems and purposes Typically addressed through multi-disciplinary research, to take into account the diversity of diverging perspectives
Strongly interdependent social and ecological dynamics	• Analyze emergent system patterns resulting from the reciprocal relationships between social and ecological system components • Well-identified research problems and purposes Typically addressed through interdisciplinary approaches	• Analyze emergent system patterns resulting from the reciprocal between social and ecological system components • Multiple diverging perspectives on the research problems and purposes Typically transdisciplinary research when values have a strong impact on the research design of the socio-ecological system; sometimes interdisciplinary if the research design can be settled outside the discussions on the value framing

conferences, and dedicated training will also provide the key mechanisms for consolidating transdisciplinary research into larger communities and organizational frameworks (Benkler, 2008). However, through such imitation of existing organizational mechanisms, although useful to partially address issues of quality management of research outputs and training of young scholars, among others, major organizational issues remain unaddressed.

Transdisciplinary research raises major questions regarding designing appropriate *institutional rules** for governing research partnerships at various levels. First, the organization of the knowledge co-production process between societal actors and scientific researchers requires rules for collaboration among research partners mobilizing heterogeneous knowledge types (Pohl et al., 2021). Second, transdisciplinary research requires appropriate rules for organizing social learning on sustainability values among actors from different sectors of activity involved in society-wide transformations (Herrero et al., 2019). Finally, to consolidate transdisciplinary research efforts beyond small niche projects, transdisciplinary research requires organizational support for competency and capacity building for researchers, students, and societal actors to allow them to successfully participate in boundary-crossing knowledge co-production efforts (Pearce et al., 2018).

The first two governance challenges for building transdisciplinary research partnerships are situated at the project level and can be illustrated through a set of questions that must be addressed by the project partners. Given heterogeneous knowledge interests in transdisciplinary research partnerships, how can one avoid each of the partners pursuing their own research agenda once a project proposal has been approved and funded? In particular, how can one create mechanisms such that research partners invest time and resources in research methods and data-gathering priorities that best suit the joint boundary-crossing research issues? What tools can be used to foster a mutual understanding of how knowledge is constructed in each of the disciplines or practitioners' communities? Moreover, how can one create the appropriate balance between acknowledging the diversity of societal values developed in different communities and organizing a dialogue on the possible convergence or accommodation between these values as a basis for successful collaboration?

Thus, to tackle these questions, beyond methodological innovations in transdisciplinary knowledge integration, transdisciplinary research will require new forms of collaboration and partnership building, along with processes of social learning among the partners to foster mutual understanding of diverse societal values and methodological perspectives. Indeed, transdisciplinary research projects generate new governance challenges as they gather scientific researchers or societal actors with different research agendas and interests who are often involved in different project contexts. For instance, a project on biodiversity in inhabited agricultural landscapes may assemble historians, sociologists, and biologists to understand the social legitimacy of various landscape management options. Hence, to successfully integrate such diverse knowledge, participating disciplinary scientists or non-academic experts must look beyond the methodologies that, at best, satisfy their interest (quantitative for some, interpretative or qualitative for others) and agree upon a set of research tasks that, at best, serve the common purpose.

Further, at a second level, transdisciplinary research faces governance challenges regarding consolidating transdisciplinary research projects in larger organizational units and capacity-building efforts. Indeed, how can one involve interdisciplinary or transdisciplinary researchers beyond small niche networks of jointly defined but specific research issues? What kind of networking activities can contribute to creating new interactions beyond such small niche networks? How can one decrease search costs to find new partners beyond the already well-known partners from prior collaborations? Finally, what kind of research resources can be shared across a heterogeneous network of boundary-crossing projects to build capacities for training and joint quality management on issues of common concern?

Indeed, to consolidate transdisciplinary research in more diverse and comprehensive research networks, researchers and science policy officials require a set of institutional mechanisms to build transdisciplinary research competences and research networks in larger communities. As will be discussed in depth in Chapter 5, such larger organizational units can be organized around cross-cutting thematic areas of sustainability transformations, be it in the fields of mobility, energy, or agrifood systems, or directly integrate researchers of various thematic communities in more generic research-enabling platforms.

To develop the various features of the enabling knowledge ecosystem for transdisciplinary research, this book is organized as follows. As highlighted throughout this chapter, research partnerships are prone to a set of governance failures. Chapter 2 reviews some of these failures and discusses the key concepts proposed to overcome them by building upon the core insights from the literature on collective action challenges in building scientific knowledge commons. Chapter 3 presents a comparative analysis of a broad set of cases of transdisciplinary research partnerships, with the view to identify core features of the knowledge co-production process that contribute to effective usable knowledge production on specific sustainability transformations. Chapter 4 probes the question of the various strategies for social learning on sustainability values among the project partners, by extending the typology of social learning situations proposed by Amartya Sen in his work on social choice. Chapter 5 uses the results of the comparative analysis at the project level in Chapters 3 and 4 to tackle the question of the institutional design of the consolidation of transdisciplinary research in larger organizational architectures. Chapter 6 briefly discusses some limits and extensions of the analysis by highlighting the importance of building synergies between various modes and types of knowledge production within and beyond academia.

As announced in the introduction, through analyzing these various aspects of the enabling knowledge ecosystem, this book aims to provide added value to both the theoretical perspectives for analyzing the governance of knowledge co-production and the comparative analysis of collective action challenges encountered in transdisciplinary sustainability research. First, in relation to the theoretical approaches, this book develops a multi-level approach to the institutional design of transdisciplinary research partnerships, building upon and extending the literature on the governance of *scientific research commons**. Second, for deepening the analysis of institutional design principles, the book provides a comparative assessment of the conditions for the successful production of usable knowledge based on a large sample of transdisciplinary research projects that encompass a broad diversity of research traditions in academia, ranging from biophysical research to socioeconomic and cultural sciences. Finally, the book uses these insights to provide an analysis of the most appropriate organizational architectures, drawing upon governance mechanisms from the literature on flexible network organizations. Overall, these different strands aim to analyze the building blocks for constructing a consistent account of the new transdisciplinary modes for organizing scientific research, where the integration of societal actors' knowledge and social learning on societal values is an indispensable part of the knowledge generation process.

Note

1 Terms defined in the glossary are marked in italic and with an asterisk upon their first appearance in the text.

References

Aarts, N. and Drenthen, M. (2020). Socio-ecological interactions and sustainable development. Introduction to a special issue. *Sustainability*, 12(17), 6967.

Arnstein, S. R. (1969). A ladder of citizen participation. *Journal of the American Institute of Planners*, 35(4), 216–224.

Benkler, Y. (2008). *The wealth of networks*. New Haven: Yale University Press.

Bergmann, M., Jahn, T., Knobloch, T., Krohn, W., Pohl, C. and Schramm, E. (2012). *Methods for transdisciplinary research: A primer for practice*. Frankfurt: Campus Verlag.

Bjurström, A. and Polk, M. (2011). Climate change and interdisciplinarity: A co-citation analysis of IPCC third assessment report. *Scientometrics*, 87(3), 525–550.

Brandt, P., Ernst, A., Gralla, F., Luederitz, C., Lang, D. J., Newig, J., Reinert, F., Abson, D. J. and Von Wehrden, H. (2013). A review of transdisciplinary research in sustainability science. *Ecological Economics*, 92, 1–15.

Byerlee, D. and Dubin, H. J. (2009). Crop improvement in the CGIAR as a global success story of open access and international collaboration. *International Journal of the Commons*, 4(1), 452–480.

Chancel, L. and Piketty, T. (2015). *Carbon and inequality: From Kyoto to Paris. Trends in the global inequality of carbon emissions (1998–2013) and prospects for an equitable adaptation fund*. Paris: Paris School of Economics.

Coolsaet, B. (2016). Towards an agroecology of knowledges: Recognition, cognitive justice and farmers' autonomy in France. *Journal of Rural Studies*, 47, 165–171.

Coolsaet, B. (Ed.). (2020). *Environmental justice: Key issues*. Abingdon: Routledge.

Costanza, R., Graumlich, L. J. and Steffen, W. (2007). *Sustainability or collapse? An integrated history and future of people on Earth*. Cambridge, MA: MIT Press.

Dedeurwaerdere, T. (2014). *Sustainability science for strong sustainability*. Cheltenham: Edward Elgar.

De Schutter, O. and Dedeurwaerdere, T. (2022). *Social innovation in the service of social and ecological transformation*. Abingdon: Routledge.

Dobson, A. (2007). Environmental citizenship: Towards sustainable development. *Sustainable Development, 15*(5), 276–285.

Dorsch, M. J. and Flachsland, C. (2017). A polycentric approach to global climate governance. *Global Environmental Politics, 17*(2), 45–64.

du Plessis, C. (2012). Towards a regenerative paradigm for the built environment. *Building Research and Information, 40*(1), 7–22.

Falk, J., Gaffney, O., Bhowmik, A. K., Bergmark, P., Galaz, V., Gaskell, N., . . . and Shalit, T. (2020). *Exponential roadmap 1.5.1*. Stockholm: Future Earth.

Fernandes, V. and Philippi Jr., A. (2017). Sustainability sciences: Political and epistemological approaches. In R. Frodeman, J. T. Klein, and R. Pacheco (Eds.), *The Oxford handbook of interdisciplinarity* (2nd ed., pp. 370–407). Oxford: Oxford University Press.

Folke, C., Carpenter, S., Elmqvist, T., Gunderson, L., Holling, C. S. and Walker, B. (2002). Resilience and sustainable development: Building adaptive capacity in a world of transformations. *Ambio, 31*(5), 437–440.

Fraser, N. (2009). *Scales of justice: Reimagining political space in a globalising world*. New York: Columbia University Press.

Goddard, J. J., Kallis, G. and Norgaard, R. B. (2019). Keeping multiple antennae up: Coevolutionary foundations for methodological pluralism. *Ecological Economics, 165*, 106–420.

Gunderson, L. H. and Holling, C. S. (2002). *Panarchy: Understanding transformations in human and natural systems*. London: Island Press.

Herrero, P., Dedeurwaerdere, T. and Osinski, A. (2019). Design features for social learning in transformative transdisciplinary research. *Sustainability Science, 14*(3), 751–769.

Hirsch Hadorn, G., Bradley, D., Pohl, C., Rist, St. and Wiesmann, U. (2006). Implications of transdisciplinarity for sustainability research. *Ecological Economics, 60*, 119–128.

Hirsch Hadorn, G., Hoffmann-Riem, H., Biber-Klemm, S., Grossenbacher-Mansuy, W., Joye, D., Pohl, C., . . . and Zemp, E. (Eds.). (2008). *Handbook of transdisciplinary research*. Dordrecht: Springer.

Huitema, D. and Meijerink, S. V. (2014). *The politics of river basin organisations: Coalitions, institutional design choices and consequences*. Cheltenham: Edward Elgar Publishing.

Jordan, A. J., Huitema, D., Hilden, M., van Hasselt, H., Rayner, T. J., Schoenefeld, J. J., . . . and Boasson, E. L. (2015). Emergence of polycentric climate governance and its future prospects. *Nature Climate Change, 5*(11), 977–982.

Kates, R. W. (2011). What kind of a science is sustainability science? *Proceedings of the National Academy of Sciences, 108*(49).

Kitcher, Ph. (2011). *Science in a democratic society*. New York: Prometheus.

Klein, J. T. (2010). A taxonomy of interdisciplinarity. In R. Frodeman, J. T. Klein and C. Mitcham (Eds.), *The Oxford handbook of interdisciplinarity* (pp. 15–30). Oxford: Oxford University Press.

Koutsoyiannis, D. and Angelakis, A. N. (2003). Hydrologic and hydraulic science and technology in ancient Greece. In B. A. Stewart, T. A. Howell (Eds.), *The encyclopedia of water science* (pp. 415–417). New York: Marcel Dekker.

Larrère, C. (1997). *Les philosophies de l'environnement*. Paris: Presses Universitaires de France.

Larrère, C. and Larrère, R. (2014). *Penser et agir avec la nature*. Paris: Editions la découverte.

Matsuyama, K. (2002). The rise of mass consumption societies. *Journal of Political Economy*, *110*(5), 1035–1070.

Mazzucato, M. (2018). *Mission-oriented research and innovation in the European Union*. Final Report. Publications Office of the European Commission, Luxembourg.

Mittelstrass, J. (2018). The order of knowledge: From disciplinarity to transdisciplinarity and back. *European Review*, *26*(S2), 68–75.

Mokyr, J. (2011). The gifts of Athena. In *The gifts of Athena*. Princeton, NJ: Princeton University Press.

National Academy of Sciences. (2005). *Facilitating interdisciplinary research*. Washington, DC: The National Academies Press.

Nelson, R. R. (Ed.). (1993). *National innovation systems: A comparative analysis*. Oxford: Oxford University Press.

Norgaard, R. B. (1984). Coevolutionary development potential. *Land Economics*, *60*(2), 160–173.

Norgaard, R. B. (1989). The case for methodological pluralism. *Ecological Economics*, *1*(1), 37–57.

OECD. (2020). *Addressing societal challenges using transdisciplinary research*. OECD Science, Technology and Industry Policy Papers 88, OECD Publishing, Paris.

Ostrom, E. (2007). A diagnostic approach for going beyond panaceas. *Proceedings of the National Academy of Sciences*, *104*(39), 15181–15187.

Pearce, B., Adler, C., Senn, L., Krütli, P., Stauffacher, M. and Pohl, C. (2018). Making the link between transdisciplinary learning and research. In *Transdisciplinary theory, practice and education* (pp. 167–183). Cham: Springer.

Petit, O., Froger, G. and Bauler, T. (2022). *Economie écologique. Une perspective européenne*. Louvain-la-Neuve: De Boeck Supérieur SA.

Pohl, C., Klein, J. T., Hoffmann, S., Mitchell, C. and Fam, D. (2021). Conceptualising transdisciplinary integration as a multidimensional interactive process. *Environmental Science and Policy*, *118*, 18–26.

Ravetz, J. (2006). *The no-nonsense guide to science*. Oxford: New Internationalist.

Rockström, J., Steffen, W., Noone, K., Persson, Å., Chapin, F. S., Lambin, E. F., . . . and Foley, J. A. (2009). A safe operating space for humanity. *Nature*, *461*(7263), 472–475.

Satcher, D. (1995). Emerging infections: Getting ahead of the curve. *Emerging Infectious Diseases*, *1*(1), 1–6.

Schlosberg, D. (2013). Theorising environmental justice: The expanding sphere of a discourse. *Environmental Politics*, *22*(1), 37–55.

Schlosberg, D., Bäckstrand, K. and Pickering, J. (2019). Reconciling ecological and democratic values: Recent perspectives on ecological democracy. *Environmental Values*, *28*(1), 1–8.

Spangenberg, J. H. (2011). Sustainability science: A review, an analysis and some empirical lessons. *Environment Conservation*, *38*, 275–287.

Stearns, P. N. (2006). *Consumerism in world history: The global transformation of desire.* New York: Routledge.

Stokes, D. E. (1997). *Pasteur's quadrant: Basic science and technological innovation.* Washington, DC: Brookings Institution Press.

Swetz, F. (1979). The evolution of mathematics in ancient China. *Mathematics Magazine, 52*(1), 10–19.

Tress, G., Tress, B. and Fry, G. (2005). Clarifying integrative research concepts in landscape ecology. *Landscape Ecology, 20*(4), 479–493.

UN. (2019). *The future is now: Science for achieving sustainable development.* Global Sustainable Development Report 2019. Independent Group of Scientists appointed by the Secretary-General of the United Nations, New York.

2

OVERCOMING COLLECTIVE ACTION FAILURES IN KNOWLEDGE CO-PRODUCTION PRACTICES

At the heart of transdisciplinary sustainability research projects lies the organization of collective action in research groups or consortia to generate common knowledge that is scientifically credible and socially relevant for addressing specific sustainability challenges. In particular, understanding real-world interdependent social and ecological system dynamics requires organizing research collaborations among specialized expert communities and societal actors involved in various fields of sustainability transformations. This chapter introduces the main collective action challenges encountered in organizing collaborative research with heterogeneous groups of knowledge holders and the proposed design principles to address gaps within the literature on the governance of knowledge commons.

Collective action problems in community-provided public goods have been studied in depth in the context of the theory of the commons. Famously, Elinor Ostrom, in her work on the governance of the commons, for which she was awarded the 2009 Nobel Prize in Economic Sciences, showed that groups of actors can effectively self-organize to produce rules to overcome collective action failures in public good provision without centralized rule-making by a state.

The approach developed in the theory of the commons shows the soundness of pursuing an alternative road to the centralized management of collective action problems and decentralized market governance based on case-by-case transactions over proprietary goods. A well-known promoter of the centralized management option is Mancur Olson (1965), who predicted the collapse of community-provided public goods without state-based supervision. Prominent examples of the alternative road of community- or network-based collection action are common pool resources, such as community forests or

DOI: 10.4324/9781032624297-3

community irrigation systems. However, Elinor Ostrom and her co-workers also broadened the study of the commons beyond the natural resource commons to so-called new commons, which include scientific research commons as an important sub-category (Hess and Ostrom, 2007).

The study of the knowledge commons boomed in the mid-1990s with the rapid spread of digital tools for conducting and disseminating research. As documented in the landmark book *Understanding Knowledge as a Commons* (ibid), scholars from various disciplines became concerned with the new collective action problems arising from large-scale collaboration in digital networks. Especially in legal scholarship, "commons" became a buzzword for the new possibilities of collaboration opened up by globally distributed information, despite the countervailing trends of the global expansion of intellectual property rights over digital network tools and the spread of password-protected fences on the Internet (Reichman et al., 2016).

More generally, within this field of the knowledge commons, scholars noticed many similarities between collective action problems encountered in governing research commons and community-managed natural resources (Hess and Ostrom, 2007). In both cases, non-state actors not only provide collective goods in the general interests that are publicly accessible on a non-exclusive basis but also exhibit so-called partial rivalry among the user communities. Such rivalry, which characterizes "impure" public goods in the standard economic approach of public goods, means that making the good available for consumption by one person might decrease its future availability for other persons (Sandler, 2004). The latter can be because the public good is depleted through use or because there is a cost for making it available in a way that corresponds to the needs or demands of given user communities.

Regarding community-managed natural resources, this rivalry can lead to the well-known "tragedy of the commons," where the absence of appropriate rules for the use of the common resource depletes the resource through overconsumption. Regarding the knowledge commons, rivalry may similarly induce a diverse set of collective action failures. As there is a cost to delivering knowledge in an appropriate format for targeted users, the lack of rules for collective action may lead to poor quality knowledge, a delay in disseminating new findings, withholding research data, or a lack of investment in new lines of research.

Scholars have extensively noted the collective action mechanisms for addressing these challenges in the case of disciplinary knowledge commons. Disciplinary communities gather researchers around a relatively similar set of core concepts and methodological approaches (Jacobs, 2017). As widely noted by scholars in science studies, such a division of labor in communities organized around common disciplinary purposes and its further specialization in sub-disciplines are highly successful in reaching a critical mass for quality assessment and review, an efficient organization of education and training, and consolidating general results in specific fields of inquiry (ibid).

The main collective action mechanism for organizing collaboration in sub-disciplinary and disciplinary communities are the disciplinary journals and disciplinary conferences that channel the contributions around a set of key approaches, concepts, and methods of inquiry (Benkler, 2008). Further, the various social networks built around the disciplinary conferences, the journals, and the informal networking of researchers from disciplinary departments of different universities contribute to building strong social norms around the so-called epistemic values or thought styles of the community (Fleck, 1979). Additionally, the institutionalization of the various disciplines and sub-disciplines into larger organizational structures is achieved through the conventional organization of research universities and research organizations in disciplinary departments. This organization is supported through available funding streams by national research foundations and other research bodies along disciplinary lines (König and Gorman, 2017).

As this short overview of the approach to collective action in disciplinary knowledge commons shows, research partners in consortia and research networks can address collective action failures in a decentralized manner via various governance mechanisms. As shown by Benkler and Nissenbaum (2006), disciplinary communities can overcome collective action failures through a combination of rules for quality assurance managed by the research communities (for peer review and research evaluation, among others) and the development of social norms. Such social norms support the sharing of research results and teaching materials among scientists based on the intrinsic motivations of individual researchers to contribute to public science (Macfarlane and Cheng, 2008; Stromberg et al., 2013).

However, even if the specific set of design rules reviewed by Benkler is also important in the transdisciplinary knowledge commons, they fail to address some of the new collective action problems that emerge in the organization of knowledge co-production. Few of the recommendations indeed specifically address challenges for governing the hybrid interdisciplinary and co-produced knowledge commons typical for transdisciplinary research. Unlike disciplinary and multi-disciplinary research consortia and communities, transdisciplinary research includes collective action arrangements with non-academic societal actors that directly affect the design of the scientific research framework and processes of social learning over societal values that are specific to each research partnership. The next sections address some of these specific governance challenges for organizing transdisciplinary knowledge co-production, which will be analyzed in the subsequent chapters.

2.1 Governance failures in transdisciplinary research

This section discusses some of the main hurdles researchers and societal actors may encounter in building effective boundary-crossing research partnerships for sustainability research. According to some scholars, part of the difficulty in further expanding the transdisciplinary research practice regards inertia, misunderstandings, and, in some cases, resistance from the existing disciplinary practices. These barriers are certainly pivotal, given the recent growth of transdisciplinary research practices relative to the long-time history of modern science. However, an important part is also related to a set of new challenges regarding the innovative nature of the collective action and decision-making arrangements required to conduct transdisciplinary research.

As documented in the general scholarly literature on knowledge commons (Benkler, 2008; Frischmann et al., 2014), effective collective action to build the scientific knowledge commons results from action at two main levels, which are also present in other forms of collective action for the decentralized provision of collective goods:

1 The first level of action is situated at the community, project, or network level (comprising research groups, research consortia, and larger research networks). At this level, scholars underline two important mechanisms that contribute to fostering decentralized collective action:

   a. The collective action agreements to guarantee the contribution of all participants to common research purposes
   b. The development of common societal value perspectives that allows for building trust, strengthening intrinsic motivations to take part in the commons, and facilitating coordinated action.

2 The second level is the consolidation of the decentralized knowledge commons in larger organizational architectures through a supportive institutional environment. As the collective action for collaborative research mainly results from action on a decentralized basis (the first level), the institutional environment does not have a "steering" or "controlling" role but mainly assumes an enabling role of decentralized dynamics. The latter can be fostered through capacity building and knowledge exchange networks.

The two levels of decentralized collective action and an enabling institutional environment are also present in the case of the transdisciplinary knowledge commons. Based on the action strategies at these two levels, one can distinguish three categories of hurdles that have to be overcome in the specific case of transdisciplinary research:

1 *The lack of contribution to common boundary-crossing research purposes*

The organization of collective action to work around common purposes is hampered by the presence of individuals with heterogeneous knowledge interests who might use the transdisciplinary process instrumentally to foster their own knowledge interests. Indeed, disciplinary researchers might use the transdisciplinary research environment merely to facilitate access to new field research within their disciplinary research agenda, or societal actors might be mainly interested in advocacy for pre-given advocacy positions.

2 *The fragmentation in an unstructured diversity of values perspectives*

The lack of relatively homogeneous societal values requires additional mechanisms to reach mutual understanding and forms of collaboration among research partners. These mechanisms are not meant to reach a consensus but to use diversity in a structured way as an asset for an improved understanding of the social possibilities of change in interdependent social and ecological systems.

3 *The isolation of many context-specific and situated research partnerships*

Innovative institutional mechanisms must be developed to bridge the many niche networks of tailor-made partnerships and foster an enabling environment of common teaching, training, and research resources for transdisciplinary research. Overcoming small niche approaches is key if researchers and societal actors aim to reach a more general understanding of system interdependencies and desirable system orientations in specific domains of sustainability transformations and types of collaborative governance arrangements.

The next sections will briefly review each of these challenges and present some ways to overcome them, as per the literature.

2.1.1 The curse of instrumentalization of the research partnership

A first set of collective action failures is related to the proneness of research partners to pursue only their own knowledge interests or habitual ways of working instead of embedding their work within a common research endeavor. This failure was, for instance, clearly identified in early experiences with transdisciplinary research on environmental risk assessment, where societal actors were mobilized in a purely instrumental way to provide increased legitimacy to expert-led knowledge generation.

According to the seminal analysis by Daniel Fiorino, such an instrumental role of stakeholder involvement in risk assessment mainly served to make the decisions based on research results more legitimate to the general public (Fiorino, 1990). Indeed, as per Fiorino (ibid), in the early 1990s, research institutions working on environmental risks were confronted with a crisis of confidence, as the lay public was increasingly unwilling to delegate decisions to experts and administrative authorities. In response, societal actors were included in risk assessment procedures to restore confidence by acknowledging societal actors' value perspectives in the expert-led assessments and reducing the probability of error through additional inputs of data and information.

More generally, in a situation of instrumental mobilization of societal actors' knowledge, the latter provides additional information or advice to a research team, but the researchers judge if these contributions are relevant or useful within their pre-defined research protocol (Mobjörk, 2010). From the point of view of disciplinary and expert-led science, the instrumental use of contextual information from societal actors is not necessarily a problem if such use is intended by and based on clear agreements among the parties. Indeed, in situations where the aim is to provide technical knowledge on system components, and the knowledge is relatively independent of specific path-dependent features and societal value choices, science can operate in a relatively autonomous sphere from the input of societal actors. In these cases, several instrumental roles may contribute to the quality of the research process, such as providing extra technical information and know-how from practice or contributing to research dissemination by translating the research results to the specific needs of certain social groups.

Importantly, even the case of instrumental participation requires transparent prior agreements with societal actors and should be distinguished from window-dressing forms of participation, where societal actors are manipulated such that researchers can more easily obtain data and information or legitimize their funding demands. A positive case in point for such transparency requirements is the international agreement on prior informed consent of indigenous and local communities in research projects on the discovery of new drugs or plant varieties for agriculture (Dedeurwaerdere et al., 2016). In other commendatory cases, such as in collaborative research projects funded by national or international research bodies, societal actors are involved in formal consultative bodies or even in the consortia agreements such that their contribution is explicitly acknowledged in the overall research process (Ahrweiler et al., 2019). Obviously, these kinds of agreements may also be important in transdisciplinary research—especially if certain societal actors are mobilized in some project components for instrumental purposes, for example, when gathering contextual information to improve the overall quality of the research outputs.

However, the involvement of societal actors in transdisciplinary partnership research is substantially different from the instrumental mobilization of contextual knowledge. The main difference with the instrumental role is that, for those parts of the research that are co-produced, societal actors contribute as substantively to the design of the research framework and the interpretation of the results as scientific researchers. The reasons for such substantive co-production are multiple. For instance, as discussed in one of the case studies in Chapter 3 regarding a living lab for the renovation of the historical city center of Cahors in Southern France, the knowledge of old building techniques by local craftsmen was essential to co-develop a research protocol for designing locally adapted bio-based materials (see the Cahors living lab project, Section 3.2.1.2). In another case to be discussed, the implementation of a vaccination campaign in Chad, researchers and nomadic pastoralists co-designed a joint human and animal vaccination campaign. This collaboration mobilized the knowledge gained from anthropological field research on the traditional communities' integrated approach to human and animal health and livestock holders' knowledge about the efficacy of the livestock vaccination campaigns (see the Chad healthcare delivery project, Section 4.3.4). In both these examples, the combination of laboratory research and joint experimentation in real-world situations allowed for integrating scientific knowledge with detailed practitioners' knowledge of technical know-how within a co-designed research framework.

2.1.2 The pitfalls of unstructured pluralism of societal values

The first governance failure shows the consequences of unequal contributions of research partners to the commonly agreed research purpose. However, successful and effective knowledge co-production also depends on mutual understanding among societal actors and scientific researchers on the specific value-laden perspectives on sustainability transformation pathways. Indeed, research partners might agree on the division of labor to address the common research questions but fail to organize a discussion on how to resolve the difference in opinion on the sustainability values used to assess the social desirability of the envisioned transformation pathways or the contextual validity of the research outcomes (Russel, 2010).

In practice, sustainability values can be highly diverse. Indeed, societal actors and researchers might each envision different ways to create synergies and co-benefits among the interrelated sustainability goals, inducing a plurality of distinct transformation pathways considered socially legitimate and relevant by the project partners (Fam and O'Rourke, 2020). Thus, to allow for effective coordination among the project partners in this situation, a minimum level of mutual understanding is required that acknowledges the diversity and employs this diversity to explore areas where converging value perspectives or common action strategies can be formulated.

Beyond the minimum level, research partners might strive for stronger forms of partial convergence around core sustainability values, depending on the history of collaboration and the perceived need for enhanced coordination to tackle the given problem situation. To designate the failure of reaching a situation of minimum mutual understanding, or of reaching the desired level of partial convergence on core sustainability values, some scholars refer to this second governance failure as "unstructured pluralism." As such, unstructured pluralism refers to a situation where a more advanced stage of social learning on sustainability values is required to address coordination needs among partners with highly diverse heterogeneous values (Spash, 2012; Popa et al., 2015).

An example of the lack of social learning in each of the core sustainability value perspectives around planetary boundaries, environmental justice, and environmental citizenship can give an initial insight into the possible consequences of the failure to structure these societal values.

For instance, regarding the planetary boundaries, in a vast five-year multi-stakeholder research project, researchers and societal actors collaborated on understanding waste management transitions in Flanders, Belgium, without concluding the research project given value disagreements (Paredis, 2011). In this case, the partners discovered quite late in the project (the last year out of five) that one group understood waste management transition as the creation of a market for reused and recycled materials, while the other aimed for reducing waste-intensive consumption practices and, thus, waste production. In this case, despite the successful knowledge integration among different societal actors, the project partners used this knowledge to understand and promote two disjointed pathways. Given these disagreements, one of the societal actor partners decided to leave the project consortium before penning the conclusion.

A second example regarding the Chad healthcare delivery project to be discussed in Chapter 4 (see Section 4.3.4) shows the challenge of a large-scale project consortium to address environmental justice issues. In this long-term research project on healthcare delivery to nomadic pastoralists in Chad, the project researchers initially failed to recognize the livelihood concerns of the pastoralist community (Bergmann et al., 2012, ch. 3; Hirsch Hadorn et al., 2008, ch. 17). This project was set up after observing that the nomadic pastoralists did not visit the state-organized local health centers. In this case, healthcare services were organized in a form that the nomads did not use, given a different cultural understanding of the organization of healthcare; hence, in practice, most of them were excluded from primary social services. As analyzed in depth in Chapter 4, it is only through partial convergence around a set of values addressing both animal and human health that the research team could set up a coordinated research approach with the pastoralists. On this basis, the program adopted a so-called one-health approach to the delivery of health services, which organizes healthcare delivery for humans and livestock in an integrated manner.

Further, the lack of clarification of environmental justice concerns of local communities in research partnerships might also be related to issues of process fairness. A telling illustration of such a situation is the transdisciplinary research on the improvement of education and access to basic social services among an immigrant population in Albuquerque, United States (Goodkind et al., 2011). In that research project, researchers evaluated the contribution of a godfathering program to the improvement of the situation of the immigrant population. However, when selecting individuals to participate in this action research project, some individuals declined to participate, as they estimated that other members of the community should first be involved and benefit from the godfathering, even if they were not originally part of the group targeted through the research protocol. Overall, the community members highlighted the lack of dialogue in the selection process of possible participants in the action research program. In response, the research team adapted the sampling procedure to these requirements of process fairness by better integrating community members in organizing the data gathering process.

2.1.3 Beyond small niche networks for boundary-crossing research

The first two governance failures of instrumentalization of the knowledge generation process and the failure of unstructured pluralism are situated at the project level. Nonetheless, to successfully build transdisciplinary knowledge commons on sustainability challenges, there is also a need to look beyond the project level. Indeed, without additional institutional efforts, project partners may remain in small niche networks around practical or theoretical problem-solving on highly specific research issues.

The small niche networks for transdisciplinary research, although already useful for addressing selected research puzzles that cannot appropriately dealt with through disciplinary methods, may fail to contribute to reliable and comprehensive transdisciplinary research commons on sustainability transformations. Indeed, if limited to small niche networks, these research projects do not address some important objectives that are part of the more general purposes of scientific research (Singleton and Straits, 2005; Willis, 2007). First, small niche projects lack a more general perspective on thematic areas of sustainability transformations and fail to contribute to a more generic understanding of human and natural interdependencies. Second, they lack the means to verify the validity of research results and research approaches in other similar contexts of sustainability challenges. Further, they do not contribute to building more generic approaches to knowledge co-production and social learning that can be used in a broader set of problem situations.

Therefore, to strengthen the overall scientific knowledge base and methodological approach that are relevant for addressing a broad diversity of sustainability issues in society-wide transformations, the small niche projects must be embedded in a larger institutional ecosystem of boundary-crossing research projects. In the context of transdisciplinary research, characterized by a heterogeneous set of highly diverse boundary-crossing projects, moving beyond small niche projects might be quite challenging. Various mechanisms to address this challenge to be discussed in more detail throughout this book include the organization of knowledge exchange in hybrid knowledge networks, social networking for identifying potential opportunities for knowledge co-production with societal actors, and training for the building of transdisciplinary research competences.

2.2   Theoretical building blocks from the multi-level approach to governing scientific research commons

This section further develops the multi-level approach for overcoming the identified collective action failures. Indeed, as underlined more generally by scholars of knowledge commons, to address the possible collective failures, appropriate strategies at, at least, two main levels (the level of decentralized collective action and the enabling institutional environment) are necessary (Ostrom, 2005, pp. 99–133).

Based on this basic model, this book will analyze three core sets of strategies for the organizational and institutional design of transdisciplinary knowledge co-production. These three strategies and the related research questions will be addressed.

First, two core strategies at the level of decentralized collective action

1   Decentralized collaborative governance strategies at the research community level (research groups, consortia, and larger research networks)

   • Analysis of the collaboration mechanisms for knowledge co-production (knowledge integration, co-management of the knowledge co-production, and co-construction of the research design)

2   Decentralized social learning mechanisms at the research community level

   • Analysis of the mechanisms of social learning over sustainability values in knowledge co-production

Second, a third strategy at the level of the enabling institutional environment

3 Enabling and consolidating the decentralized dynamics through a supportive institutional environment

- Analysis of the integration of the boundary-crossing project networks into broader enabling networks for transdisciplinary research

Given the historical importance of the scholarship on collective action based on the rational actor perspective, this chapter will introduce these various strategies from the perspective of the so-called second-generation theory of collective action (Ostrom, 1998). This perspective helps to introduce a simplified model of the two-level approach, which will then be gradually enriched and broadened in the specific chapters dedicated to each of the collective action strategies and mechanisms.

The proposed model does not address the higher level of the overarching institutions of research policy that impact the choices that can be made in universities and research organizations for building the enabling environments and organizing transdisciplinary project work. This does not mean that this overarching higher level is not important, as clearly shown in the systematic review of multi-level institutional analysis by Hollingsworth (2000). However, to address the issues of reform of research policy, a deeper understanding of the design requirements at the level of the organization of boundary-crossing research projects and the level of the enabling environment in research organizations is first required. Except for some short indications in Chapter 5, the analysis of governance and institutional design in this book will therefore mainly focus on the levels of the project organization and the enabling institutional environment at institutions of higher education.

2.2.1 Organizing collaboration mechanisms for knowledge co-production

Based on the similarities of the collective action challenges between natural resource and knowledge commons, scholars have adopted a broad approach to community-produced collective goods. From a theoretical perspective, commons can be defined as resources that are jointly used and managed by groups of varying sizes and interests (Hess and Ostrom, 2007, p. 5). This approach also applies to the case of transdisciplinary knowledge co-production, where the research partners collaborate in the production, use, and dissemination of usable knowledge on specific sustainability transformation pathways.

The previous section highlighted an important collective action failure in the case of transdisciplinary knowledge commons, which is the instrumentalization of the partnership for one's research purposes. This failure is related to the challenge of overcoming the tendency of research partners to follow their own disciplinary or practical knowledge interests instead of contributing their efforts and resources to solving common boundary-crossing research questions.

This collective action failure of common knowledge production, which may induce under-provision of the common good, is a feature that is also somewhat present in interdisciplinary research consortia. In the case of interdisciplinary consortia, neglecting to invest time and resources in the common interdisciplinary research questions is in part related to the lack of incentives to produce knowledge beyond disciplinary interests. Two main hurdles can be mentioned. First, the expected contributions to the common interdisciplinary research framework do not necessarily contribute to the state of the art in the disciplinary specialization, and, second, they do not always fit the specialized disciplinary standards for data gathering.

This so-called under-provision is an important collective action challenge recognized in the broader scholarship on the building of knowledge commons in large-scale collaborative research. Michael Madison highlights the latter in the case studies of the companion volume on *Governing Knowledge Commons* (Frischmann et al., 2014). As stated by Madison, without proper governance mechanisms, producers of knowledge resources "will fail to invest in creating new goods or in preserving them, either on their own or in combination with others, because of uncertain[ty] [in] their ability (either individually or collectively) to earn returns that justify the investment" (Madison, 2014, p. 219).

Hence, to address these problems in interdisciplinary research collaborations, researchers have set up various governance mechanisms to foster collective action around standards of open science, research accreditation, and joint efforts in common quality management. For instance, Yochai Benkler shows in his landmark work on "the power of networks" how scientists in interdisciplinary fields of research follow common standards of open science and joint quality standards by participating in various social networks at scholarly conferences and expert groups (Benkler, 2008). Another leading political economy scholar of the historical emergence of the science commons, Joel Mokyr, highlights the crucial role of formal and informal peer review practices as a tool for collective quality management ever since the emergence of the modern scientific societies in the 17th and 18th centuries (Mokyr, 2011).

Nevertheless, regarding the transdisciplinary research commons, these governance mechanisms are not sufficient to build an effective knowledge commons. Indeed, regarding transdisciplinary research projects, a single scientist does not operate within a larger community, as in the case of disciplines or interdisciplinary fields of research. Rather, they are involved in a set of different research projects, each of which comprises members of distinct disciplinary communities and societal actor groups.

For instance, a researcher on the transition toward sustainable food systems may collaborate in one project with health professionals and researchers in bio-medical and nutrition sciences; in another project, they may collaborate with agronomists and economists, and in yet another project, with a representative of the local municipality and a political scientist. Each project mobilizes different combinations of disciplinary and practical knowledge that require building agreements on the contribution of partners with different knowledge interests to the common knowledge co-production process.

A centralized, top-down solution to this challenge is unlikely to provide sufficient guarantees to ensure the collaboration of all partners to contribute to common research endeavors. For instance, research-funding bodies may require evidence for effective collaboration with societal actors in knowledge production as a condition for the allocation of funding. However, as shown in comparative analyses of climate change research projects by de Jong et al. (2016), such contractual obligations may attract projects that involve societal actors as window dressing, assigning them a role while not necessarily giving them influence. It forms part of the general issues with participation, as highlighted by Sherry Arnstein in her classic work on citizen involvement in planning processes in the United States: "There is a critical difference between going through the empty ritual of participation and having the real power needed to affect the outcome of the process" (Arnstein, 1969, p. 216).

As per de Jong et al. (2016), true participation in joint knowledge generation requires more direct co-management by the participating scientists and societal actors of the various aspects of the research process, similar to the co-management arrangements to overcome collective action problems in the natural resource commons. For instance, scientific researchers and societal actors as project partners can collaborate on the joint definition of research goals and core research questions. Regarding research design, both partners can make valuable contributions to the selection of cases and data sources. During the research, they may contribute data that would otherwise be challenging to obtain and provide access to facilities and study sites. In communicating research results, their involvement may help to consider local contexts and communicate research results clearly. Ideally, all research partners should play a role in each phase of the process, as the impact on the production of usable knowledge has been shown to increase with the number of phases in which they have a role (Pohl and Hirsch Hadorn, 2007; Peer and Stoeglehner, 2013).

Notably, scholars of transdisciplinary research distinguish different degrees of involvement in the co-management of the knowledge co-production process. This involvement can be quite strong, as in the case of co-decision-making in a common governing board or joint supervision by scientific researchers and societal actors of the Ph.D. research fellows of the project. It can also rely on weaker forms, such as through specific collaborations on agreed-upon real-world test cases or agreements for joint involvement in data gathering. Per the perception of the danger of a lack of dedication of time and resources to the common endeavor, the partners might decide to invest in stronger (thus, more demanding) or weaker and less demanding forms of co-management.

In some cases, when the initial motivations of all partners to address a common research question are strong, they may consider that the risk of instrumentalization is not high. For instance, in a well-documented successful large-scale transdisciplinary research project on community health approaches in the province of North Karelia, Finland, there was a clear intrinsic motivation of all partners to contribute knowledge to understanding the interdependencies between environmental factors, change in social practices, and individual behavior and health outcomes (Puska et al., 2009). In such cases, the co-management processes may be lightweight. In this case, the co-management process was mainly organized around specific tasks for joint data gathering on the common research issues and joint analysis of the research results.

When the risk of instrumentalization is high, as in the case of the participation of disenfranchised social groups, research partners are likely to make stronger investments in co-managing various components of the research process. One prominent example of such a situation of strong power differentials will be discussed in Chapter 4, regarding the project co-led by ATD Quart Monde on food assistance in Brussels, Belgium. In this case, the research partners adopted a strong co-decision-making approach called "merging of knowledge," developed by the non-profit association ATD Quart Monde. It is used for building transdisciplinary research partnerships to overcome situations of extreme poverty. In this methodology, given the important power differentials, persons living in poverty are involved at all stages through co-decision on the question to be addressed, joint data gathering, permanent discussion and adjustment on the research methods to be chosen, and common writing of the research outputs. By involving persons living in poverty as "situational experts," this project contributed to a more multi-dimensional approach to food assistance, in particular by underlining the importance of respect for the dignity of each recipient of food assistance as a key "soft" value that is often not at the heart of poverty research.

Overall, the main lesson of the literature on collective action for investment in common knowledge production in transdisciplinary research is the importance of the collaboration of scientific researchers and societal actors in the governance of the research process. As analyzed in depth in Chapter 3, this collaboration process goes beyond the conventional stage of knowledge integration between science and practice. The collaboration also includes the co-management of various steps of the co-production process and the active involvement in research co-design (Lang et al., 2012; Norström et al., 2020). Per the perceived danger of instrumentalization, the research partners may decide to invest more time and resources in the deliberation on one or several of these aspects of the collaboration process.

2.2.2   Social learning on the sustainability values

The organizational perspective on the partnership among scientific researchers and societal actors is only one lens through which one can approach the challenges of collaborative governance of the research process. A second important aspect that contributes to the effective governance of the commons is the mutual learning on partially convergent or at least mutually compatible societal values perspectives. As shown in several review papers on knowledge integration by leading scholars in sustainability research, social learning that seeks to reach mutual understanding on a diversity of societal values plays a key role in successful transdisciplinary knowledge co-production (Pohl et al., 2021).

In her later work during the mid-1990s, Ostrom (1998) developed the role of convergence around societal values in contributing to in-depth collective action. For instance, in the review paper on the "Second generation theory of collection action," Ostrom (ibid) shows how communities that develop mutual learning around societal values successfully decrease the costs (regarding time, organizational means, and material resources) invested in organizing coordination among the community members. Indeed, these societal values create patterns of behavior that, if recognized by the other members, allow for anticipating behavior and common action strategies around the agreed-upon rules more effectively. In the case of the community management of natural resource commons analyzed by Ostrom (1990), societal values evolve through two types of mechanisms. First, communities gradually adopted societal values through a process of trial-and-error experimentation throughout the history. Second, when societal values became more diverse, they further evolved through processes of public deliberation to impartially assess their respective validity through rational argumentation.

This second type of evolution of societal values through deliberation is most relevant to the case of transdisciplinary research partnerships. Indeed, regarding transdisciplinary research commons, the role of deliberation among the research partners is likely to be crucial, as the actor networks are highly heterogeneous and changing. As will be discussed in depth in Chapter 4, this deliberation on societal values among the project partners can strive to reach stronger or weaker forms of partial convergence over key sustainability values. The latter hinges on the perceived need for convergence—which depends on the complexity of the coordination needs among the project partners— and on the history of trust building through previous collaborations.

For instance, convergence among societal values can be absent at the beginning of a project amid strong conflicting interests. In such cases, partners may decide to focus first on creating the conditions for mutual understanding of the legitimate and relevant perspectives of the various project partners. In other situations, the partnership may start with high levels of mutual understanding, but the addressed sustainability transformations may nevertheless require identifying the areas of convergence on societal values for organizing coordinated action. In the latter case, the social learning process may strive to identify such areas of convergence and clarify the remaining areas of divergence. These different mechanisms will be analyzed in depth in Chapter 4.

2.2.3 Collaborative platforms for enabling the integration of polycentric knowledge networks

The second level of collective action strategies reaches beyond the decentralized strategies at the project level to the building of larger organizational architectures for enabling transdisciplinary research. As argued, to build a more encompassing knowledge base on sustainable interdependent social and ecological system dynamics, an appropriate institutional environment is required to enable the building of generic capacities for transdisciplinary research.

The challenge of fostering interactions among a broad diversity of knowledge co-production activities, beyond the individual boundary-crossing project networks, shows many similarities to the general idea of building a polycentric network of commons in Elinor Ostrom's analysis. According to Ostrom (2010), beyond the level of specific commons-based initiatives, a major governance feature of successful and enduring commons is their embedding in larger polycentric networks. These networks provide a higher level of integration among the local commons that contributes to their long-term successful operation through various collaborative arrangements. As shown in the broader research on network governance (Sørensen and Torfing, 2007), such institutional arrangements can be limited to only parts of the overall network, such as the creation of network clusters for the sharing of knowledge, or be more generic, such as through the building of generic competences for collaboration and co-management.

Regarding transdisciplinary research, the challenge is to build capacities for researchers and societal actors to conduct transdisciplinary research in highly diverse problem contexts involving different combinations of conceptual approaches and partners with different knowledge backgrounds. Therefore, the enabling institutional environment must create incentives for research partners to look beyond their specialized project networks and to build bridges with other field-specific knowledge co-production processes.

For instance, the review papers by Veronica Boix-Mansilla et al. (2016) on interdisciplinary collaborations and the review paper by Christian Pohl et al. (2021) on transdisciplinary research underline the importance of such boundary-crossing institutional enabling mechanisms. First, they underline the importance of decentralized learning by research partners across hybrid boundary-crossing initiatives through the creation of so-called trading zones or boundary objects (Boix-Mansilla et al., 2016, p. 573; Pohl et al., 2021, p. 23). These spaces for decentralized learning cluster participants around overlapping research activities in a way that is "plastic enough to be interpreted differently by relevant actors yet robust enough to maintain . . . unity across contexts" (Boix-Mansilla et al., 2016, p. 580). Further, participation in these bridging networks promotes the acquisition of transdisciplinary research competences via mastering a diversity of socio-ecological research methods and frameworks that can be used to analyze a broad set of context-specific transformation pathways.

Despite the similarities between the various enabling mechanisms for polycentric networking in the cases of natural resource commons and transdisciplinary knowledge commons, it is important to highlight an important difference between these two cases. Natural resource commons addresses communities that manage well-identified natural resource systems with rather homogeneous shared societal values that evolved gradually to adapt resource management strategies to local contexts. Regarding transdisciplinary research projects, the definition of the socio-ecological system is not identified in advance, as it strongly depends on the problem framing, and societal values tend to be highly heterogeneous among the project partners.

Further, to apply the polycentric network concept developed by Ostrom and other scholars of network-based governance to the case of transdisciplinary research commons, the collaboration agreements must involve a strong degree of active deliberation on the network boundaries, the co-construction of the topics to be addressed, and the value perspectives to be included. Therefore, the various proposed network-bridging and competence-building activities must also be actively co-constructed with both societal actors and scientific researchers. As will be discussed in-depth in Chapter 5, the latter can be implemented via practicing interdisciplinary and transdisciplinary research co-design in the teaching of transdisciplinary methods, the involvement of societal actors in identifying potential research topics or creating thematic clusters for the sharing of knowledge.

2.3 Promoting synergies among various styles of transdisciplinary research practice

The multi-level analysis of collective action for contributing to knowledge commons shows that the building of transdisciplinary research commons relies on a distinct set of design principles. These design principles are different from the case of specialized disciplinary research commons, as they introduce new standards of evidence, such as the integration of societal actor knowledge in the co-construction of research design and social learning on societal values at the project level. Likewise, at the level of the supporting institutional environment, the accent is more on the development of capacities for boundary-crossing work and network-bridging instead of the consolidation of research results around relatively consistent common disciplinary concepts and methodological approaches.

As shown in the discussion of three main strategies to overcome collective action failures, transdisciplinary scholars mobilize a variety of mechanisms to ensure the effective contribution of all research partners to knowledge co-production. In theory, research projects that combine each of these strategies show the highest chance of effective co-production of usable knowledge on sustainability transformations. In practice, however, given limits of resources or different initial experiences among the project partners, projects often focus on one of the strategies or a combination of strategies deemed most relevant for improving upon the problem situation.

The choice of these strategies and mechanisms is influenced in large part by a broader understanding of the relationship between knowledge generation in transdisciplinary research projects and the contribution to solving sustainability issues in interdependent socio-ecological systems. In this context, based on a literature review and an analysis of a representative set of 31 transdisciplinary research projects at their research institute, Flurina Schneider and her colleagues identified three main pathways of impact generation (Schneider et al., 2019) (see Figure 2.1).

The most well-known pathway is rooted in the assumption that transdisciplinary co-production of knowledge is a cognitive process leading to new knowledge, understanding, and propositions that can subsequently be used

FIGURE 2.1 Research styles within transdisciplinary research contributing to sustainability transformations

Figure by the author, based on an adaptation of theoretical concepts developed in Schneider et al. (2019).

to inform societal actors for decision-making. As stated by Schneider et al. (2019), in this pathway, the generated knowledge is seen as "a substance to be transferred from the project to other people," where it can trigger action (ibid, p. 29).

The project review by Schneider et al. (2019) identified two other important understandings of impact pathways that play a role in transdisciplinary research practices. The second pathway is the generation of societal impact by promoting capacities for collaborative governance among research partners with heterogeneous societal values. In this understanding, transdisciplinary knowledge is "conceived as the emergent property of interactions and is situated in coordinated actions rather than as a substance that can be removed from the social context where it was created" (ibid, p. 30). The third pathway focuses on the building of individual competences for boundary-crossing analysis via transformative educational practices or shared learning in communities of practice (ibid, p. 31). The research partners can use the acquired competences in various research projects or decision-making in societal practices.

Given these different understandings of the impact pathways, the spread of transdisciplinary research practices does not induce a well-identifiable and unified new research practice. Rather, researchers developed different approaches and research traditions within the enterprise of transdisciplinary research. As in the case of disciplinary research commons, these different approaches and research traditions can be understood as different *research styles*.* Following the historical epistemology approach of Ian Hacking (2012), research styles are characterized by common problem interests and approaches to tackle research problems. That is, via the differentiation in different research styles, the key organizing concepts of transdisciplinary sustainability science (interdisciplinary analysis of interdependent social and ecological dynamics and partnership research with societal actors) yield various research traditions with interrelated but distinct research interests (Sciortino, 2017).

Obviously, the various collective action challenges play a role in each of the three research styles identified by Schneider et al. (2019). However, some challenges are more critical in certain research styles than others. Therefore, in the subsequent chapters, we will analyze each of the collective action challenges in the context of one research style (see Figure 2.2).

First, as noted, the most well-known research style is related to the production of usable knowledge outputs that can subsequently be transferred to support societal actors in decision-making. Moreover, this research style is formulated in one of the most cited papers in the field (Lang et al., 2012), which defines transdisciplinary research as a "reflexive, integrative, method-driven scientific principle aiming at the solution or the transition of societal problems and concurrently of related scientific problems by differentiating

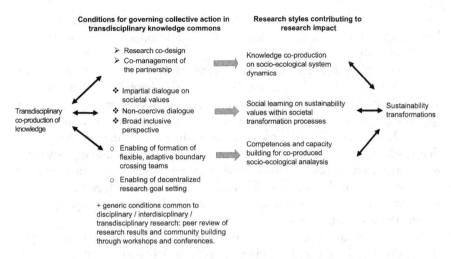

FIGURE 2.2   Key conditions for governing collective action in each of the three styles of transdisciplinary research practice. The detailed analysis of each condition is the subject of Chapters 3, 4 and 5.

and integrating knowledge from various scientific and societal bodies of knowledge" (ibid, p. 27). In particular, as highlighted by many scholars, understanding issues and solving problems in the practical-life world of societal actors through transdisciplinary research requires matching the knowledge co-knowledge process with legitimate actors' purposes in the problem field and the available real-world options for change. Therefore, transdisciplinary research in this perspective must integrate three main types of knowledge: (1) systems knowledge, (2) target knowledge (regarding the purposes of social practices), and (3) transformation knowledge (regarding the real-world options for change) (Hirsch Hadorn et al., 2008, p. 28; Lang et al., 2012, p. 26; Schneider et al., 2019, p. 29; Karrasch et al., 2022).

Although researchers can encounter a diverse set of governance challenges, a core collective action challenge to tackle in this first research style is the tendency toward the instrumentalization of the usable knowledge focus. As noted in the analysis in this chapter, research partners can instrumentalize the common endeavor for their scientific or advocacy purposes without dedicating time and resources to co-producing a common problem understanding, research approach, and methodological framework. Disciplinary researchers may be confronted with different methodological requirements for field research, laboratory work, or modeling. Societal actors may also have different priorities when mobilizing resources for promoting action strategies that address different aspects of desirable sustainability transformations. In this context, organizing deliberation throughout the research process to align the partners around a common research design is crucial to provide usable knowledge on feasible and scientifically reliable options for society-wide transformations.

The overall objective of the first style of transdisciplinary research practice is to produce scientifically reliable and usable knowledge that matches, at best, the legitimate and most relevant sustainability value perspectives in the specific problem area. Although social learning on sustainability values occurs during such research projects, the main focus in the analysis of this first research style is on collective action for matching the usable knowledge to the given set of sustainability values in the problem area. An important presupposition of the analysis of this first style of research is the existence of a sufficient level of mutual understanding of the given value perspectives among the research partners.

When the mutual understanding is insufficient, the collaboration between the actors may be seriously hampered and research partners may decide to focus the research partnership in the first instance on improving this mutual understanding as a condition of fruitful collaboration before embarking upon usable knowledge production. The second style of research practice identified by Schneider et al. (2019) addresses this second challenge by organizing a "social learning process that enhances the participants' collective agency and potential for joint action toward sustainability" (ibid p. 30). In this understanding of transdisciplinary research practice, one major collective action challenge is organizing deliberation to foster mutual understanding among the project partners on sustainability values. An important goal of this second style therefore is to overcome the collective action problems regarding the unstructured diversity of societal value perspectives. As noted, such unstructured diversity may lead to fragmentation or the unreflective uptake of certain normative orientations based on path-dependent habits (potentially perpetuating existing rent-seeking behavior). The main issue is the establishment of mutual understanding through a process of impartial and inclusive dialogue, where the societal value positions are submitted to public argumentation and critical deconstruction of ideology and dominant knowledge structures.

Finally, the research styles directed toward usable knowledge production and social learning within societal transformation processes can benefit from a supportive institutional environment. Such an environment is especially important to further disseminate transdisciplinary practices beyond small niche projects. Important features of this institutional capacity building for transdisciplinary research can also be the specific target of research projects, for instance, via organizing competence building or knowledge exchange on research in different situations of sustainability transformations. This third concern is addressed in part through the third research style identified by Schneider et al. (ibid), directed toward building transdisciplinary research competences.

As stated by Schneider et al. (ibid, p. 31), the underlying assumption in this third style of research practices is that when research partners "engage in transdisciplinary work, including joint experimentation, learning, and self-reflection, they develop competences (knowledge, skills, values, and attitudes) that enable them to better tackle sustainability challenges and opportunities in their life and work." Obviously, the example of transdisciplinary teaching, where students must design and implement a partnership research project (e.g., as a part of their master thesis) is a good case in point of such competence-building research practices.

In the analysis in Chapter 5, this third research style will be considered more broadly as designating transdisciplinary research practices that contribute to various kinds of capacity building in the institutional environment. Competence building is one of the mechanisms; other enabling mechanisms to be considered include research practices to consolidate knowledge, such as meta-research for a better understanding of certain transdisciplinary process features and exploratory research projects or workshops to connect interested actors and initiate new co-production or social learning processes. Regarding the collective action problems discussed, these practices specifically presuppose the formation of integrated polycentric networks that can support research activities in a larger ecosystem of boundary-crossing research and knowledge exchanges.

As noted from this short outline, each of the subsequent chapters will address the collective action challenges in the context of one style of transdisciplinary research practice, respectively organized around one aspect of the impact pathways of transdisciplinary research. As mentioned, in practice however, research partners often combine various aspects of the research styles to organize successful transdisciplinary research. The latter can be the case within a given project or through a sequence of different projects that build upon the outcomes of the previous project work. Therefore, the analysis of the different research styles must be considered in the context of a broader research ecosystem, where, through the creation of synergies and interactions among research teams involved in various transdisciplinary research practices, the different knowledge co-production, social learning, and institutional capacity-building challenges can be successfully addressed.

References

Ahrweiler, P., Gilbert, N., Schrempf, B., Grimpe, B. and Jirotka, M. (2019). The role of civil society organisations in European responsible research and innovation. *Journal of Responsible Innovation*, 6(1), 25–49.

Arnstein, S. R. (1969). A ladder of citizen participation. *Journal of the American Institute of Planners*, 35(4), 216–224.

Benkler, Y. (2008). *The wealth of networks*. New Haven, CT: Yale University Press.

Benkler, Y. and Nissenbaum, H. (2006). Commons-based peer production and virtue. *Journal of Political Philosophy*, *14*(4), 394–419.

Bergmann, M., Jahn, T., Knobloch, T., Krohn, W., Pohl, C. and Schramm, E. (2012). *Methods for transdisciplinary research: A primer for practice*. Frankfurt: Campus Verlag.

Boix-Mansilla, V., Lamont, M. and Sato, K. (2016). Shared cognitive—emotional—interactional platforms: Markers and conditions for successful interdisciplinary collaborations. *Science, Technology and Human Values*, *41*(4), 571–612.

Dedeurwaerdere, T., Melindi-Ghidi, P. and Broggiato, A. (2016). Global scientific research commons under the Nagoya Protocol: Towards a collaborative economy model for the sharing of basic research assets. *Environmental Science and Policy*, *55*, 1–10.

de Jong, S. P., Wardenaar, T. and Horlings, E. (2016). Exploring the promises of transdisciplinary research: A quantitative study of two climate research programmes. *Research Policy*, *45*(7), 1397–1409.

Fam, D. and O'Rourke, M. (Eds.). (2020). *Interdisciplinary and transdisciplinary failures: Lessons learned from cautionary tales*. Abingdon: Routledge.

Fiorino, D. J. (1990). Citizen participation and environmental risk: A survey of institutional mechanisms. *Science, Technology and Human Values*, *15*(2), 226–243.

Fleck, L. (1979 [1935]). *Genesis and development of a scientific fact*. Chicago: The University of Chicago Press.

Frischmann, B. M., Madison, M. and Strandburg, K. (Eds.). (2014). *Governing knowledge commons*. Oxford: Oxford University Press.

Goodkind, J. R., Githinji, A. and Isakson, B. (2011). Reducing health disparities experienced by Refugees Resettled in Urban areas: A community-based transdisciplinary intervention model. In M. Kirst et al. (Eds.), *Converging disciplines: A transdisciplinary research approach to urban health problems* (pp. 41–55). New York; Dordrecht; Heidelberg; London: Springer Science and Business Media.

Hacking, I. (2012). Language, truth and reason' 30 years later. *Studies in History and Philosophy of Science*, *43*(4), 599–609.

Hess, C. and Ostrom, E. (Eds.). (2007). *Understanding knowledge as a commons: From theory to practice*. Cambridge MA: MIT Press.

Hirsch Hadorn, G., Hoffmann-Riem, H., Biber-Klemm, S., Grossenbacher-Mansuy, W., Joye, D., Pohl, C., . . . and Zemp, E. (Eds.). (2008). *Handbook of transdisciplinary research*. Dordrecht: Springer.

Hollingsworth, J. R. (2000). Doing institutional analysis: Implications for the study of innovations. *Review of International Political Economy*, *7*(4), 595–644.

Jacobs, J. A. (2017). The need for disciplines in the modern research university. In R. Frodeman, J. T. Klein and R. Pacheco (Eds.), *The Oxford handbook of interdisciplinarity* (pp. 35–39). Oxford: Oxford University Press.

Karrasch, L., Grothmann, T., Michel, T. A., Wesselow, M., Wolter, H., Unger, A., . . . and Siebenhüner, B. (2022). Integrating knowledge within and between knowledge types in transdisciplinary sustainability research: Seven case studies and an indicator framework. *Environmental Science and Policy*, *131*, 14–25.

König, Th. and Gorman, M. E. (2017). The challenge of funding interdisciplinary. In R. Frodeman, J. T. Klein and R. Pacheco (Eds.), *The Oxford handbook of interdisciplinarity* (pp. 513–524). Oxford: Oxford University Press.

Lang, D. J., Wiek, A., Bergmann, M., Stauffacher, M., Martens, P., Moll, P., . . . and Thomas, C. J. (2012). Transdisciplinary research in sustainability science: Practice, principles, and challenges. *Sustainability Science*, 7(1), 25–43.

Macfarlane, B. and Cheng, M. (2008). Communism, universalism and disinterestedness: Re-examining contemporary support among academics for Merton's scientific norms. *Journal of Academic Ethics*, 6(1), 67–78.

Madison, M. J. (2014). Commons at the intersection of peer production, citizen science, and big data: Galaxy Zoo. In B. M. Frischmann et al. (Eds.), *Governing knowledge commons* (pp. 209–254). New York: Oxford University Press.

Mobjörk, M. (2010). Consulting versus participatory transdisciplinarity: A refined classification of transdisciplinary research. *Futures*, 42(8), 866–873.

Mokyr, J. (2011). The gifts of Athena. In *The gifts of Athena*. Princeton, NJ: Princeton University Press.

Norström, A. V., Cvitanovic, C., Löf, M. F., West, S., Wyborn, C., Balvanera, P., . . . and Österblom, H. (2020). Principles for knowledge co-production in sustainability research. *Nature Sustainability*, 3(3), 182–190.

Olson, M. (1965). *The logic of collective action: Public goods and the theory of groups*. Cambridge, MA: Harvard University Press.

Ostrom, E. (1990). *Governing the commons: The evolution of institutions for collective action*. Cambridge: Cambridge University Press.

Ostrom, E. (1998). A behavioral approach to the rational choice theory of collective action: Presidential address, American Political Science Association, 1997. *American Political Science Review*, 92(1), 1–22.

Ostrom, E. (2005). *Understanding institutional diversity*. Princeton, NJ: Princeton University Press.

Ostrom, E. (2010). Beyond markets and states: Polycentric governance of complex economic systems. *American Economic Review*, 100(3), 641–672.

Paredis, E. (2011). *Transition management as a form of policy innovation. A case study of Plan C, a process in sustainable materials management in Flanders*. Working Paper. Flemish Policy Research Centre on Sustainable Development, Ghent University, Ghent.

Peer, V. and Stoeglehner, G. (2013). Universities as change agents for sustainability–framing the role of knowledge transfer and generation in regional development processes. *Journal of Cleaner Production*, 44, 85–95.

Pohl, C. and Hirsch Hadorn, G. (2007). *Principles for designing transdisciplinary research*. Munich: Oekom Verlag.

Pohl, C., Klein, J. T., Hoffmann, S., Mitchell, C. and Fam, D. (2021). Conceptualising transdisciplinary integration as a multidimensional interactive process. *Environmental Science and Policy*, 118, 18–26.

Popa, F., Guillermin, M. and Dedeurwaerdere, T. (2015). A pragmatist approach to transdisciplinarity in sustainability research: From complex systems theory to reflexive science. *Futures*, 65, 45–56.

Puska, P., Vartiainen, E., Laatikainen, T., Jousilahti, P. and Paavola, M. (2009). *The North Karelia project: From North Karelia to national action*. Helsinki: National Institute for Health and Welfare.

Reichman, J. H., Uhlir, P. F. and Dedeurwaerdere, T. (2016). *Governing digitally integrated genetic resources, data, and literature: Global intellectual property strategies for a redesigned microbial research commons*. Cambridge: Cambridge University Press.

Russell, J. Y. (2010). A philosophical framework for an open and critical transdisciplinary inquiry. In V. A. Brown, J. A. Harris and J. Russell (Eds.), *Tackling wicked problems* (pp. 31–60). Abingdon: Routledge.

Sandler, T. (2004). *Global collective action*. Cambridge: Cambridge University Press.

Schneider, F., Giger, M., Harari, N., Moser, S., Oberlack, C., Providoli, I., . . . and Zimmermann, A. (2019). Transdisciplinary co-production of knowledge and sustainability transformations: Three generic mechanisms of impact generation. *Environmental Science and Policy*, *102*, 26–35.

Sciortino, L. (2017). On Ian Hacking's notion of style of reasoning. *Erkenntnis*, *82*(2), 243–264.

Singleton, R. A. and Straits, B. C. (2005). *Approaches to social research*. Oxford: Oxford University Press.

Sørensen, E. and Torfing, J. (Eds.). (2007). *Theories of democratic network governance*. Heidelberg: Springer.

Spash, C. L. (2012). New foundations for ecological economics. *Ecological Economics*, *77*, 36–47.

Stromberg, P. M., Dedeurwaerdere, T. and Pascual, U. (2013). The heterogeneity of public ex situ collections of microorganisms: Empirical evidence about conservation practices, industry spillovers and public goods. *Environmental Science and Policy*, *33*, 19–27.

Willis, J. W. (2007). *Foundations of qualitative research: Interpretive and critical approaches*. Thousand Oaks, CA: Sage Publishing.

3

GENERATING ACTIONABLE KNOWLEDGE OUTPUTS THROUGH COLLABORATIVE RESEARCH CO-DESIGN

To respond to the urgent sustainability challenges, scientific researchers organize a wealth of projects based on integrating contextual knowledge from societal actors in the production of knowledge outputs (Norström et al., 2020). This effort is reflected in the vast amount of scientific journal papers produced on knowledge integration in sustainability research. However, such research efforts do not always induce the production of usable knowledge on real-world sustainability transformation pathways.

The hypothesis in this chapter is that to produce usable knowledge outputs for sustainability transformations, sustainability researchers must strengthen the collective action arrangements to co-construct a common research framework for socio-ecological analysis. This investment in research co-design is needed to provide additional guarantees for the alignment of heterogeneous knowledge interests and value-laden perspectives around a common research purpose. These guarantees extend beyond the well-researched conditions of the integration of societal actors' knowledge and perspectives in knowledge generation processes.

Thus, to test the hypothesis on the importance of co-constructing the research design, this chapter considers a broad sample of cases that covers different levers of transformation in socio-ecological systems, ranging from technological and socioeconomic levers to policy and sociocultural change. Covering the various levers of societal transformation aims to provide evidence of the organization of research co-construction with societal actors that are, potentially, of concern to a broad set of transdisciplinary research traditions on interdependent social and ecological system dynamics.

The analysis in this chapter will proceed in three steps. The first section presents a sample of in-depth case studies of transdisciplinary research

DOI: 10.4324/9781032624297-4

and applies a basic model of research co-design to the comparative analysis of success or failures in usable knowledge production. The second section deepens this preliminary analysis via an overview of knowledge co-production in five research clusters dealing with distinct levers of sustainability transformations. The third section concludes by showing how this analysis of knowledge co-production fits with the more general epistemological framework of pragmatist constructivism.

3.1 Usable knowledge production on sustainability transformations

3.1.1 A model of research co-design for delivering usable knowledge outputs

To conduct a preliminary analysis of the production of usable knowledge, this section discusses the key features of research co-design and a basic model of various types of usable knowledge outputs developed from the existing scholarly literature on the societal impacts of transdisciplinary research.

3.1.1.1 Collaboration for knowledge integration, process co-management, and research co-design

As acknowledged by scholars of transdisciplinary research, effective production of usable knowledge outputs requires intensive collaboration among scientific researchers and societal actors for knowledge integration from various sources in combination with a form of co-management of the knowledge generation and dissemination processes. These two types of collaboration mechanisms are also highlighted in a review paper by 36 co-authors working on sustainability research published in *Nature Sustainability* (Norström et al., 2020). Norström et al. (ibid) first highlight various mechanisms of knowledge integration between scientific researchers and societal actors. This first type respectively aims at producing knowledge situated in a particular context or issue (context-based), integrating multiple ways of knowing and doing (pluralistic) and articulating shared goals related to the challenge at hand (goal-oriented). The second type of mechanism relates to the iterative and collaborative character of the co-management process. As stated by the authors, the "act of engagement across domains and disciplines can be as important for the pursuit of sustainability as the production of knowledge." This mechanism of "process co-management" emphasizes that co-production produces more than just knowledge. It develops capacity, builds networks, fosters social capital, and implements actions that contribute to sustainability (ibid, p. 2).

The need to combine mechanisms for knowledge integration with the co-management by the scientific researchers and societal actors is a common thread in the literature on transdisciplinary co-production (see also section 2.2.1). However, this perspective on knowledge co-production does not specify the conditions under which the collaboration leads to elaborating a common framework for analyzing interdependent socio-ecological transformation dynamics. The contextual and pluralist knowledge integration mechanisms identified by Norström et al. (ibid) may be successfully implemented without co-designing the interdisciplinary framework for the analysis of the socio-ecological system dynamics. Thus, such a process might produce usable knowledge outputs that are co-produced among the scientific researchers and societal actors in a pluralist and context-specific way but that only address separate components of the overall sustainability issues.

To address the challenge of common knowledge production on specific interdependent dynamics between social and ecological system dynamics, this chapter considers an additional type of mechanism to be considered in the knowledge co-production process: the co-construction of the interdisciplinary research design among the scientific researchers and societal actors. Indeed, to understand the specific coupled dynamics between the social and ecological dimensions of sustainability transformations, scientific researchers and societal actors must match the research design to the real-world possibilities of interdependent socio-ecological transformations. Therefore, the design of interdisciplinary frameworks cannot be separated from the understanding of the given value-related perspectives on real-world transformation pathways.

The key additional challenge, therefore, is to understand how heterogeneous knowledge sources and research styles can fit into a common research design that reflects specific feasible and desirable sustainability transformation pathways. In this context, researchers can benefit from the systematic analysis of research design practices in the broad field of mixed methods research. Mixed methods are used in many specific areas of interdisciplinary research, such as geography or landscape ecology. However, in transdisciplinary research on socio-ecological systems, they are omnipresent.

In a review paper on mixed methods research, Joseph Maxwell and Diane Loomis summarize five key ingredients of successful mixed methods research that can be adapted to the purposes of transdisciplinary co-design (Maxwell and Loomis, 2003). Figures 3.1 and 3.2 schematically represent them, respectively, for the cases of disciplinary and interdisciplinary research.

The central component of the research design with mixed methods is the design of interrelated and compatible research question among the research partners: What specifically do the researchers want to understand by conducting the research? What questions will the researcher attempt to answer? However, as illustrated in Figure 3.1, to fruitfully combine various methods

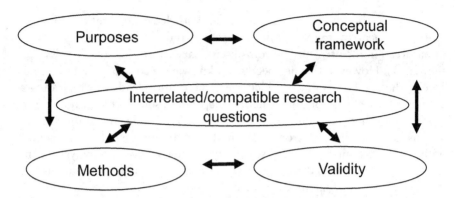

FIGURE 3.1 Research co-design among researchers in multi-method disciplinary research

Figure by the author, based on an adaptation of the concepts developed in Maxwell and Loomis (2003).

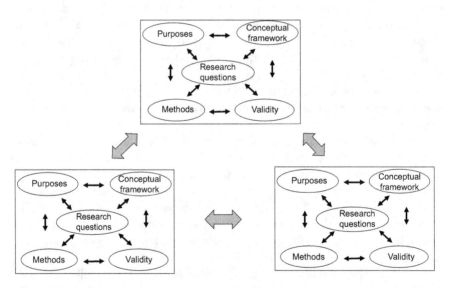

FIGURE 3.2 Research co-design among researchers in interdisciplinary research

in a common research design, the researchers must agree upon a set of other design elements. Four additional design elements are underlined in the review by Maxwell and Loomis (ibid): (1) the conceptual framework that gathers the contributions of the various disciplines in a common model, (2) the criteria of validity and the limits of each of the knowledge types, (3) the available approaches and techniques to collect and analyze the data, and (4) the commonly agreed-upon goals of the study.

Regarding interdisciplinary research on sustainability problems, the co-construction of the different design elements must be coordinated among the different disciplines. Indeed, to be relevant, interdisciplinary framework research must look beyond the analysis of the single components, which are often better addressed through purely disciplinary research, and look at the interactions between the natural, social, and human science features of the problem at hand.

In this context, to make the heterogeneous knowledge perspectives among the various disciplines mutually consistent, the research partners must organize a form of reciprocal learning between the various disciplines, sometimes qualified as reciprocal reference (Jaeger and Scheringer, 1998) or reciprocal critique (Becker and Jahn, 2003). This reciprocal learning can take the form of adjustments at the level of selection of methods that allow for knowledge transfer from one discipline or knowledge type to another or adjustments at the level of conceptual background assumptions, data collection methods, and sampling strategies.

Without such reciprocal adjustment of knowledge perspectives, there is no guarantee for an effective contribution to a common research endeavor. Indeed, scholars approaching the same socio-ecological reality through different disciplinary approaches use different conceptual frameworks to build their research objects, even when addressing the same real-world phenomena (Sciortino, 2017). In such a context there is a danger that the various disciplines focus on one aspect of reality per the disciplinary state of the art and the skills of the disciplinary researchers involved, instead of selecting the disciplinary variables and the various research questions in the function of the common transdisciplinary framework (Ostrom, 2007; Wuelser and Pohl, 2016). Therefore, the different conceptual choices by the project partners in constructing their research objects must be adjusted to bring them in line with a common object of inquiry.

In the context of transdisciplinary research, the research co-design must satisfy an additional requirement, as the co-design must consider the research participation of societal actors. Indeed, the various aspects of the research co-design must accord with the societal actor and scientific researcher perspectives on the identification of the socio-ecological problem situation and their perspectives on sustainability values. Figure 3.3 illustrates the additional requirements.

In summary, the key question scientific researchers and societal actors must address for successful co-design is to clarify and collectively decide how the various approaches to methodology, validity, research purpose, conceptual framing, and the identification of the most relevant research questions can be integrated into a common transdisciplinary framework. Failure to do

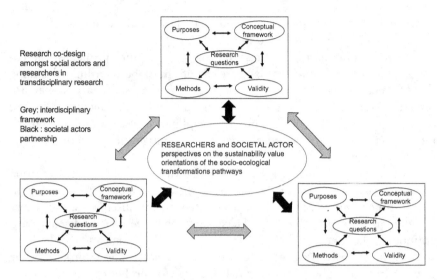

Research co-design amongst social actors and researchers in transdisciplinary research

Grey: interdisciplinary framework
Black : societal actors partnership

FIGURE 3.3   Research co-design between researchers and societal actors in trans-disciplinary research

so may still yield interesting knowledge on disjointed aspects of the over-all socio-ecological system dynamics, which might be of interest to individual disciplinary researchers or societal actors. However, such a disjointed approach is likely to be of poor use to understanding the dynamics of change in interdependent social and ecological systems in a socially relevant and legitimate manner.

3.1.1.2   Factoring in a broad variety of societal effects of transdisciplinary research

The short review on collaboration mechanisms for usable knowledge production on specific socio-ecological transformation pathways shows the importance of combining collaboration for knowledge integration, process co-management, and research co-design. To analyze their contribution to effective transdisciplinary research, the basic model used in this chapter considers three main categories of knowledge outputs to analyze the contribution of the various mechanisms of collaboration. The first category covers scientific research outputs on socio-ecological relationships, and the second, the dissemination through peer-reviewed scientific publications. The third category covers different usable knowledge outputs that can support decision-making by societal actors, as illustrated in Figure 3.4.

First, as in the case of interdisciplinary research on sustainability issues, the goal is to produce knowledge to better understand the world in a scientifically

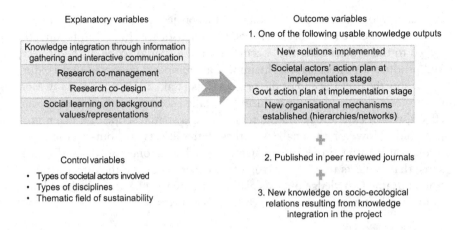

FIGURE 3.4   Core variables of the comparative case study design of transdisciplinary research projects. For details on the scales used for coding the
variables, see Annex 3.

reliable manner. Such usable knowledge can be produced through applied
and basic research. As highlighted in the introduction, both applied and
basic research practices are present in transdisciplinary research. Applied
transdisciplinary research provides knowledge that contributes directly to
improving the understanding of specific problem situations. On the other
hand, basic transdisciplinary research contributes by building more general
knowledge on socio-ecological dynamics, which may yield new approaches
and problem-solving in the long term (Rosenberg, 2010). In the case studies
below, the contribution to such improved understanding from applied and
basic research will be assessed through evidence of peer-reviewed publications
from the projects that address social and ecological system interdependencies.

Second, to assess the contribution of the improved understanding to usable knowledge for decision-making by societal actors, this chapter considers
a broad variety of usable knowledge outputs. The analysis will evaluate the
possible contribution to three distinct categories of usable knowledge outputs highlighted in a series of review papers on usable knowledge production
in transdisciplinary research (Walter et al., 2007; Wiek et al., 2014; Mitchell
et al., 2015; Schneider et al., 2019). These categories include contributions
to (1) new knowledge for the implementation of solutions and improvement
of the situation; (2) promoting knowledge integration among the actors by
translating the research results in integrated strategy and planning documents, for both societal actors and policy makers; and (3) building new actor
networks, leading to new organizational initiatives.

An important feature of this basic model of usable knowledge outputs
must be mentioned before proceeding. Following other authors, for the

consistency of the comparison among the projects, the analysis considers essentially so-called first-order effects. Such first-order effects can be directly linked to the project activities, occur within the spatial scope of the project, and produce the effect within the immediate temporal context—that is, during or shortly after the end of the project (Lux et al., 2019, p. 184). However, the projects also produce more diffuse, so-called second- or third-order social effects, which extend beyond the temporal and spatial scope of a given project (ibid). However, the analysis of these latter effects falls outside the scope of the comparative project assessment. Nevertheless, one can reasonably presume that projects that show strong first-order effects on the direct production of usable knowledge outputs also contribute to enhancing the likelihood of the production of second- and third-order effects.

3.1.2 A sample of in-depth case studies on transdisciplinary research processes

To grasp the contribution of the various mechanisms of knowledge co-production, this chapter presents a comparative assessment of a sample of well-documented transdisciplinary research projects via a unique "most different" case study sampling process covering a broad variety of thematic areas of sustainability research.

The initial cases in the sample were identified through a keyword search on "transdisciplinarity and sustainability" and "participatory research and sustainability" in four scholarly journals. The purpose of the keyword search was to identify publications on case studies of research projects that were based on interdisciplinary sustainability analysis and involved research collaborations among scientific researchers and societal actors. Based on an initial reading of the journal publications and the available project documents, a further selection was made to keep only projects that (1) were interdisciplinary across the natural and social or the natural and human sciences and (2) effectively integrated knowledge from societal actors on the sustainability transformations into the analysis. Only journal publications that provide an in-depth analysis of the organizational features of the full research process in the journal publication (in addition to the presentation of the results) or in the supplementary material were selected. For the selected projects, all available project materials (other journal publications and web documents) were consulted to complete the analysis.

In a second step, to cover a variety of different thematic approaches to sustainability transformations, the sample considered cases that address five different levers of change, ranging from technological and socioeconomic levers to policy and sociocultural change, as detailed below. Whenever the initial selection process did not yield a sufficient number of papers dealing with one of these levers (with a minimum of five in each lever), the sample was completed based on a general keyword search in a broader set of journals on that specific lever of change combined with the keyword "transdisciplinary" in Google Scholar. Annex 2 lists the cases that resulted from the sampling process.

As can be seen, the sampling process used a minimalistic characterization of transdisciplinary sustainability research based on the two core features of (1) interdisciplinary modeling of interdependent socio-ecological systems and (2) integration of scientific and practitioner knowledge in the research process. The sample from this process contained a sufficiently broad variety of failed and successful cases, with different degrees of success, in usable knowledge production to allow for a qualitative comparative analysis of the institutional design features for overcoming collective action failures (see, e.g., Rihoux and Ragin (2008) for an analysis of sample size for Medium N qualitative comparative analysis).

Further, the sampling of a set of highly diverse cases from within the five levers of change decreases the potential bias from an overly strong representation in the sample of a specific methodological approach or thematic field of society-wide transformation. In particular, the sample covers a diversity of methodological approaches for integrated boundary-crossing research that are mobilized to analyze the various levers of change, including technology living labs, multi-criteria analysis, community-based survey methods, and participatory qualitative research. The projects in the sample also covered a broad variety of thematic fields of sustainability transformations, including sustainable food and agriculture, sustainable mobility, energy, and housing.

As noted, to analyze successful knowledge co-production, the sample addresses cases from within five clusters that focus on a specific lever of sustainability transformations in socio-ecological systems. These clusters are based on the knowledge-based sustainability transformations framework elaborated in the 2019 Global Sustainability Report (UN, 2019). According to this report, societal transformations can be accelerated through actions based on different levers, respectively:

Biophysical levers

1 Fostering technological innovation from a socio-technical systems perspective
2 Planning sustainable resource use in society-wide sectors of activity (e.g., energy, mobility, and housing)

Socioeconomic and policy levers

3 Designing socioeconomic regimes for sustainability transformations
4 Developing policy and governance for implementing new socioeconomic regimes

Sociocultural levers

5 Including the diversity of sociocultural perspectives in the sustainability transformation pathways

The consideration of these different levers allows covering a broad diversity of knowledge integration challenges in the case study sample. For instance, the analysis of the first lever requires combining technical knowledge with socioeconomic and sociocultural variables. Other cases, dealing with the fifth cluster, require combining knowledge of sociocultural practices with knowledge of the broader socio-ecological system-wide changes and challenges that impact the transformation of these practices.

The challenges encountered in organizing research co-design can differ per lever of change. For instance, in transdisciplinary research on socio-technical transitions, researchers may find it relatively easy to integrate general ethical perspectives as a constraint on the choices of future technological innovation pathways. Indeed, such considerations do not necessarily directly impact the technical component of the research design, as long as the envisioned innovations stay within the set of socially acceptable ethical perspectives. However, addressing the change in habits and impacts on social meanings of each of the technological pathways is likely to require a more in-depth reciprocal learning process between disciplines. In the latter case, the question of patterns of the use of technology in specific sociocultural contexts and technical choices must be analyzed in close relation to each other. In other cases, the co-design of the sociocultural dimensions of the socio-ecological pathway may be the first entry point for the research partners, while the integration of the technical or economic system dimensions requires stepping outside of the research partners' comfort zone.

Although most scholars recognize the importance of these five levers of change in addressing major sustainability challenges, they often fail to organize effective co-design processes with the various disciplines and societal actors involved. Therefore, the remainder of this chapter discusses the challenges of organizing a broad interdisciplinary approach to the analysis of levers, the benefits from research co-design in the building of partnerships among researchers and societal actors, and organizing appropriate forms of co-management for conducting such transdisciplinary partnership research.

3.1.3 Aggregate results from the in-depth case study analysis

An elementary coding of the key explanatory and usable knowledge outcome variables (see Figure 3.4) of the case studies of the sample confirms, at an aggregative level, the overall importance of knowledge co-production processes. In particular, the analysis strongly supports the role of the two mechanisms of research co-design and co-management with the societal actors reviewed above.

Even though the authors of the publications on these case studies labeled the projects explicitly as transdisciplinary sustainability research or participatory sustainability research, some projects in the sample are, in reality, at the level of a pure aggregation of different types of knowledge for academic scientific research purposes without significant knowledge co-production with societal actors. Indeed, all the projects in the sample used contextual information from societal actors and resulted in peer-reviewed publications, but not all led to one or several co-produced usable knowledge outputs related to common research questions among the partners on socio-ecological transformation dynamics.

The analysis shows that, of the 44 transdisciplinary research projects, only 29 co-produced at least one of the types of usable knowledge outputs on specific socio-ecological transformation pathways that resulted from the integration of knowledge from the scientific researchers and societal actors. In this sub-sample of 29 projects, all projects explicitly organized co-construction activities of the research design with societal actors and a form of co-management among researchers and societal actors in the knowledge production process. Specifically, the amount and strength of usable knowledge outputs increase with the strength of the knowledge co-production features, as illustrated in Figure 3.5 (for an overview of the average results on the

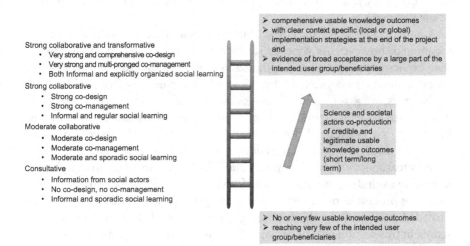

FIGURE 3.5   Aggregate results of the coding of the case studies of transdisciplinary sustainability research. Co-produced knowledge outputs (right side of the figure) resulting from increasing comprehensiveness of the science and societal actors partnership (left side of the figure). The ladder schematically represents the increasing strength of the partnership, according to comparative case study analysis (for a detailed overview, see Annex 2).

importance of these features and the detailed coding scale used for the analysis, see Annex 2). In practice of course, not all individual projects have the means to organize comprehensive research co-design and/or social learning. Nevertheless, the analysis clearly indicates the benefit of doing so and the need to imagine different means to strengthen the knowledge co-production features, including through the networking of different projects (sequentially or in clusters) or through the integration of knowledge co-production in training activities at institutions of higher education. Therefore, even if the analysis in this chapter is based on the comparison of individual project outcomes, the findings also show the need to explore the embedding of these projects in broader polycentric networks for transdisciplinary knowledge co-production. The latter will be further developed in the discussion on the building of integrated boundary-crossing organizational networks in Chapter 5.

The other 15 transdisciplinary research projects did not produce any of the usable knowledge outputs within the time frame of the project in direct relation to specific socio-ecological transformations in a significant manner. Some mention this explicitly as a failure or a challenge that remains to be addressed. All these projects produced peer-reviewed scientific publications from the partnership processes and mentioned the contextual information gathering with societal actors as an appropriate definition of transdisciplinary research. None of the projects in this sub-sample of 15 mentions co-construction of research design or co-management as a governance feature of the partnership.

A note of caution for the correct interpretation of these results needs to be mentioned, however. As we only selected projects in our case study sample that explicitly provide an in-depth analysis of the knowledge co-production process, and as we consulted a broad set of supplementary material for each of the cases, we assume that the omission of co-management or research co-design with societal actors is an indication that these features were absent or in any case considered not sufficiently significant in the overall process. In case of doubt on the completeness of the available information on these process features in the project publication and supplementary material, projects were excluded from our sample for the outset (cf. the explanation of the sampling process above). Nevertheless, in spite of the careful analysis of the provided documents on the process design and its evaluation, the results presented in this section should be considered as an average trend over the entire sample of 44 cases. This trend is clearly strongly significant but needs to be further substantiated through additional comparative analyses and in-depth qualitative research on isolated cases. The presentation of in-depth research on illustrative cases presented in the subsequent section aims to contribute to this deepening of the results.

Levels of comprehensiveness of science and social actors participation in transd. sust. research

Strong collaborative and transformative
- Very strong and comprehensive co-design
- Very strong and multi-pronged co-management
- Both Informal and explicitly organized social learning

Strong collaborative
- Strong co-design
- Strong co-management
- Informal and regular social learning

Moderate collaborative
- Moderate co-design
- Moderate co-management
- Moderate and sporadic social learning

Consultative
- Information from social actors
- No co-design, no co-management
- Informal and sporadic social learning

Multi-stakeholder user/beneficiary driven science, with active co-design, co-interventions and co-research (ex. Community health case §3.2.4)

Multi-stakeholder user/beneficary driven science, with active co-design and co-interventions (ex. Enkanini §3.2.5)

Multi-stakeholder research alliance with active research co-design (ex. Street design §3.2.2; Climpol §3.2.3)

Participatory action research: co-interventions with active research co-design (ex. Cahors § 3.2.1)

FIGURE 3.6   Examples of types of transdisciplinary research in the case study sample, with varying degrees of strength of co-design, co-management and social learning; case study names refer to the detailed case study sections in Annex 2.

The next section will therefore further build on this elementary comparative analysis to better understand the benefits of various components of knowledge co-production in transdisciplinary research through a series of selected cases out of the sample of 29 transdisciplinary projects that produced effective, usable knowledge outputs. Obviously, the various transdisciplinary research projects are extremely diverse, as they cover different areas of sustainability transformations and involve highly diverse societal actors. Thus, as one can expect, there is no optimal design of the process for organizing knowledge co-production with societal actors but rather a set of diverse types of approaches, as illustrated in the right column of Figure 3.6. Nevertheless, all successful projects in the sample show strong evidence of the explicit organization of research co-management and research co-design with the view to developing integrated interdisciplinary frameworks of socioecological system dynamics that match legitimate and relevant societal value perspectives in the specific field of sustainability transformations.

3.2 Collaborative research co-design across technological, socioeconomic, and cultural levers of sustainability transformations

The next sections illustrate cases of research co-design across various levers of change to foster sustainability transformations, ranging from the analysis of technological and biophysical levers of change to socioeconomic and sociocultural levers. For each lever, scholars widely documented the failures of the mere aggregation of disciplinary approaches for understanding interdependent social and ecological dynamics and proposed specific methodologies for interdisciplinary analysis of sustainability transformation pathways. Therefore, each section first presents a specific methodology of interdisciplinary analysis before discussing the various attempts in the selected cases for integrating knowledge co-production processes with societal actors in this interdisciplinary approach.

Moreover, to illustrate the role of co-design in transdisciplinary research, each section addresses a different aspect of the co-design framework developed based on the analysis of Maxwell and Loomis (2003) (see Figure 3.2). Specifically, the selected case studies respectively show the role of co-construction of the following aspects of the research design:

Co-designing "Validity of data collection and analysis"

- Historic City Centre Living Lab case study: Co-design of data collection from various methodological perspectives to match available data sources on social possibilities to use bio-based materials (in Section 3.2.1).

Co-designing "Research purposes"

- Future Streets case study: Co-design of the research purposes of dynamic systems modeling to match the research framework to diverse sociocultural perspectives (in Section 3.2.2).

Co-designing "Methods"

- Sustainable Mobility case study: Co-design of a research method to match this method to the analysis of the feasible transformation options of the sustainable mobility strategy of a municipality (in Section 3.2.3).

Co-designing "Research questions"

- Environmental Health case study: Iterative co-design of research questions through different rounds of community surveying that reveal the case-specific social and ecological interdependencies (in Section 3.2.4).

Co-designing "Conceptual frameworks"

- Energy Poverty in Informal Urban Settlements: Co-design of a new conceptual framework that better matches the key societal actors' perspectives on sustainable energy transformations (in Section 3.2.5).

Each of the case-study sections is structured as follows. The section first recapitulates some of the key arguments for moving toward an interdisciplinary and social-actor partnership-based approach to the sustainability problems in the analysis of a given lever of change. In the second step, a case study illustrating a specific aspect of research co-design in that lever of change is presented. In the third step, other cases from the case study sample are presented to further illustrate the contribution of co-design processes around the different sustainability value orientations of planetary resilience, environmental justice, and environmental citizenship.

3.2.1   User and citizen co-design of technological levers of change

3.2.1.1   From the laboratory to interdisciplinary socio-technical transformation research

The first lever of society-wide sustainability transformations, also prominently present in the popular media and policy debates on sustainability, is technological innovation and product development (UN, 2019). However, technological innovation on its own is neutral toward achieving sustainability objectives. On the one hand, well-designed technologies can increase resource efficiency and contribute to transformation pathways for living within the boundaries of the planet. On the other hand, technological innovation is a major driver of the development of ever-new products for individual consumption, which might further add to the already existing dependency on the use of natural resource inputs, such as energy or non-renewable materials in contemporary mass consumption societies.

For instance, innovations in consumer products, such as digital platforms for car sharing, LED lighting systems, or less-energy-consuming water boilers, have brought important cost benefits to consumers but without a proven shift in behavior toward overall less resource-intensive consumption patterns (Ceschin and Gaziulusoy, 2016). In particular, researchers estimate that 78% of discarded products still function properly when replaced (Van Nes, 2003). The reasons include new trends in fashion, the desire for societal status, or changing user needs (Van Nes, 2003; Cooper, 2004, 2016). Moreover, for products that consume energy, user behavior mainly determines the level of energy consumption (Tang and Bhamra, 2009). Further, regarding industry-led innovations, emission and waste reduction technologies in industrial production processes, even when they offer cost-effective alternatives to current practice, often fail to engage the company shareholders or to mobilize the technical staff in developing new competences to implement the envisioned changes on a wider scale (Stindt et al., 2016).

Therefore, the first challenge for sustainability research focused on technological innovation and product development is to move from a disciplinary product-centered research approach to an interdisciplinary analysis of inter-dependent technological and social dynamics. How can sustainable product or service innovations be developed that address environmental challenges and promote sustainable behavior by producing co-benefits with social and economic sustainability dimensions? How can new technologies be developed for the factory floor while generating effective participation of all the relevant actors in the re-organization of production and supply chains? Further, how can the broad range of concerned societal stakeholders be associated with the dissemination of technologies that promote environmental, social, and economic sustainability in an integrated manner?

In response to these challenges, researchers in engineering and biophysical sciences and societal actors have developed a broad set of interdisciplinary methods for user-centered research and technological innovation processes. Indeed, given the initial impetus in the 1990s by early initiatives, such as the living lab initiated at the Massachusetts Institute for Technology in the United States (ENoLL, 2019), researchers have developed user-centered technologi-cal innovation methods to orient these toward advancing social, environmen-tal, and economic sustainability in an integrated socio-technological systems approach. Labeled in the literature with different terms such as "sustainable living labs," "design for sustainability," or "product service system" innova-tions, these approaches share a focus on involving users and other relevant actors along value chains in technological design and innovation processes (Ceschin and Gaziulusoy, 2016)

The interdisciplinary challenge of the socio-technological systems approach to address sustainability issues is to integrate product-related improvements with other sustainability dimensions, such as through an analysis of behav-ioral changes, psychological factors, business models, governance of innova-tion, and inclusive economic development goals. Nevertheless, to produce usable knowledge in specific transformation pathways, societal actors must be involved in this integrated and multi-dimensional approach. Indeed, each research project must zoom in on a subset of these sustainability dimensions when building the research partnership. Per the most urgent challenges iden-tified, to promote desirable and feasible real-world sustainability transfor-mations, researchers and societal actors must prioritize certain scientific and societal outcomes and organize the various phases of the knowledge co-pro-duction process accordingly.

3.2.1.2 A living lab for sustainable renovation in the historic city center of Cahors, France

The research on energy refurbishment technologies in the historic city of Cahors in France aptly illustrates the contribution of co-constructing research design in user-centered research on technological innovation

(Cruchon, 2019). As in many other cities, the development in recent decades of suburban areas has led to the depopulation of the city center and a lack of investment in the refurbishment of historic dwellings (Claude et al., 2017). In response, to revitalize the city center, the municipality launched in 2015 a renovation program while promoting sustainable building techniques based on the sourcing of locally available bio-based materials and the conservation of valuable historical heritage.

Even though the project partners agreed on the general sustainability values that guided the project (around the use of bio-based materials and preservation of historical heritage), they still faced the challenge of matching the activities in the research project to real-world social possibilities for transformation in the local building sector that reflects these values. Indeed, in the broader context of the building sector, many refurbishment solutions are based on conventional solutions with mass-produced non-renewable materials proposed by the industrialized building sector (ibid). In this context, a more systematic integration of artisan knowledge with expertise in the refurbishment of a historical building remains a considerable challenge to be addressed. Moreover, government programs for financial support of energy refurbishment are based on a theoretical diagnosis of energy performance, which is not well adapted to the situation of old buildings (ibid, p. 122). The standard governmental energy performance requirements can encourage renovators to favor solutions that contradict the preservation of the historical heritage, for instance, by changing windows and doors. Finally, despite being one of the green energies with high economic potential and the broad availability of these materials, the industry and market for bio-based materials remain poorly coordinated and lack overall recognition.

Thus, to address these issues, the municipality and the researchers from the University of Toulouse established a living lab on new refurbishment technologies that are better adapted to the thermal renovation of old historic buildings while enhancing the skills of local craftsmen. This living lab implemented a knowledge co-production process by involving local artisans, end-users, local authorities, and material producers in the design of an interactive process of data gathering combining refurbishment of buildings in real-world test sites in Cahors, laboratory measurement, and socio-historical analysis. In contrast with classical interdisciplinary and expert-based approaches, participants in the living lab could develop sustainable technologies in a real-life context, where political, ecological, socioeconomic, and technological dimensions must be integrated.

The overall research process included a first phase of more conventional interdisciplinary framework building and a second transdisciplinary phase of knowledge co-production and research co-design. First, to involve the stakeholders in the definition of the research frame and the choice of the materials to be tested, the Cahors living lab organized a set of co-creation workshops during the 2017–2018 period in the context of the overall ENERPAT project (2018). They yielded an interdisciplinary framework that considered various theoretical aspects to implement the bio-based sustainable building pathway. This specific socio-ecological pathway required considering multiple dimensions in the choice of the materials and energy, such as the moisture regulation efficiency of the bio-based materials, the shape and orientation of the building on the test sites, the climate and geographical conditions of the region, and socioeconomic and cultural factors of historical building practices (Claude et al., 2017).

Second, to match these choices to the real-world possibilities for implementation in the specific context of the Cahors living lab, the partners designed a process of data collection that integrated the various constraints of the test sites. Given the collaboration with local artisans and their empirical knowledge of vernacular techniques, the partners designed an iterative process of on-site prototyping of bio-based materials, laboratory measurements, and field-testing of using the materials in building renovation. The archaeologist from the city council brought expert knowledge on the architectural and socioeconomic features of the historical building practices. Based on these combined inputs, various on-site experiments were performed (e.g., moisture measurements and testing the sealing of the doors) by researchers and students to improve the proposed refurbishment solutions.

The project resulted in some direct exploitable research results, such as the development of mixes of Earth and natural fiber with the desired properties for use in historical buildings. These results were communicated through public events in 2018 and 2019 with various researchers and actors in the sustainable building sector. Beyond these events and the scientific publications on the properties of bio-based building materials, the project team also notes more indirect results that impact the social practices in the building sector. First, the project produced guidelines on various aspects of improving the energy efficiency of buildings in historic city centers. Second, for the federation of artisans and the local small building firms, the project allowed for upgrading the status and the recognition of their work. In particular, the project has shown that the artisans can contribute to solutions with many co-benefits for the environment, the creation of new social bonds in old city centers, and the conservation of historic patrimony.

3.2.1.3 Co-designing socio-technical research for understanding real-world sustainability transformations

The living lab approach in Cahors is part of the cases in the sub-sample on the technological lever of change. Within this sub-sample, other successful cases also consider the need for co-construction of various aspects of the research design with societal actors.

A first group of cases in this sub-sample focuses—in line with the Cahors case—on sustainability values regarding planetary boundaries and responsibility for living beings and ecosystems. These cases clearly show the limits of purely technical eco-design to foster sustainability transformations (Toffolini et al., 2021). For instance, the twin research projects, Capflor (2011–2020) and SALSA (2013–2015) (Goutiers et al., 2016; Lacombe et al., 2017), by the French National Agricultural Research Institute clearly show the need for partnership research to consider societal actors' perspectives on understanding different pathways that integrate planetary boundaries in agro-ecological innovations.

The Capflor project started when a group of farmers aimed to limit the external inputs of feed for their livestock by promoting "on farm" fodder production on the surrounding grasslands while decreasing the use of fertilizers on these grasslands. In this context, the farmers sought a seed mix that would be more productive, biodiverse (for pollination services), and include legumes, such as clover and alfalfa (for nitrogen fixation). Given the absence of a tradition of using complex mixed grasslands in France, they resorted to buying complex seed mixes from Switzerland, where researchers and farmers at Agroscope developed seed mixes through a user-driven research platform with farm test fields. However, this initial attempt failed, as the seeds were not adapted to the specificities of the local farming practices and the understanding of desirable sustainability transformations by the local farmers.

A more integrated understanding that is more sensitive to the local context of feasible and desirable socio-technical innovations was needed to transition toward diverse grassland management. Hence, the twin projects Capflor and SALSA organized a set of workshops among researchers, farmers, and local organizations to identify the key agronomic, environmental, economic, and social decision-making criteria that should be used in designing and evaluating a transition to a diversified grassland system. The project organized field experiments with the farmers, which led to developing seed mixes adapted to the local context that better matched the desirable transformation pathways.

For instance, the research team was able to broaden the set of sustainability targets for sustainable grassland management. The resulting pathways did not only consider diversified grassland systems with high biodiversity outcomes but also consider other pathways of grassland diversification with lower biodiversity outcomes, which provided an equally high level of fodder autonomy but higher perceived work satisfaction by the involved farmers. Another tangible output of this knowledge co-production process is the effective uptake of more sustainable grassland management by the farmers in the area, relative to a much lower uptake in other areas where no partnership research has been conducted (Ribeiro et al., 2017, p. 34; Apaba, 2014).

Other cases in this sub-sample on the technical lever of change focus on research co-design between the researchers and societal actors to frame the environmental justice issues. Indeed, many socio-technical innovations do not apply to all income groups or low-income markets (Crul and Diehl, 2008, p. 129). In the latter contexts, researchers highlight the need to focus on specific issues that are different from the high-income markets, such as the desirability of the technical innovations by low-income groups, capacity building for effective use, and affordability (Gomez Castillo et al., 2012, p. 129; Ehrenfeld, 2008, p. 135).

For instance, in Tanzania, a research project on the installation of local off-grid photovoltaic solar cell systems induced a re-framing of the problem issue to investigate from a purely technical one to a socioeconomic evaluation of the adaptation of the photovoltaic system to the local energy needs. Through this project, the off-grid solar system was combined with building a locally managed and owned biomass generator operating during peak electricity demand, using vegetable oil from local jatropha nuts (Chionidou, 2008). Similar initiatives of off-grid or micro-grid electricity provision have been promoted worldwide. However, as illustrated by many failures, to be successful, they should be designed around local needs and capacities instead of promoting specific products or technologies (Wilson and Zarsky, 2009).

Overall, as shown by various reviews of sustainable living labs (Ceschin and Gaziulusoy, 2016; McCrory et al., 2020), the researchers involved in co-construction processes for socio-technical research have gradually expanded their sustainability focus. The earlier approaches mainly dealt with environmental aspects. Subsequently, social and economic sustainability aspects, such as labor conditions, integration of marginalized people, or inclusive governance of socio-technical change, were increasingly integrated (Ceschin and Gaziulusoy, 2016, p. 145).

What these evolutions show is that the development of transdisciplinary partnership research on the technical levers of change is not just based on a rejection of conventional scientific methods. Rather, the evolution shows an integration of existing tools and methods in a new way of organizing the research process. Therefore, the failures of "ivory-tower" science to analyze the role of technical levers of sustainability transformations should not induce a call for less science and less knowledge but more and better science by enhancing existing methods with new principles of knowledge co-production. As illustrated by the cases, such co-production involves knowledge integration among researchers and societal actors and research co-design to consider the socially relevant and legitimate perspectives on sustainability values.

3.2.2 *Participatory modeling of sustainable resource use in society-wide sustainability transformations*

3.2.2.1 *From optimization modeling to participatory modeling of socio-ecological system dynamics*

The second biophysical lever highlighted in the 2019 Report (UN, 2019) regards actions for improving the sustainable use of natural resources in society-wide sustainability transformations (e.g., transformations in the mobility, energy, or housing sector). In this context, to produce biophysical analyses of resource use that also provide a match to knowledge on specific socially desirable and feasible transformation pathways, researchers developed a broad range of participatory modeling approaches. This section discusses how knowledge co-production can be successfully integrated into this brand of sustainability research.

Since the publication in 1972 of the influential computational models in the book *The Limits to Growth* by Dennis Meadows and her co-authors at MIT, computational modeling of system dynamics has been improved and has become a key research tool for understanding the evolution of resource use in complex socio-ecological systems (Meadows, 2009). Grounded in systems theory, system dynamics models typically analyze networks of cause–effect relations among the elements of a system and feedback loops that stabilize or amplify changes in the system through time. This simulation of system-wide effects of networks of causal relations and feedback processes makes system dynamics modeling well suited to exploring emergent system-level behavior of integrated socio-ecological systems and assessing the implications of management or policy interventions in these systems (Schlüter et al., 2019).

In practice however, the use of these models may yield fancy simulations and sophisticated results of resource use at the expense of a proper understanding of the value-related perspectives of researchers and societal actors on the overall orientation of the system dynamics (Vennix, 1999). Indeed, researchers who produce computational models may have trouble organizing the active involvement of societal actors in the co-design of the research framework, analysis, or interpretation of the results. In such circumstances, even though the models may formally consider technically feasible pathways for sustainable resource use in society-wide transformations, they are likely to fail to match the socially legitimate and relevant perspectives of societal actors on real-world transformation processes.

Hence, to answer these concerns, participatory modeling aims to address a double challenge. First, it aims to combine the respective strengths of quantitative and qualitative dynamic modeling tools, as these approaches complement each other (Smetschka and Gaube, 2020). On the one hand, quantitative computational models used in socio-ecological analyses provide accurate measurable results on the general system-level results that can be compared across cases. On the other hand, many of the core social sustainability concerns, such as strengthening social bonds or work-life balance, cannot be captured in quantitative measures and are better approached through qualitative research. Second, participatory modeling also actively involves societal actors in the research design. As will be shown through the below case studies in our sample, by co-designing the quantitative and the qualitative variables of the system models, participatory modeling allows for reaching a better understanding of the real-world outcomes of the action strategies envisioned by societal actors to tackle specific sustainability issues.

3.2.2.2 Self-explaining people-friendly street design in Auckland, New Zealand

The Future Streets project in Auckland, New Zealand, is a good illustration of the outcome of a series of transdisciplinary research projects based on participatory systems dynamic modeling and community surveying. The project was headed by a multistakeholder consortium from the regional transportation planning authority (Auckland Transport), the New Zealand Transport Agency, local community leaders, various local transportation consultancies, and university researchers (Mackie et al., 2018). The Future Streets project was inspired by a previous pilot project on traffic calming in Point England, Auckland. The pilot project modified local streets by making them more environmentally friendly, removing line marking, placing plants and artwork to slow motorists, and reinforcing a sense of place. Five years after this pilot project, the likelihood of accidents had more than halved, with more pedestrians and cyclists using local streets (ibid, 2018).

The idea of broadening this pilot project to a set of social interventions for redesigning the streets in the Māngere neighborhood in Auckland stems from several years of collaborative research. The Māngere area has a large indigenous population. The area was selected because of the high number of fatal and serious car crashes in the neighborhood. The choice of the various priority interventions in the area was based on intensive community consultation and insights from a series of projects that were conducted from 2014 to 2016.

The main result from the research co-design processes in the project was a broadening of the initial research purpose of the pilot project (initially mainly related to road safety) toward addressing biodiversity-related and sociocultural objectives in the street design proposals that were subsequently analyzed in the participatory modeling exercise. In particular, based on a vast number of community engagement meetings, the project identified the main social well-being factors highly valued by the community: environmental health, neighborhood connections, a sense of neighborhood safety, and ease of access to employment, goods, and services (Macmillan and Mackie, 2016). Through this process, the researchers also engaged with cultural values that are important to the indigenous communities of the neighborhood. The latter led to road improvements that reflect the identity of the Māngere people. Some of these improvements are colored pathways that refer to shark oil traditionally used by Māori (Kōkowhai—yellow), the use of endemic plant species to slow traffic, and signposts for wayfinding and culturally relevant landmarks (Mackie et al., 2018).

For the initial participatory systems dynamics study in 2014, the research team created a stakeholder group of 16 people from public authorities, citizens from various social groups, researchers, and representatives of indigenous communities from the Māori and Pacific people (Macmillan et al., 2014). The constitution of a representative, comprehensive stakeholder group, with connections to the local and regional policy was considered a key condition of a successful participatory modeling process. Among others, the creation of a comprehensive stakeholder group allowed for a continuous process of confidence building with societal actors.

On this basis, the project team organized two rounds of dynamic system modeling. First, in 2014, the team developed a detailed quantitative model of the impacts of three different active mobility infrastructures on bicycle use, cyclist injuries, and air pollution (Macmillan et al., 2014). Second, in 2016, the team integrated this analysis into a broader dynamic system model that also considers the economic, environmental, and sociocultural drivers of sustainable mobility solutions. This model helped to build a common understanding of a multi-dimensional approach to the proposed transformations (Macmillan et al., 2016, 2020).

From a societal perspective, self-explaining road design in the Māngere area of Auckland is the most visible project outcome. This street design aims to calm traffic on local roads via self-explanatory features that reflect the sociocultural concerns of the research partners, particularly the local indigenous communities. Overall, through careful selection and ongoing collaboration with the non-academic project partners in a socially inclusive way, the project team could generate a high level of uptake of the research results by the local actors.

3.2.2.3   Co-designing participatory modeling frameworks for matching feasible and socially desirable transformation pathways

Some additional cases for this second sub-sample on biophysical levers of change in socio-ecological systems allow for illustrating the importance of research co-construction among scientific researchers and societal actors.

One project that ranked high in matching the research design with the diversity of the sustainability values of the key societal actors was the

NATCAP project in Belize, Central America. The NATCAP project provided data-intensive modeling of ecosystem health and fisheries revenue in Belize, a coastal state in Central America (Verutes et al., 2017; Arkema et al., 2019). A six-year collaboration (2010–2016) between the research consortium of NATCAP and the Coastal Zone Management Body allowed for building relationships, making scientific advances, and strengthening local planning capacity. The latter was especially challenging, as it involved addressing the competition among societal actors for limited space, mainly for oil exploration, aquaculture, fisheries, coastal real estate development, and conservation of unique mangrove ecosystems.

Through joint data gathering among scientists and various Coastal Advisory Committees, the project could explore alternative strategies to over-intensive coastal real estate development. These strategies focused on two sustainability transformation pathways considered desirable and feasible by the main societal actors. The first pathway was protecting sensitive habitats in the unique mangrove ecosystem. The second pathway aimed at safeguarding the operations of the small-scale coastal lobster fisheries, which is the economic activity in the area that is most compatible with the various sustainability values.

In other projects in this sub-sample, the research co-design resulted in the revision of the overall strategies to be prioritized through the modeling exercise. For instance, the TERIM project provided an agent-based model that simulated the interactions of various stakeholders in the energy system in the Weiz-Gleisdorf region in Austria (Binder et al., 2014). The discussion on the project design induced a strong shift in the understanding of action priorities by the multistakeholder steering board of the energy region Weiz-Gleisdorf. Initially focused on reaching regional energy sufficiency through local biomass, the research team gradually shifted the focus toward reducing energy demand through renovation as the main action priority. Moreover, within this new research purpose, the project gathered new evidence on the importance of social networking among house owners for motivating sustainable energy choices and fostering behavioral change, which was not foreseen in the initial research design.

The sub-sample of participatory biophysical modeling cases also highlights the role of research co-design in considering environmental justice values. A potential benefit of research co-design among societal actors and researchers on sustainability values is promoting equity in participation and empowering more marginal actors to bring their knowledge to the modeling process. For instance, the participatory design of a computational model for the sustainable management of a community forest in Larzac, Southern France, revealed the contribution of practices of woodcutting by small-scale farmers, as it contributes to their economic subsistence and provides tangible biodiversity benefits. In the first round of simulations, such practices were not included, as they were considered contrary to science-based rational forest management by the regional forest administration (Simon and Etienne, 2010).

In general, the various cases in this sub-sample show that participatory systems dynamics modeling can create a better match of the modeling frameworks with socially desirable and feasible transformation pathways. In practice, as the understanding of the appropriate action strategies may evolve with the intermediary results of the participatory modeling process, researchers must update and adjust the computational models in various rounds of model design. The first phase, building the model, requires input from a broad range of people and an initial understanding of the main causal interactions in the socio-ecological system. In the next phases, the computation of the model in a series of test runs allows for tackling the limitations and flaws of the initial intuitive mental models of societal actors and researchers to capture the dynamics of complex systems (Videira et al., 2010). Therefore, research co-design in the field of participatory modeling shows the importance of the ongoing commitment of the researchers and societal actors throughout the process in a series of iterations between computational modeling and participatory workshop discussions.

3.2.3 Multi-criteria assessment of socioeconomic levers of change

3.2.3.1 From quantitative cost-benefit analysis to participatory multi-criteria assessment

As can already be seen in the discussion of the biophysical levers of change, socioeconomic policies are key to the dissemination or upscaling of technical solutions for accelerating sustainability transformations. Therefore, developing an appropriate framework of socioeconomic policy planning and decision-making is a key to achieving the social transformations necessary for implementing sustainable development goals. It is the third major lever of change in the 2019 Global Sustainability Report (UN, 2019).

As shown by economics and sustainability science scholars, conventional quantitative cost-benefit analysis fails to provide an adequate framework for analyzing multi-dimensional economic policy and decision-making (Scrieciu, 2007; Salas-Molina, 2019). In the context of economic theorizing, the limits of quantitative approaches have been extensively documented in the literature on social cost-benefit analysis (Nussbaum, 2000; Masur and Posner, 2011). Indeed, conventional cost-benefit analysis adopts a quantitative approach to the economic and social dimensions, for example by calculating a monetary equivalent to assess societal values. At best, this approach can provide information on the efficiency of a policy measure at a certain moment of time in a given context of consensual societal values (Masur and Posner, 2011). Nevertheless, the approach is less well equipped to account for the broad scope of intangible social benefits that drive sustainability transformations, such as the building of more inclusive and just societies (ibid).

In response to these well-known failures of conventional cost-benefit analysis to address broader social dimensions of sustainability transformations, scholars have developed a set of multi-criteria decision support tools (Abaza and Baranzini, 2002). These tools consider quantitative and qualitative criteria, and, through an interactive and structured knowledge-gathering process on the criteria, organize a dialogue among researchers and societal actors on the value-laden choices among the many social welfare and social well-being outcome targets. This section draws upon the sub-sample cases within the thriving research tradition of multi-criteria assessment to illustrate the role of research co-design processes in usable knowledge production on socioeconomic levers of change in sustainability transformations.

3.2.3.2 Sustainable mobility in Potsdam, Germany

The ClimPol research group at the Institute for Advanced Sustainability Studies in Potsdam, Germany, provides a good illustration of a highly successful research partnership on socioeconomic mobility planning from an integrated sustainability perspective. The group developed a study in cooperation with international research partners, the federal government, the state of Brandenburg, and local business and society partners. The team worked from 2015 to 2016 on a multi-criteria assessment of policies to address widespread air pollution in the Potsdam area, while recognizing the importance of the social dimension of mobility transitions beyond the more conventional technological and economic perspectives.

Much research on transport and pollution is still conducted through expert-led multi-disciplinary science. As shown in a review of scholarly work by the ClimPol project team, most mobility decision-support tools are based on researches that analyze the various aspects of mobility planning through separate research frameworks, whether through models for analyzing traffic planning, air quality, or carbon emissions mitigation (von Schneidemesser et al., 2017, p. 3). For instance, time efficiency surveys in traffic planning focus on individual route planning, which places a heavy focus on time gains that can be made by various mobility choices, without considering measures to stop the circle of increasing travel speed, travel distances, and energy consumption (BFS and ARE, 2017; Hoppe and Michl, 2017). Other studies use cost-benefit analysis to compare the costs of mobility choices with various benefits regarding the satisfaction of individual mobility needs and pollution impacts but without considering the broader benefits on urban welfare or quality of life, which cannot be captured entirely in quantitative measures (Delhaye et al., 2017). Given this separate analysis of the various dimensions, the results fail to provide an integrated understanding of society-wide mobility transformations.

Thus, to support multi-dimensional decision-making on mobility transitions, the research group on mobility and climate developed a multi-criteria assessment jointly with scientists, practitioners, and decision-makers, between 2015 and 2017 (Schmale et al., 2015, 2016). This assessment included environmental considerations and considerations for road safety, eco-mobility, and quality of life.

As stated by the project team, to successfully address complex urban transportation challenges, it is necessary to adapt the multi-criteria assessment methods to include available sources of knowledge on local and regional feasible sustainability transformation options. Practical knowledge can be used to judge, for example, the feasibility of local travel options, while discussions with societal actors can play a role in clarifying value choices regarding social equity in urban planning. On the other hand, scientific knowledge can contribute to the various quantitative and qualitative assessments of environmental, economic, and social impacts.

In the first phase, the project team gathered roughly 10 representatives from various departments of the municipality's administration, one person from the state province, one from the ministry of environment, and two natural scientists. This working group framed collaboratively the main research questions and developed the multi-criteria assessment process.

The project worked with a list of socioeconomic policy measures in the municipalities' planning stage. The measures were assessed by a set of criteria that considered impacts on six categories: air quality, climate change, noise emissions, road safety, eco-mobility, and quality of life. The integrated participatory assessment was applied in a one-day workshop. Before the workshop, the team studied the indicators for assessing the various criteria and gathered the best available scientific data on these indicators. At the workshop, breakout groups ranked the various measures. The resulting scores were statistically analyzed by the scientists and presented to the participants in the various working groups. Further discussions, adjustments, plausibility checks, and decisions on weighting the various criteria were conducted within the plenary workshop meetings.

Initially, the city's "urban- and climate-friendly mobility" initiative identified over 75 specific measures in the planning or pre-implementation stage in 2013. With so many measures, it was challenging to maintain an overview of the synergies, overlaps, or counter-productivity of the measures and assess the priorities within the limited city's budget.

At the end of the project, the research team listed the measures of the initiative that were ranked as very high and high priority. The very high priority group included extensions of park-and-ride facilities (connecting to public transport and cycling-walking paths), the overall enhancement of infrastructure for public transport and cycling, limiting parking spaces in the city to discourage driving, and creating a mobility agency. Most measures were assessed based on the reference data and previous experience. Through the participatory process, expert input was combined with other considerations, such as the public acceptance of the new policies and contextual features related to the real-world options for urban re-design. Based on the project results, the municipality adjusted its planning to implement all the high and very high priority measures from the final project ranking.

3.2.3.3 Co-designing sustainability evaluation frameworks for participatory multi-criteria assessments

In the ClimPol research project, the key focus is on the design of sustainable mobility that integrates social and environmental value concerns. In this case, most of the criteria related to desirable city development were assessed through qualitative scales, while the air pollution data was gathered through quantified pollution measurements.

The quantitative part of the multi-criteria assessment is more prominent in its other applications. For instance, one case in the Transport Innovation Deployment for Europe (TIDE) Handbook on Impact Assessment addresses a multi-criteria assessment of congestion charging measures, introduced in cities such as London, Stockholm, or Milan (TIDE, 2015, p. 35). In this multi-criteria assessment, even many behavioral impacts, such as changes in travel time or the share of walking and cycling, could be quantified, based on structured surveys on the impact of congestion charging measures introduced in various pilot cities. However, other research aspects, such as the equity of the scheme regarding the various population groups could not be quantified, as they involved value-related choices. Thus, even though the project was focused on the quantitative criteria, this key societal value required involving the societal-actor partners in the design of the empirical methodology of the project, dealing with data collection on the social equity implications of the congestion charging measures.

As shown in the various case studies presented in the TIDE handbook, by involving societal actors in co-designing quantitative and qualitative data collection methods, multi-criteria assessment has evolved into a powerful tool for integrated sustainability assessment of the socioeconomic lever of change. Scholars developed improvements to make the weighting of the various criteria more reliable. The direct weighting of the importance of the criteria, as in the ClimPol case, has the advantage of very low resource requirements and high transparency of the process. More resource-intensive techniques introduce pairwise comparisons of the criteria in the weighting procedure and several techniques to check the consistency among the assessment scales, often using a software (for an overview, see, for instance, Németh et al., 2019).

For complex assessment processes, some of the technical improvements will be useful. However, regardless of the choice among these techniques, the participatory nature of the process remains an essential attribute and the improvements must be evaluated accordingly. Therefore, when co-designing the research protocol, the research partners must carefully consider the balance between the increasing complexity of the computational algorithms that can be used with the transparency and the quality of the research co-construction.

3.2.4 Multistakeholder policy implementation research

3.2.4.1 From idealized sampling standards to real-world field research on policy impacts

Sustainability scholars highlight innovations in public sector governance toward increased stakeholder participation as an important fourth lever to address the current global ecological and social crisis (UN, 2019). This strengthening of multistakeholder governance aims to foster enhanced cooperation among a multitude of actors who drive sustainability transformations, often operating at different scales of governance.

According to the outcomes of an international expert workshop on multistakeholder governance, held in Zürich in June 2017, the capacity of multistakeholder governance can be best enhanced by integrating the various knowledge inputs at the various stages of the policy cycle. It can be achieved through a combination of strategies, such as considering system characteristics at the policy formulation stage, building conflict resolution and leadership skills at the implementation stage, and fostering adaptive and generic learning at the evaluation stage of the policy cycle (Hitziger et al., 2019). Conventional disciplinary ivory-tower science seems ill-equipped to generate the knowledge base to support such highly interactive and evolving multistakeholder policy design and implementation processes.

A stylized paradigmatic case of a classic disciplinary ivory-tower science approach can illustrate the challenges of analyzing multistakeholder policy implementation processes in interdependent social and ecological systems. For instance, prominent research tools in the social sciences for obtaining data on the impacts of policy interventions, so-called random controlled trials, have become popular to analyze the impact of policy interventions over the last decades (Banerjee and Duflo, 2011). In these methods, scientists randomly allocate individuals to several groups that are subject to different interventions and compare the measured responses. Copied on the model of laboratory science, these real-world trials, while appropriate to analyze the effect of specific measures on specific groups, fail to capture the multiple interdependent socio-ecological features and the heterogeneous perspectives of multiple societal actors in real-world sustainability policies.

First, in random trials, to control for possible bias between different situations of various individuals, the number of individuals to include rapidly increases with the number of policy measures or variables to be included in the analysis (Black, 1996). Therefore, in practice, to keep the number of individuals to include in the study within reasonable limits, random controlled trials must focus on one or a few dimensions of the problem to be addressed. The case of the successful North Karelia health prevention research on coronary heart diseases in the sub-sample of cases is a good example of the importance of this methodological constraint. Indeed, in this case, a random approach to sampling was abandoned in favor of a more feasible and robust multi-dimensional case study approach to health surveying (Puska et al., 1983). Second, for rigorous control, the researchers must apply the interventions to a unique and complete group of people belonging to a given category (e.g., school students, members of associations, and inhabitants of a region) and in similar contexts (Melia, 2015). The latter is rarely the case in the implementation of policy measures for multi-dimensional sustainability transformations. Finally, the method requires comparing the results with a control group that does not benefit from the envisioned policy interventions. Nevertheless, in some situations, isolating a control group that does not benefit from proposed policy interventions is ethically inappropriate (Goodkind et al., 2011; cf. the Montréal case study in the sub-sample) or unrealistic (Puska et al., 1983).

In contrast to the laboratory-like random controlled trials, to understand multistakeholder policy implementation processes, researchers must address the multiple dimensions of sustainability transformations in an integrated manner (Poteete et al., 2010). Typically, such integrated approaches will use tools that combine quantitative and qualitative field surveying over multiple dimensions or rely on thick and contextual fieldwork. Indeed, to analyze multistakeholder policies for sustainability, researchers must consider the impact of policy interventions on interdependent social and ecological system features, which cannot be separated from each other as in random controlled trials. Overall, to gather reliable scientific data and information and support effective policy implementation of integrated sustainability transformations, researchers and societal actors must integrate knowledge on multiple system dimensions and from the perspective of a diversity of evolving societal actor perspectives

3.2.4.2 Community health surveying of asthma prevalence in New York

A well-documented case illustrating the failures of ivory tower, disciplinary research for data gathering on policy implementation in multistakeholder governance contexts is Jason Coburn's study of environmental health in the

Williamsburg neighborhood of New York City, in southeast Manhattan (Corburn, 2005). The context of this study is the involvement of disenfranchised population groups in policies for addressing the increase of asthma prevalence in urban areas with high levels of pollution (Flies et al., 2019).

Gathering data on asthma prevalence can be challenging, as patients do not systematically search for or have access to formal medical care, especially in low-income urban neighborhoods. In this context, through improvements in mix-methods research (i.e., combining conventional quantitative surveys and qualitative community-led data collection and intervention studies), public health researchers have identified general trends in the evolution of asthma prevalence. They established correlations with environmental factors such as exposure to major traffic and industry-related pollutants (New York City Mayor's Office, 2015, p. 190). Nevertheless, as shown in the Williamsburg neighborhood case, documented by Corburn, such general aggregated data must be refined with the knowledge of the specific socio-ecological path-dependent evolutions in the problem field if policymakers and societal actors want to understand the specific causal pathways leading to high asthma incidence and formulate policies for the most impacted social groups.

In 1992, a conflict over the operation of an incinerator in the heavily industrialized Williamsburg neighborhood led to a highly contested neighborhood health study. In this study, researchers from the City University of New York Medical School (CUNY-CHASM), along with the New York City Department of Health (DOH), analyzed the statistics produced by the local neighborhood hospital (Kaminsky et al., 1993). Accordingly, the research team concluded that there may not be a major asthma problem in the neighborhood. As noted by Corburn in his fieldwork on the 1992 study, from the outset, the residents dismissed the methodology of the epidemiological study for using hospitalization data from a local hospital, which many residents from local communities rarely, if ever, visited, and for failing to disaggregate results by age, gender, ethnicity or type of daily activities (Corburn, 2005, p. 119).

By ignoring crucial local knowledge, the CUNY-CHASM/DOH study compiled poor scientific evidence and, more importantly, failed to identify the appropriate research questions to understand the causes of the health concerns in the community. In response to the community concerns, El Puente, a local community organization, together with Community Information and Epidemiological Technologies (CIET), a non-profit research consultant specialized in community-based survey tools, organized three community-wide surveys between 1995 and 1999. Through these surveys, the researchers could show high asthma rates among sub-groups of the community, most prominently among school children and women aged over 45, which previously did not appear in any statistics. Follow-up focus groups could relate this high prevalence to the women's occupations in laundries, dry cleaners, beauty salons, or sweatshop-like textile factories.

As documented by Corburn, none of the major scientific results of the study could have been obtained by a traditional top-down, principal investigator-led, epidemiological study into asthma prevalence and its environmental causes. Two processes served the successful generation of reliable and usable knowledge: the organization of collaborations between researchers and societal actors in the production of various types of knowledge and the organization of effective research co-design.

First, the collaboration between researchers and societal actors at all stages of the project was crucial in reaching successful scientific and societal outcomes of the project. The main reason is that the research team, trained by El Puente and CIET, had to act as community health workers, not just survey administrators, to overcome distrust (Corburn, 2005, p. 127). Particularly, to organize the collaboration in data gathering, El Puente recruited 10 community members with a personal or family stake in asthma and trained them with the help of the New York City DOH and public health professionals from Hunter College at the City University of New York.

Second, per Cecilia Iglesias-Garden, one of the coordinators of the research team, to understand the specific causal pathways leading to health concerns, health workers must speak credibly about more issues than just asthma and pollution. If the researchers could not address questions related to health and social issues other than asthma and pollution, the residents were not going to trust them or talk to them. Therefore, the survey team decided to focus the first round of surveying on the multi-dimensional social welfare and well-being issues of the community.

The results of the survey in the first year were discussed with the community members, which led to the identification of topics for investigation for the next year of fieldwork (Corburn, 2005, p. 121). Using this kind of iterative process, the information gathered during one phase provided the starting point for a critical dialogue on the analysis of the results, their local relevance, and the selection of follow-up research questions. It led to three major surveys, conducted between 1995 and 1999. The first focused on the general community problems related to environmental health issues and general community concerns. The second targeted specific categories of the population with identified asthma problems, such as women and school children. The third helped improve the understanding of the efficacy of traditional remedies widely used in the immigrant communities of the neighborhood.

The results of these studies were widely publicized and induced a series of peer-reviewed publications in high-profile medical journals (Ledogar et al., 1999, 2000). Beyond these scientific results, the project induced various health interventions that significantly advanced the situation of the population. For instance, after learning from the second round of surveying that adults, particularly women, exposed to pollution in laundries and dry cleaning in the community also suffered from asthma, an asthma plan for adults was developed by the community organization. Another innovative community outcome was the initiation of a program addressed to professional healthcare providers to inform them about asthma home remedies and their cultural significance in immigrant communities. Further, beyond the community-specific initiatives, the research project also contributed to advancing the research tradition of community health surveys, adding to the body of the partnership methodologies in public health research worldwide.

3.2.4.3   Co-designing socio-ecological systems analysis in policy implementation research

As shown in the case study of community health surveys documented by Corburn (2005), involving societal actors in research co-design at various moments of the research process contributes to successful usable knowledge production in multistakeholder governance contexts. In general, such transdisciplinary co-design helps societal actors to address the integration challenge of the various knowledge types mobilized in multistakeholder governance at various moments of the policy cycle (Hitziger et al., 2019).

Another transdisciplinary research project on multistakeholder policy implementation cases that illustrates this challenge is the so-called cascade model of ecosystem services (Spangenberg et al., 2014). Typically, as shown through a review of recently published studies, most research on ecosystem services starts with the identification of natural processes that support the production of various ecosystem services (Menzel and Teng, 2010). Only in a later phase are stakeholders included to discuss the recommendations from the analysis (see, e.g., Cowling et al., 2008). By separating the biophysical identification of ecosystem services from their social valuation by local stakeholders, researchers suggest that the ecosystem services can be defined without reference to ongoing societal debates on societal values in the specific implementation context. However, to make ecosystem service research useful in highly diverse multistakeholder policy implementation contexts, the values and the needs of local users should guide the process from the beginning. Therefore, as illustrated by the cascade model developed by Spangenberg et al. (2014), users of the ecosystem should be engaged early in the design of the research process. In the cascade model, societal actors are directly involved in a sequence of research steps with the scientific researchers in attributing the use value to various ecosystem functions, identifying real-world ecosystem service potentials related to these use values, and analyzing how the potentials can be mobilized and appropriated via appropriate policy planning and implementation.

Similarly, regarding environmental justice concerns, multistakeholder policy implementation research should combine objective measurements of the distribution of outcomes for the various social groups with an improved understanding of how individuals perceive justice and injustice of distributional outcomes. For instance, in a research project on implementing payment schemes for ecosystem services, Adrian Martin and his team at Sussex University found that local respondents mostly preferred an egalitarian approach to distributing the payments (each household receiving the same amount). Such a contextual understanding is contrary to dominant utilitarian ideas, which hold that payments according to the household's contribution to the service provision would be fairer (Martin, 2017, p. 158). This context-based analysis of local conceptions of justice is crucial to understand how social legitimacy can be built around the contextual implementation of general and more abstract principles of justice. The organization of broad stakeholder participation in defining the general framework for assessing various approaches to equity and justice can contribute to strengthening the social legitimacy of the envisioned policies for ecosystem service provision (ibid).

As highlighted in the introduction to this section, multistakeholder governance approaches raise a set of challenges that must be addressed for effective policymaking on multi-sectoral and multi-actor sustainability issues. These challenges are related to building capacities for knowledge integration among the involved actors. As illustrated through the case studies, transdisciplinary research approaches that actively organize research co-design can contribute to building such knowledge integration capacity required for improved coordination and cooperation among various stakeholders.

3.2.5 Including the diversity of sociocultural perspectives on sustainability transformations

3.2.5.1 From expert-driven qualitative data collection to community-based qualitative research

The fifth lever of change identified in the Global Sustainability report is the inclusion of the diversity of sociocultural perspectives on change (UN, 2019). Thus, to strengthen the science base to understand the sociocultural perspectives on sustainability transformations, scientists mobilize the broad diversity of qualitative sources at their disposal, ranging from direct statements contributed by the participants in workshops, textual sources in paper and online media, informal reports by civil society and policy organizations, and photo and video material (Singleton and Strait, 2005, ch. 11).

Although this is sometimes less obvious, qualitative research is not automatically based on knowledge co-production processes nor easily integrated within interdisciplinary research frameworks. A key undertaking in this context for researchers is to integrate qualitative research methods with knowledge co-production processes on the various social and ecological dimensions of the ongoing sustainability transformations. To successfully use these methods in transdisciplinary sustainability research, qualitative research on sociocultural levers of change must consider how global and system-wide social and ecological issues interact with the sociocultural dynamics. Indeed, through the multi-level and multi-sectoral nature of sustainability issues, such as climate change or the biodiversity extinction crisis, civil society and organized collectivities are increasingly confronted with evolutions in other sectors of activity that question their value perspectives and problem understandings. Thus, the sociocultural perspectives of such actors are continuously questioned, applied, and evaluated from the perspective of multi-sectoral and multi-level system-wide changes.

Further, similar to the analysis of the other levers of change, to produce usable knowledge on the various sociocultural drivers and barriers, scholars must integrate these conventional qualitative research methodologies in partnership research processes that contribute to a socially relevant and legitimate research framing of the sustainability issues. Indeed, qualitative research methods are also used in conventional expert-led research processes without research co-design (Willis, 2007). A quick "Google Scholar" search for publications that use methods such as focus groups or qualitative systems modeling shows that many non-participatory uses and expert-led uses of such tools have been developed. A prominent example of non-participatory uses includes the so-called focus groups used in marketing research (Belk, 2007). Group-based assessment of new consumer products in focus groups is a powerful method to uncover participants' emotional and nonverbal reactions and observe group-based imitation behavior. In such cases, the focus group is not used in the context of knowledge co-production but as an improved data collection method for the marketing researcher and a useful qualitative complement to statistical user surveys.

3.2.5.2 *Energy poverty in the informal urban settlements of Enkanini, South Africa*

The case of qualitative research on energy poverty in an informal urban settlement in South Africa aptly illustrates the role of research co-design in qualitative research on sociocultural perspectives on change (Smit et al., 2018, 2019). In this case, a follow-up research project of a successful public-private partnership for small-scale off-grid solar energy provision led to deepen the engagement with the potential community of beneficiaries.

The initial framework of the off-grid solar energy project focused on the lack of technical infrastructure as the key explanatory factor of energy poverty. Through a process of co-construction in a series of follow-up research projects, this perspective was reframed in terms of a lack of involvement of all social groups in social innovations related to energy infrastructure, energy saving, and access to affordable technologies. These follow-on projects lead to highlight the importance of strengthening community control and decision over energy choices (so-called energy democracy) (Bloem et al., 2021). In particular, a set of participatory workshops with energy poor households showed the potential benefits for the community of a more meaningful and representative engagement of women in co-designing socio-technological innovations (Smit at al., 2018, 2019).

The Enkanini informal settlement in South Africa is an illegal settlement at 30 km from Cape Town, established in 2006 on land owned by the municipality of Stellenbosch. By 2015, approximately 8,000 people lived in Enkanini in approximately 2,000 rudimentary shacks (Van Breda and Swilling, 2019). They provide labor to the neighboring cities, mainly in services and government, such as cleaning and security work. Moreover, the inhabitants organize a small but vibrant informal economy offering a range of products and services, such as the sale of food and beverages, hair and beauty salons, and childcare facilities (Smit et al., 2018).

The crux of the Enkanini case is the lack of provision of basic infrastructure services to this informal settlement by the local government, mainly in the areas of electricity, water, and waste management (Van Breda and Swilling, 2019). The problems from this lack of services include high levels of vermin invasions (especially rats), indoor air pollution from paraffin and candle use, frequent fires and floods, and the associated increased health risks mentioned earlier.

Since 2010, a group of Master students and researchers at the Centre for Sustainability Transitions of Stellenbosch University have partnered with inhabitants of the settlement to set up a series of research projects on improving basic services (Bloem et al., 2021). After two years of applied research in Enkanini, iShack (which stands for "improved shacks"), a social enterprise, was established. This initiative brought solar panels to 767 households between 2011 and 2016 and was widely advertised as a major solution to decentralized renewable energy provision in off-grid settlements (Ambole et al., 2019). It benefitted from a two-year funding for a pilot project by the Bill and Melinda Gates Foundation and was subsequently supported by a zero-interest loan of the Development Bank of Southern Africa and a subsidy from the municipality of Stellenbosch.

In spite of the success of this social enterprise, major challenges for addressing the energy poverty in the community remain. Indeed, the focus on a single technological solution has failed to generate a broader uptake by the community. Only 27% of the dwellings stepped into the solar panel scheme, and most inhabitants who took part in the scheme continued to rely on gas or kerosene (so-called paraffin) for their main energy needs. Second, by providing support to this initiative through a basic electricity subsidy for solar energy, the municipality has awakened fears in the population that this support would be used to postpone a more structural solution to the needs of developing basic infrastructure services in the informal settlement.

Hence, to better understand these issues, researchers conducted a series of follow-up research projects, which illustrate the use of research co-design with societal actors in qualitative research methods. These projects aimed at better understanding the local energy system in the Enkanini settlement, from the point of view of the various social groups. The following projects highlighted, in particular, the potential benefits of a more meaningful representation of women in local social innovation: the participatory integrated assessment project (PARTICIPIA, 2013–2016); the qualitative systems dynamic mapping project, funded by the Southern African Systems Analysis Centre (2016–2018); and the project on Co-Designing Energy Communities with Energy-Poor Women (funded by "Leading Integrated Research for Agenda 2030" from 2017 to 2019) (Smit et al., 2018, 2019).

In the first project, PARTICIPIA, researchers organized a three-day workshop together with the community members to collaboratively design a framework for analyzing the possible pathways to address the energy poverty situation. These workshops involved the main energy user groups: solar users, users with contracts for indirect access to the grid of the neighboring township, and users of traditional off-grid sources of gas and kerosene. The main shift in the design of the conceptual framework realized by the mutual learning in this initial workshop was a shift from a focus on technical solutions for energy provision to a recognition of the sociocultural and aspirational factors that drive the energy behavior of these various groups of inhabitants.

For instance, women are searching for solutions that are affordable and less time consuming regarding access to fuel sources for livelihood activities such as cooking to free time for income-generating activities. Other inhabitants sought alternatives to kerosene (paraffin), as it "smokes and burns the eyes" (Smit et al., 2019, table 3). Thus, despite divergent opinions on the (dis)advantages of the solar solution, the participants converged on the importance of a deeper engagement of the population in social innovations around energy use and the strengthening of the community organization to involve all members in these social innovations.

These insights were further deepened in the subsequent research projects. A qualitative systems design mapping (Hovmand, 2014) helped identify a set of interrelated feedback loops in the local energy system between energy-saving behavior, access to technologies, and infrastructure improvements, which indicate possible pathways for improving upon the current situation (Batinge et al., 2021). These pathways integrate the idea of a deeper engagement of the main users of the energy solutions in innovation, such as via the involvement of women in community co-design of appliances for cooking and refrigerating that generate energy savings and address their main livelihood concerns. Combined with governmental support for making the solutions accessible to the largest number, a dynamic of change can be initiated.

The results of the initial participatory assessment of the problem dimensions and the qualitative systems dynamic mapping project led to a series of peer-reviewed publications (Smit et al., 2018, 2019). Moreover, the research results were used in various strands of follow-up research on the implementation of the envisioned organizational changes. From a political perspective, the results of the research project were used in the organization of a policy seminar in 2017 in the context of the project on "Co-Designing Energy Communities with Energy-Poor Women." In this policy seminar, policymakers from different levels of government, community members, and researchers discussed the various relations between energy, health, and gender that were highlighted in the research project. One institutional proposition that resulted from the seminar is to organize increased multi-level coordination between the regional government (Western Cape government) and the Stellenbosch municipality to address the identified livelihood challenges (Ambole et al., 2019).

3.2.5.3 Co-designing socio-ecological systems analysis in community-based qualitative research

Many of the case studies in the sub-sample on understanding sociocultural dynamics explicitly address environmental justice issues. Indeed, qualitative research, combined with research co-design of common relevant and legitimate research questions, offers some key ingredients that are conducive to promoting the effective participation of disenfranchised social groups in sustainability research.

Another example in this sub-sample that addresses environmental justice issues is the research project on food assistance and food waste in the Brussels Region, Belgium. This project was conducted from October 2018 to March 2019 by ATD Quart Monde, the Federation of social services of the Brussels Region, and an interdisciplinary research team at the University UCLouvain and the University of Antwerp. The proposed protocol for organizing qualitative research on food assistance for people living in poverty was based on the method of "merging of knowledge" developed in various research programs co-conducted by ATD Quart Monde (Ferrand, 1999; ATD Quart Monde, 2016; Godinot and Walker, 2020; Osinski, 2020). In this protocol, persons living in poverty are directly involved as situation experts on equal footing with co-researchers from social assistance services and university researchers (Joos-Malfait et al., 2019).

Further, to co-design the research framework, the project first organized a workshop to co-construct the main research question. The discussion in this workshop led to re-framing the initial focus of the project, which initially focused on new urban food-sharing initiatives and their potential to contribute to food assistance. However, food donation often fails to address the basic aspirations for social inclusion and improved livelihood opportunities for persons living in poverty (ibid). In particular, this first co-design workshop showed that the free provision of food cannot be separated from the creation of spaces where persons living in poverty can access resources that can contribute to lifting them out of poverty. Accordingly, the research purpose was reframed in terms of the question of the contribution of different solutions of food assistance to enhanced dignity of the urban poor and access to new opportunities to lift them out of poverty.

The ATD Quart Monde project on food assistance and food waste subsequently organized four successive workshops and a collaborative process of writing the project report with the persons living in poverty and local social welfare workers (ibid). One main result of this group-based qualitative research is that an excessively strong conditionality in food aid delivery creates competition for satisfying the eligibility conditions among groups of people in poverty, which goes against the community spirit of solidarity and mutual support that otherwise prevails. Further, the research shows that, even though an increase in the diversity of food items is a real concern, the most important demands are related to the defense of their broader socioeconomic rights to work, housing, education, and culture. Finally, participants in the workshops identified alternative channels for distribution, such as neighborhood restaurants and social groceries, as places with a more humane way of food distribution and offering protective spaces for discussing opportunities for multi-dimensional learning and capacity building.

Other examples in the sub-sample illustrate the contribution of the knowledge co-production process in qualitative research to identifying sociocultural perspectives that drive citizen engagements in sustainability transformation processes. For instance, the methodology of future visioning workshops, developed in particular by the scholars of the Dutch Research Institute for Transition, is a well-known research tool for organizing group-based qualitative research on the involvement of citizens and so-called change agents in disruptive innovations for sustainability (Loorbach and Rotmans, 2010).

The method of future visioning aims to elaborate new perspectives on sustainability transformations that are disruptive of the existing status quo by combining the exploration of desirable futures and the analysis of social possibilities of change. In the first step, the research partners organize a workshop on the visioning of a desirable long-term future. This visioning process is informed by existing system diagnosis and analysis and a discussion on legitimate sustainability orientations. The key point of this workshop for future visioning is that, by referring to the long-term desirable future, the group identifies research perspectives that go beyond business-as-usual and are not constrained by vested interests (Roorda et al., 2014, p. 10, p. 30).

Next, starting from this common strategic vision, the research team organizes a group-based qualitative research process for identifying solutions, innovation pathways, and societal change agents that contribute to disruptive transformations. One tool often used in this context is "backcasting," which is an iterative method that takes the desired future as a starting point (e.g., 50 years from now) and proceeds step-by-step back in time, identifying at each time interval the incremental innovation needed to foster progress toward the desired end goal.

One case of this sub-sample of qualitative research projects on sociocultural levers applied a future visioning method, which is the MUSIC project (Mitigation in Urban Context, Solutions for Innovative Cities, 2010–2015). In this project, city officers, together with local stakeholders, organized visioning workshops on climate change mitigation initiatives in six different cities to identify innovations and mobilize change agents for disruptive transformation (Tillie et al., 2012). In the city of Ghent, the backcasting exercise led to embedding radical innovations such as neighborhood initiatives for temporary car-free streets into a larger narrative of Ghent as a climate-neutral city. Since this first qualitative research project, the social movement has spread to other neighborhoods, and the creation of temporary "living streets" has now been recognized as a legitimate tool within sustainability mobility policies in the city.

The examples of transdisciplinary research projects from the sub-sample of research on sociocultural levers of change illustrate the need to integrate discussions on broader system-wide transformations in the research co-design of qualitative approaches to sociocultural perspectives. This research co-design is conducive to better understanding the impact of system constraints on the evolution of sociocultural perspectives on change and enhancing the capacities of societal actors to address multi-scale social justice issues and build more comprehensive visions for supporting multi-scale civic activism. Further, from the Enkanini energy poverty and the ATD Food Assistance case, partnership-based research approaches to qualitative research effectively empower disenfranchised social groups to actively participate in knowledge co-production. The latter topics, which concern the broader issues of capacity building for knowledge co-production, will be further developed in Chapters 4 and 5.

3.3 A pragmatist constructivist approach to knowledge co-production

Research partners embarking upon usable knowledge production on sustainability transformations must mobilize different types of knowledge to cover the coordination needs arising in the management of coupled social and ecological systems. Indeed, the interdependent dynamics often cross different societal sectors of activities and involve very heterogeneous societal actors. Therefore, these research endeavors are inherently collaborative and pluralist, as highlighted in the review paper on knowledge co-production in sustainability research by Norström et al. (2020), discussed in the introduction to this chapter.

At first glance, specialized multi-disciplinary approaches seem to adequately address the needs for organizing such research on sustainability transformations involving heterogeneous types of knowledge and values. Indeed, multi-disciplinary collaborations can mobilize different types of specialized expertise to understand the various social and natural system dimensions.

However, such multi-disciplinary and multi-method approaches, as shown through the analysis of the case studies, are likely to be insufficient for, at least, two reasons. First, the mere juxtaposition of specialized disciplinary analysis of social and ecological system dimensions does not allow for capturing the case-specific systemic interaction processes among the dimensions. The latter requires identifying the interactions at the overall system level and focusing on a subset of desirable and feasible transformation pathways within the space of possible interaction dynamics, and accordingly adjusting the research design in each of the mobilized disciplines in a coordinated manner.

Second, the different value-laden perspectives are not just different ways of evaluating independently existing social and ecological interaction dynamics. Rather, the researchers and societal actors are active participants in the debate over sustainability values, and how they frame the socio-ecological system dynamics is already a result of their prior value-laden perspectives on the unsustainable problem situation.

For instance, to conduct a survey or other forms of field research or identify key actors and societal values reliably, the project partners require a research framework. Regarding interdependent social and ecological systems, such a research framework will have a different focus per the specific pathways that the research team decides to analyze. The latter choice already involves prior decisions on how to characterize the initial problem situation and how to evaluate the sustainability values that define the overall orientation of the societal transformations analyzed in the research.

Transdisciplinary research aims to address this double need for analyzing specific socio-ecological interdependencies and understanding the value-laden orientations through knowledge co-production between scientific researchers and societal actors. As discussed, this knowledge co-production involves knowledge integration and co-management of the research process and the co-design of the various aspects of the research framework. The latter includes identifying socially relevant research questions, the conceptual framework, the legitimate purposes, and the research methodology.

This approach, which recognizes the pragmatic need for collaboration among many perspectives and the co-construction of a common framework for collaborative research, has been characterized in the literature as an example of a pragmatist constructivist position to the learning of common frameworks for collaboration (Reich, 2009; Klein, 2018, p. 14; Boix-Mansilla, 2017). From the pragmatist constructivist view, collaborative learning does not yield a unified final framework, such as in some theoretical approaches to interdisciplinary research that foster methodological unification and the building of new common conceptual categories (Klein, 2010). Rather, the result is an inherently pluralistic framework, hence respecting the various heterogeneous disciplinary research styles and non-academic approaches to knowledge. Further, the adopted framework is characterized as purposeful and accepted by the partners regarding the purpose of a given inquiry into unsustainable problem situations while remaining provisional (i.e., open for further adjustment based on subsequent learning on the systems features and the sustainability values).

In her literature review on learning from a perspective of philosophical pragmatism, Boix-Mansilla characterizes the validity of this pluralistic, purposeful, and provisional framework as one of "reflective equilibrium" between prior perspectives of the partners and new insights gained through social deliberation processes (Boix-Mansilla, 2017). Other prominent scholars of philosophical pragmatism characterize the validity of these provisional frameworks as based on the convergence of the perspectives to a position that "cannot be improved under present circumstances" (see, e.g., Misak, 2000, p. 95).

In this perspective, both scientific knowledge and knowledge from societal actors influence the purposeful learning of common perspectives that do justice to the diversity of perspectives on sustainability transformations. Indeed, pragmatist constructivism does not require a prior privileged perspective, whether being a priority given to the perspective of the scientific researchers or societal actors. Therefore, various types of knowledge contribute to improving the purposeful and provisional common framework, whether it is scientific knowledge on the social and natural system features, laypersons' experiential knowledge on case-specific dynamics, or the deliberation on value perspectives.

The over three decades of research on collaborative planning by Judith Innes and David Booher allows for illustrating the role of the various types of knowledge inputs in the pragmatist constructivist perspective. In their review of 30 years of experience with research for collaborative planning, Judith Innes and David Booher (2010) indicate at least three reasons that knowledge co-production between researchers and societal actors is needed to understand sustainability transformations.

First, understanding ongoing system-wide transformations in specific problem fields requires gathering lay knowledge from involved actors to understand the unique characteristics of the interactions in the socio-ecological systems. As elaborated by Innes and Booher, the latter is grounded in a combination of "first-hand experience, conversations with those with direct knowledge, conversations that help individuals to make sense of what is happening, and logic based on familiarity with comparable situations" (Innes and Booher, 2010, p. 171). Thus, to access this experiential knowledge, quantitative surveying must be combined with qualitative research methods that are better equipped to address thick case-specific knowledge and with informal exchanges to access difficult-to-codify information on the system.

One example discussed by Innes and Booher aptly illustrates the contribution of such integration of experiential knowledge (ibid, pp. 176–177). After the nuclear catastrophe of Chernobyl in 1986, researchers working in the United Kingdom initially failed to anticipate the long-term impact of the radioactive fallout on lambs. They could only map the full extent of the nuclear radiation fallout by integrating the knowledge of local sheep farmers. The farmers' knowledge of the local soils was essential to understanding the dissemination of the radioactive cesium particles in the environment. Similarly, as discussed in the case study on pollution-related asthma in New York City, researchers initially missed important context-specific local knowledge. In both cases, researchers only reached an integrated understanding of the socio-ecological interactions by combining scientific analysis with participatory observation and informal exchange on experience-based insights of local societal actors.

The second reason highlighted by Innes and Booher on why knowledge co-production is important is the need for learning on the plurality of value-related perspectives on interdependent socio-ecological systems. Innes and Booher provide a telling illustration of the failure to integrate different perspectives on desirable and feasible socio-ecological pathways through the case of research projects on Potato Farming in the Peruvian Andes. By neglecting the contributions of indigenous knowledge systems and institutions for seed exchange and improvement, major studies failed to understand how the knowledge from traditional innovation systems is a major resource to build upon to overcome the current deadlocks of the high-input industrial farming system (ibid, p. 178).

The third reason knowledge co-production is important, according to Innes and Booher, directly touches on the issues of environmental justice and the recognition of marginalized voices (ibid, p. 170). In practice, this third reason often overlaps with the first two arguments around knowledge co-production: the integration of experiential knowledge and the integration of the plurality of value-related perspectives on interdependent socio-ecological systems. In some cases, differences in power between societal actors or societal actors and researchers lead to overshadowing the voices of social groups that are part of the research project. In other cases, researchers must factor in the possible social or political consequences of the sharing of experiential knowledge for the individuals affected by social transformation processes. In these circumstances, to consider such marginalized knowledge perspectives, Innes and Booher suggest that researchers mobilize less intrusive methods of information gathering and "be proactive in encouraging and assisting those marginalized populations to participate meaningfully and to recognize that their local knowledge is useful" (ibid, p. 170).

The analysis by Innes and Booher of the various reasons for knowledge co-production with societal actors resonates with the broader pragmatist constructivist perspective. Indeed, pragmatist constructivism underlines not only the importance of knowledge co-production but also the importance of referring to the practical context of ongoing societal transformations to create transversality and dialogue among project partners with heterogeneous disciplinary perspectives and diverging societal value orientations (cf. also Hirsch Hadorn, 2004). Thus, both analyses call for a crucial complement of abstract scientific knowledge with knowledge coming from practice.

In short, pragmatist constructivism underlines the important role of societal actors and researchers as active agents of transformations, who bring specific views to the research partnership on the most relevant problems and the desirable sustainability orientations. As active agents, societal actors and researchers introduce a pluralist and open-ended perspective on the sustainability transformation pathways, which directly affects the enterprise of sustainability science (Klenk and Meehan, 2015). Therefore, to design adequate scientific frameworks for analyzing real-world socio-ecological dynamics, research partners should mutually learn the various legitimate and relevant perspectives on specific transformation pathways. As discussed in this chapter, this can be achieved by combining the integration of different knowledge types from scientific researchers and societal actors, and by involving societal actors in the co-management of the research process and the active research co-design of the various aspects of the framework for analysis.

References

Abaza, H. and Baranzini, A. (Eds.). (2002). *Implementing sustainable development: Integrated assessment and participatory decision-making processes.* Cheltenham: Edward Elgar Publishing.

Ambole, A., Musango, J. K., Buyana, K., Ogot, M., Anditi, C., Mwau, B., . . . and Brent, A. C. (2019). Mediating household energy transitions through co-design in urban Kenya, Uganda and South Africa. *Energy Research and Social Science, 55,* 208–217.

Apaba. (2014). *Recherche d'autonomie fouragère*. Fiche technique 9. Association pour la Promotion de l'Agriculture Biologique de l'Aveyron (APABA), Rodez; Fédération Régionale des Agriculteurs Biologiques Midi-Pyrénées (FRAB), Toulouse.

Arkema, K. K., Rogers, L. A., Toft, J., Mesher, A., Wyatt, K. H., Albury-Smith, S., . . . and Samhouri, J. (2019). Integrating fisheries management into sustainable development planning. *Ecology and Society, 24*(2), 1.

ATD Quart Monde. (2016). *La démarche du Croisement des savoirs et des pratiques avec des personnes en situation de pauvreté*. Montreuil-sous-Bois: Repères (août 2016).

Banerjee, A. and Duflo, E. (2011). *Poor economics. A radical rethinking of the way to fight global poverty*. New York: PublicAffairs.

Batinge, B., Musango, J. K., Ceschin, F., Ambole, A., Smit, S. and Petrulaityte, A. (2021). Modelling gendered innovation for the security of energy services in poor urban environments. *Systems Research and Behavioral Science*, 1–18.

Becker, E. and Jahn, T. (2003). Umrisse einer kritischen Theorie gesellschaftlicher Naturverhältnisse. In Gernot Böhme und Alexandra Manzei (Hrsg.), *Kritische Theorie der Technik und der Natur* (pp. 91–112). München: Fink.

Belk, R. W. (Ed.). (2007). *Handbook of qualitative research methods in marketing*. Cheltenham; Northampton: Edward Elgar Publishing.

BFS and ARE. (2017). *Verkehrsverhalten der Bevölkerung. Ergebnisse des Mikrozensus Mobilität und Verkehr 2015*. Neuchâtel: Bundesamt für Statistik (BFS) and Bundesamt für Raumentwicklung (ARE).

Binder, C. R., Absenger-Helmli, I., Bedenik, K., Chappin, E., Dijkema, G., Goetz, A., . . . and Vilsmaier, U. (2014). TERIM—Transition dynamics in energy regions: An integrated model for sustainable policies. In *Tagungsband 15. Klimatag: 2–4 April 2014* (pp. 78–79). Innsbruck: Universität Innsbruck.

Black, N. (1996). Why we need observational studies to evaluate the effectiveness of health care. *British Medical Journal, 312*(7040), 1215–1218.

Bloem, S., Swilling, M. and Koranteng, K. (2021). Taking energy democracy to the streets: Socio-technical learning, institutional dynamism, and integration in South African community energy projects. *Energy Research and Social Science, 72*, 101906.

Boix-Mansilla, V. (2017). Interdisciplinary learning: A cognitive-epistemological foundation. In R. Frodeman, J. T. Klein and R. Pacheco (Eds.), *The Oxford handbook of interdisciplinarity* (2nd ed., pp. 261–275). Oxford: Oxford University Press.

Ceschin, F. and Gaziulusoy, I. (2016). Evolution of design for sustainability: From product design to design for system innovations and transitions. *Design Studies, 47*, 118–163.

Chionidou, E. (2008). Power for Africa: Solar hybrid systems for rural electrification. *Solarmagazine* (online brochure available through calaméo.com). Solarthemen Media GmbH. https://fr.calameo.com/books/00142283957a4595c0712. Accessed 7 February 2023.

Claude, S., Ginestet, S., Bonhomme, M., Moulène, N. and Escadeillas, G. (2017). The living lab methodology for complex environments: Insights from the thermal refurbishment of a historical district in the city of Cahors, France. *Energy Research and Social Science, 32*, 121–130.

Cooper, T. (2004). Inadequate life? Evidence of consumer attitudes to product obsolescence. *Journal of Consumer Policy, 27*(4), 421–449.

Cooper, T. (2016). The significance of longevity. In T. Cooper (Ed.), *Longer lasting products: Alternatives to the throwaway society* (pp. 3–38). Abingdon; New York: Routledge.

Corburn, J. (2005). *Street science: Community knowledge and environmental health justice.* Cambridge, MA: MIT Press.

Cowling, R. M., Egoh, B., Knight, A. T., O'Farrell, P. J., Reyers, B., Rouget'll, M., . . . and Wilhelm-Rechman, A. (2008). An operational model for mainstreaming ecosystem services for implementation. *Proceedings of the National Academy of Sciences of the United States of America, 105*(28), 9483–9488.

Cruchon, J. (Coord.). (2019). *Retour d'expériences. Cahors, Porto, Vitoria-Gasteiz.* Brochure du projet ENERPAT SUDOE. https://www.envirobat-oc.fr/IMG/pdf/guide_retourexperience_enerpat_fr2.pdf.

Crul, M. and Diehl, J. C. (2008). Design for sustainability (D4S): Manual and tools for developing countries. *Proceedings of the 7th annual ASEE global colloquium on engineering education, Cape Town* (pp. 19–23). Washington: American Society for Engineering Education.

Delhaye, E., De Ceuster, G., Vanhove, F. and Maerivoet, S. (2017). *Internalisering van externe kosten van transport in Vlaanderen: Actualisering 2016.* Study Commissioned by Vlaamse Milieumaatschappij (MIRA). Transport and Mobility Leuven, Leuven.

Ehrenfeld, J. (2008). *Sustainability by design: A subversive strategy for transforming our consumer culture.* New Haven, CT: Yale University Press.

ENERPAT. (2018). *Expérimentation en matière d'éco-rénovation du patrimoine bâti ancien.* https://enerpatsudoe.fr/. Accessed 11 January 2023.

ENoLL. (2019). *Short history of living labs-research and policy context.* European Network of Living Labs, 29 August 2019. ENoLL Office, Brussels.

Ferrand, F. (1999). *Le croisement des savoirs—Quand le Quart Monde et l'Université pensent ensemble.* Ivry-sur-Seine: Editions de l'atelier.

Flies, E. J., Mavoa, S., Zosky, G. R., Mantzioris, E., Williams, C., Eri, R., . . . and Buettel, J. C. (2019). Urban-associated diseases: Candidate diseases, environmental risk factors, and a path forward. *Environment International, 133,* 105–187.

Godinot, X. and Walker, R. (2020). Poverty in all its forms: Determining the dimensions of poverty through merging knowledge. In *Dimensions of poverty* (pp. 263–279). Cham: Springer.

Gomez Castillo, L., Diehl, J. C. and Brezet, J. C. (2012). *Design considerations for base of the pyramid (BoP) projects* [Conference presentation]. Cumulus Conference 2012, 24–26 May, Helsinki, Finland [s.l., s.n.].

Goodkind, J. R., Githinji, A. and Isakson, B. (2011). Reducing health disparities experienced by refugees resettled in urban areas: A community-based transdisciplinary intervention model. In M. Kirst et al. (Eds.), *Converging disciplines: A transdisciplinary research approach to urban health problems* (pp. 41–55). New York; Dordrecht; Heidelberg: Springer Science and Business Media.

Goutiers, V., Charron, M. H., Deo, M. and Hazard, L. (2016). Capflor®: un outil pour concevoir des mélanges de prairies à flore variée. *Fourrages, 228,* 243–252.

Hirsch Hadorn, G. (2004). Unity of knowledge in transdisciplinary research for sustainability. In *Encyclopedia of life support system (EOLSS-UNESCO).* Oxford: EOLSS Publishers Co.

Hitziger, M., Aragrande, M., Berezowski, J. A., Canali, M., Del Rio Vilas, V., Hoffmann, S., . . . and Rüegg, S. R. (2019). EVOlvINC: Evaluating knowledge integration capacity in multistakeholder governance. *Ecology and Society*, 24(2), art36.

Hoppe, M. and Michl, T. (2017). *Transforming the Swiss mobility system towards sustainability*. Working Paper. Zurich University of Applied Science, ZHAW School of Engineering, Zurich.

Hovmand, P. S. (2014). Group model building and community-based system dynamics process. In P. S. Hovmand (Ed.), *Community based system dynamic* (pp. 17–30). Heidelberg: Springer.

Innes, J. E. and Booher, D. E. (2010). *Planning with complexity: An introduction to collaborative rationality for public policy*. Abingdon: Routledge.

Jaeger, J. and Scheringer, M. (1998). Transdiszipinarität. Problemorientierung ohne methodenzwang. *Global Astrometric Interferometer for Astrophysics*, 7(1), 10–25.

Joos-Malfait, V., Myaux, D. and Osinski, A. (Coord.) (2019). *L'expérience de l'aide alimentaire. Quelles alternatives. Rapport d'une recherche en croisement des savoirs*. Fédération des Services Sociaux (FdSS), Bruxelles.

Kaminsky, M., Klitzman, S., Michaels, D. and Stevenson, L. (1993). *Health profile of cancer, birth defects, asthma, and childhood lead poisoning in Greenpoint/Williamsburg*. Second Report, June 1993. Greenpoint Environmental History Project, Brooklyn Public Library, Center for Brooklyn History, New York City.

Klein, J. T. (2010). A taxonomy of interdisciplinarity. In R. Frodeman, J. Thompson Klein and C. Mitcham (Eds.), *The Oxford handbook of interdisciplinarity* (pp. 15–30). Oxford: Oxford University Press.

Klein, J. T. (2018). Learning in transdisciplinary collaborations: A conceptual vocabulary. In *Transdisciplinary theory, practice and education* (pp. 11–23). Cham: Springer.

Klenk, N. and Meehan, K. (2015). Climate change and transdisciplinary science: Problematizing the integration imperative. *Environmental Science and Policy*, 54, 160–167.

Lacombe, C., Couix, N. and Hazard, L. (2017). *Envisager l'accompagnement du changement des systèmes agricoles vers l'agroécologie comme un processus co-conçu. Cas de la co-conception locale d'un outil de diagnostic agroécologique des fermes ovin-lait dans le Sud-Aveyron* [Conference presentation]. 7ième Colloque du réseau "Des Outils pour Décider Ensemble" (OPDE), 26–27 October (Montpelier). HAL - Archive ouverte de l'Institut national de recherche pour l'agriculture, l'alimentation et l'environnement (INRAE), Paris.

Ledogar, R. J., Garden-Acosta, L. and Penchaszadeh, A. (1999). Building international public health vision through local community research: The El Puente—CIET partnership. *American Journal of Public Health*, 89(12), 1795–1797.

Ledogar, R. J., Penchaszadeh, A., Garden, C. C. and Garden, I. (2000). Asthma and Latino cultures: Different prevalence reported among groups sharing the same environment. *American Journal of Public Health*, 90(6), 929–935.

Loorbach, D. and Rotmans, J. (2010). The practice of transition management: Examples and lessons from four distinct cases. *Futures*, 42(3), 237–246.

Lux, A., Schäfer, M., Bergmann, M., Jahn, T., Marg, O., Nagy, E., Ransiek, A. C. and Theiler, L. (2019). Societal effects of transdisciplinary sustainability research—How can they be strengthened during the research process? *Environmental Science and Policy*, 101, 183–191.

Mackie, H., Macmillan, A., Witten, K., Baas, P., Field, A., Smith, M., . . . and Woodward, A. (2018). Te Ara Mua—Future Streets suburban street retrofit: A researcher-community-government co-design process and intervention outcomes. *Journal of Transport and Health*, 11, 209–220.

Macmillan, A., Connor, J., Witten, K., Kearns, R., Rees, D. and Woodward, A. (2014). The societal costs and benefits of commuter bicycling: Simulating the effects of specific policies using system dynamics modeling. *Environmental Health Perspectives*, 122(4), 335–344.

Macmillan, A., Davies, M., Shrubsole, C., Luxford, N., May, N., Chiu, L. F., . . . and Chalabi, Z. (2016). Integrated decision-making about housing, energy and wellbeing: A qualitative system dynamics model. *Environmental Health*, 15(1), 23–34.

Macmillan, A. and Mackie, H. (2016). Optimising low carbon mobility for health and equity. In D. Hopkins and J. Higham (Eds.), *Low carbon mobility transition*. Oxford: GoodFellow Publishers.

Macmillan, A., Smith, M., Witten, K., Woodward, A., Hosking, J., Wild, K. and Field, A. (2020). Suburb-level changes for active transport to meet the SDGs: Causal theory and a New Zealand case study. *Science of the Total Environment*, 714, 136–678.

Martin, A. (2017). *Just conservation: Biodiversity, wellbeing and sustainability*. Abingdon: Routledge.

Masur, J. S. and Posner, E. A. (2011). Climate regulation and the limits of cost-benefit analysis. *California Law Review*, 99, 1557.

Maxwell, J. A. and Loomis, D. M. (2003). Mixed methods design: An alternative approach. In A. Tashakkori and C. Teddlie (Eds.), *Handbook of mixed methods in social and behavioral research* (Vol. 1, pp. 241–272). Thousand Oaks, CA: Sage Publishing.

McCrory, G., Schäpke, N., Holmén, J. and Holmberg, J. (2020). Sustainability-oriented labs in real-world contexts: An exploratory review. *Journal of Cleaner Production*, 277, 123202.

Meadows, D. H. (2009). *Thinking in systems: A primer*. Abingdon: Earthscan.

Melia, S. (2015). Do *randomised control trials offer a solution to 'low quality' transport research?* [Conference presentation]. 47th Annual Universities' Transport Study Group (UTSG) Conference, 1 January. University College London, London.

Menzel, S. and Teng, J. (2010). Ecosystem services as a stakeholder-driven concept for conservation science. *Conservation Biology*, 24(3), 907–909.

Misak, Ch. (2000). *Truth, politics, morality*. London: Routledge.

Mitchell, C., Cordell, D. and Fam, D. (2015). Beginning at the end: The outcome spaces framework to guide purposive transdisciplinary research. *Futures*, 65, 86–96.

Németh, B., Molnár, A., Bozóki, S., Wijaya, K., Inotai, A., Campbell, J. D. and Kaló, Z. (2019). Comparison of weighting methods used in multicriteria decision analysis frameworks in healthcare with focus on low-and middle-income countries. *Journal of Comparative Effectiveness Research*, 8(4), 195–204.

New York City Mayor's office. (2015). *One New York: The plan for a strong and just city*. Public Sector Information. New York Department of Health and Mental Hygiene (DOHMH), New York.

Norström, A. V., Cvitanovic, C., Löf, M. F., West, S., Wyborn, C., Balvanera, P., . . . and Österblom, H. (2020). Principles for knowledge co-production in sustainability research. *Nature Sustainability*, 3(3), 182–190.

Nussbaum, M. C. (2000). The costs of tragedy: Some moral limits of cost-benefit analysis. *The Journal of Legal Studies*, 29(S2), 1005–1036.

Osinski, A. (2020). Evaluating transition pathways beyond basic needs: A transdisciplinary approach to assessing food assistance. *Food Ethics*, 5(1), 1–34.

Ostrom, E. (2007). A diagnostic approach for going beyond panaceas. *Proceedings of the National Academy of Sciences*, 104(39), 15181–15187.

Poteete, A. R., Janssen, M. A. and Ostrom, E. (2010). *Working together. Collective action, the commons and multiple methods in practice*. Princeton, NJ: Princeton University Press.

Puska, P., Salonen, J. T., Tuomilehto, J., Nissinen, A. and Kottke, Th. E. (1983). Evaluating community-based preventive cardiovascular programs: Problems and experiences from the North Karelia project. *Journal of Community Health*, 9, 49–64.

Reich, K. (2009). Constructivism: Diversity of approaches and connections with pragmatism. In L. A. Hickman, S. Neubert and K. Riech (Eds.), *John Dewey between pragmatism and constructivism*. New York: Fordham University Press.

Ribeiro, E., Croisel, B. and Belleil, A. (2017). *Les prairies à flore variée*. La Grande Motte: ABioDoc.

Rihoux, B. and Ragin, C. C. (2008). *Configurational comparative methods: Qualitative comparative analysis (QCA) and related techniques*. Thousand Oaks, CA: Sage Publishing.

Roorda, C., Wittmayer, J., Henneman, P., Van Steenbergen, F., Frantzeskaki, N. and Loorbach, D. (2014). *Transition management in the urban context: Guidance manual*. Rotterdam: Dutch Research Institute for Transition (DRIFT), Erasmus University Rotterdam.

Rosenberg, N. (2010). Why do firms do basic research (with their own money)? In N. Rosenberg (Ed.), *Studies on science and the innovation process: Selected works of Nathan Rosenberg* (pp. 225–234). Singapore: World Scientific Publishing Company.

Salas-Molina, F. (2019). A formal specification of multicriteria economics. *Operational Research*, 21, 2627–2650.

Schlüter, M., Müller, B. and Frank, K. (2019). The potential of models and modeling for social-ecological systems research. *Ecology and Society*, 24(1), 31.

Schmale, J., Von Schneidemesser, E., Chabay, I., Maas, A. and Lawrence, M. G. (2016). Building interfaces that work: A multi-stakeholder approach to air pollution and climate change mitigation. In J. L. Drake, Y. Y. Kontar, J. C. Eichelberger, S. T. Rupp and K. M. Taylor (Eds.), *Communicating climate-change and natural hazard risk and cultivating resilience* (pp. 65–76). Heidelberg: Springer.

Schmale, J., Von Schneidemesser, E. and Dörrie, A. (2015). An integrated assessment method for sustainable transport system planning in a middle-sized German city. *Sustainability*, 7(2), 1329–1354.

Schneider, F., Giger, M., Harari, N., Moser, S., Oberlack, C., Providoli, I., . . . and Zimmermann, A. (2019). Transdisciplinary co-production of knowledge and sustainability transformations: Three generic mechanisms of impact generation. *Environmental Science and Policy*, 102, 26–35.

Sciortino, L. (2017). On Ian Hacking's notion of style of reasoning. *Erkenntnis*, 82(2), 243–264.

Scrieciu, S. S. (2007). The inherent dangers of using computable general equilibrium models as a single integrated modelling framework for sustainability impact assessment. A critical note on Böhringer and Löschel (2006). *Ecological Economics*, *60*(4), 678–684.

Simon, C. and Etienne, M. (2010). A companion modelling approach applied to forest management planning. *Environmental Modelling and Software*, *25*(11), 1371–1384.

Singleton, R. A. and Straits, B. C. (2005). *Approaches to social research*. Oxford: Oxford University Press.

Smetschka, B. and Gaube, V. (2020). Co-creating formalized models: Participatory modelling as method and process in transdisciplinary research and its impact potentials. *Environmental Science and Policy*, *103*, 41–49.

Smit, S., Musango, J. K. and Brent, A. C. (2019). Understanding electricity legitimacy dynamics in an urban informal settlement in South Africa: A community based system dynamics approach. *Energy for Sustainable Development*, *49*, 39–52.

Smit, S., Musango, J. K., Kovacic, Z. and Brent, A. C. (2018). Towards measuring the informal city: A societal metabolism approach. *Journal of Industrial Ecology*, *23*(3), 674–685.

Spangenberg, J. H., von Haaren, C. and Settele, J. (2014). The ecosystem service cascade: Further developing the metaphor. Integrating societal processes to accommodate social processes and planning, and the case of bioenergy. *Ecological Economics*, *104*, 22–32.

Stindt, D., Sahamie, R., Nuss, C. and Tuma, A. (2016). How transdisciplinarity can help to improve operations research on sustainable supply chains—A transdisciplinary modeling framework. *Journal of Business Logistics*, *37*(2), 113–131.

Tang, T. and Bhamra, T. A. (2009). *Improving energy efficiency of product use: An exploration of environmental impacts of household cold appliance usage patterns* [Conference paper]. 5th International Conference on Energy Efficiency in Domestic Appliances and Lighting-EEDAL'09, 16–18 June, Berlin, Germany. Deutsche Energie-Agentur GmbH (dena), Berlin.

TIDE. (2015). *Impact assessment handbook. Practitioners' handbook for cost benefit and impact analysis of innovative urban transport measures*. (Cré, I., Vancluysen, K, coord.). Transport Innovation Deployment for Europe (TIDE). Tide-innovation.eu.

Tillie, N., Aarts, M., Marijnissen, M., Stenhujs, L., Borsboom, J., Rietveld, E., . . . and Lap, S. (2012). *Rotterdam. People make the inner city*. Rotterdam: Gemeente.

Toffolini, Q., Capitaine, M., Hannachi, M. and Cerf, M. (2021). Implementing agricultural living labs that renew actors' roles within existing innovation systems: A case study in France. *Journal of Rural Studies*, *88*, 157–168.

UN. (2019). *The future is now—Science for achieving sustainable development*. Global Sustainable Development Report 2019. Independent Group of Scientists appointed by the Secretary-General of the United Nations, New York.

Van Breda, J. and Swilling, M. (2019). The guiding logics and principles for designing emergent transdisciplinary research processes: Learning experiences and reflections from a transdisciplinary urban case study in Enkanini informal settlement, South Africa. *Sustainability Science*, *14*(3), 823–841.

Van Nes, N. (2003). *Replacement of durables: Influencing product life time through product design* [PhD Thesis]. Rotterdam: Erasmus University Rotterdam.

Vennix, J. A. (1999). Group model-building: Tackling messy problems. *System Dynamics Review: The Journal of the System Dynamics Society*, *15*(4), 379–401.

Verutes, G. M., Arkema, K. K., Clarke-Samuels, C., Wood, S. A., Rosenthal, A., Rosado, S., . . . and Ruckelshaus, M. (2017). Integrated planning that safeguards ecosystems and balances multiple objectives in coastal Belize. *International Journal of Biodiversity Science, Ecosystem Services and Management, 13*(3), 1–17.

Videira, N., Antunes, P., Santos, R. and Lopes, R. (2010). A participatory modelling approach to support integrated sustainability assessment processes. *Systems Research and Behavioral Science, 27*(4), 446–460.

Von Schneidemesser, E., Kutzner, R. D. and Schmale, J. (2017). A survey on the perceived need and value of decision-support tools for joint mitigation of air pollution and climate change in cities. *Elementa: Science of the Anthropocene, 5*, 68.

Walter, A. I., Helgenberger, S., Wiek, A. and Scholz, R. W. (2007). Measuring societal effects of transdisciplinary research projects: Design and application of an evaluation method. *Evaluation and Program Planning, 30*(4), 325–338.

Wiek, A., Talwar, S., O'Shea, M. and Robinson, J. (2014). Toward a methodological scheme for capturing societal effects of participatory sustainability research. *Research Evaluation, 23*(2), 117–132.

Willis, J. W. (2007). *Foundations of qualitative research: Interpretive and critical approaches.* Thousand Oaks, CA: Sage Publishing.

Wilson, E. and Zarsky, L. (2009). *Power to the poor: Sustainable energy at the base of the pyramid.* London: International Institute for Environment and Development (IIED).

Wuelser, G. and Pohl, C. (2016). How researchers frame scientific contributions to sustainable development: A typology based on grounded theory. *Sustainability Science, 11*(5), 789–800.

4

SOCIAL LEARNING AMONG ACTORS WITH INCOMMENSURABLE VALUE PERSPECTIVES ON SUSTAINABILITY TRANSFORMATIONS

The second research style in transdisciplinary research focuses on the mechanisms for fostering social learning on societal values among the research partners. As indicated by Schneider et al. (2019), even though social learning also plays a role in the first research style focused on usable knowledge production, there is a key difference with the research projects that specifically identify social learning as the key goal of the research partnership. In this second research style, the learning is not only oriented toward matching pre-existing societal values that drive specific sustainability transformation processes in the given problem context through collaborative co-design. Rather, societal values emerge from the interactions among the researchers and societal actors who collaborate in the various stages of the research process.

A good illustration of this second research style is the agent-based participatory modeling of an irrigation system with local farmers in Thailand (Barnaud et al., 2008, 2010). The main purpose of the transdisciplinary research project was to improve the mutual understanding among the participants of their value-laden perceptions of a problem situation. In this case, a proposed sustainability improvement method based on the introduction of erosion-resistant perennial crops exacerbated social tensions around equitable access to agricultural water, as these crops require intense irrigation. To address this situation of high distrust among the farmers, the objective of the participatory modeling was to "facilitate communication and coordination among stakeholders across institutional levels while taking into account the diversity of interests at the grassroots level" (Barnaud et al., 2008, p. 562). To this purpose, the researchers organized a set of role-playing games in various villages that allowed to visualize and discuss the socio-ecological relationships highlighted by the simulation model. This role-playing game facilitated

DOI: 10.4324/9781032624297-5

a "different form of communication, which allowed less powerful villagers to raise their problem and to create a collective awareness of its existence" (Barnaud et al., 2010, p. 66).

Therefore, in the context of this second style of transdisciplinary research, social learning is not a product that can be separated from the social context of interactions among the research partners, as was the case with the analysis of usable knowledge products. Rather, social learning aims to address failures in mutual understanding among the project partners and create the conditions for productive collaboration (Schneider et al., 2019).

The latter also accords with the general scholarly literature on social learning. As stated, for instance, by Mark Reed and his colleagues in a review paper on this literature, social learning is a process that is defined by improved understanding and the embedding of this new understanding in social networks (Reed et al., 2010). According to their review, social learning can be defined through a combination of three process features: a process (1) leading to a change in understanding; (2) resulting from the exchange of ideas, arguments, and information; and (3) going beyond the individual and becoming situated in wider social units and communities of practice.

The analysis in this chapter is based on the sub-set of cases in our overall sample, where social learning on sustainability values plays an important role (see a detailed list in Annex 2). The selected cases explicitly reported failures to collaborate given a lack of structuring of the diversity of societal value perspectives among the project partners and the lack of organized processes to overcome these failures. To analyze these cases, this chapter adopts a representative case study approach based on a clustering of the cases in different types of social learning processes. Indeed, instead of focusing on generic features of social learning on sustainability values across all the cases, which is unlikely to do justice to the different social learning needs in the different projects, it seems more relevant to cluster the cases according to distinct learning needs and types of structuring of societal value perspectives among the project partners.

Further, to investigate the observed types of social learning in the case study sample, the chapter proceeds in two steps. First, the chapter reviews the key theoretical insights from deliberative approaches to social learning in complex social choice situations. These deliberative approaches are introduced through the work of Bryan Norton on environmental conflict management. Second, the various forms of social learning are further analyzed through the deliberative approach to social choice in the framework of analysis elaborated by Amartya Sen. The choice of this latter framework is based on the similarities between Amartya Sens' diagnosis of social choice problems and the social learning challenges in transdisciplinary research. In both cases, societal actors are confronted with the need to structure the diversity of societal value perspectives to improve collaboration among actors with mutually incompatible value rankings. Based on these similarities, the types of social learning elaborated in the deliberative approach to social choice by Sen will be briefly reviewed and subsequently adapted to better match the type of coordination failures observed in our case study sample of transdisciplinary research.

4.1 Building common perspectives for research collaboration in highly diverse societal value settings

A key insight from the research on social learning in transdisciplinary sustainability research is that working with a diversity of societal values is not necessarily an obstacle to successful collaboration among project partners (Pohl and Hirsch Hadorn, 2007). Nevertheless, comparative analysis of social learning in transdisciplinary research projects shows that coordination among the project partners is greatly facilitated by some level of agreement on a part of these societal values, without necessarily striving for a consensus over the entire value set (Herrero et al., 2019). Therefore, the focus on social learning in transdisciplinary research aims to strengthen such agreements in a collective and adaptive search for appropriate partnership composition and areas of convergence among project participants.

As highlighted, the need for such deeper agreements on some sustainability values depends on the sustainability issues at hand and the type of actors involved in the partnerships. Given this diversity of situations, no standard of convergence can fit all situations beyond a diversity of degrees of convergence per project needs. This section aims to introduce the discussion on the diversity of such agreements in the context of sustainability research to build a typology that can guide further case study analyses.

The lively debates in environmental philosophy on the balancing of multiple legitimate sustainability goals is a good starting point to introduce this discussion. For instance, Bryan Norton, in his reference work on the philosophy of adaptive ecosystem management (Norton, 2005) develops a vision of environmental management as a process of evaluating multiple goals, which remains open for revision given further evidence. Precisely, this process of evaluation is an iterative process. Adaptive ecosystem management is based on evaluating various arguments for combining ecological and social system values, and, subsequently, on a further refinement of these values, reviewing the evidence of various impacts of decisions made based on these arguments.

The starting point of the analysis of Norton is his personal experience with failures in the management of public programs of wetland management at the US Environmental Protection Agency in the early 1970s. As stated by Norton, given the functional specialization of the departments in the Agency, only ecologists sat on the committee for the wetland policy (ibid, p. 35). Therefore, the committee had no definition of a wetland that included considerations of economic value or sociocultural values associated with the wetlands for the surrounding population. According to Norton, consequently, the management models used by the Agency failed to develop models that are useful in complex public decisions, which include considerations of ecology, economic opportunities, and social acceptance of environmental regulations.

Moreover, to contrast this technocratic approach with an adaptive approach to wetland management, Norton cites the case of a successful social learning process on land and water use around the Platte River in Colorado, United States. As in many situations of biodiversity protection, in this case, the top-down designation of river habitat to be protected resulted first in over a decade of protests by homeowners close to the river bank and water users, including threats to multiply individual court cases to contest the application of the habitat protection rulings to individual land plots. Given such threats, the US Fish and Wildlife service granted a temporary continuance of activities, provided that serious and fruitful negotiations were undertaken by all interested parties to seek approval for a river basin-wide solution (Norton, 2015, p. 242).

Norton highlights two main mechanisms that contributed to a successful agreement on the key principles to organize habitat protection. First, parties identified areas of convergence and divergence on the values that should guide collective decision-making. Such convergence does not mean all parties adhered to these values. However, at least, they could understand and accept the provisional validity within the space of common action. One area of agreement was the importance of protecting the rare species of Whooping Crane whose river habitat was endangered. The other area was to orient the choice of land acquisition for habitat protection first to land plots with lower economic development value.

Second, within this space of convergence, the parties still had different perspectives on many details of habitat protection. Parties held different views on the need (or not) to actively improve the river habitat, such as by regulating the flow of the river or building small ponds. Moreover, opinions diverged on house development plans on the riverbank, which contribute to the tax revenues of the municipalities. Nevertheless, to explore common action strategies within this diversity of perspectives, the parties adopted a social learning approach based on scientific experimentation and monitoring. Through a common research protocol for real-world testing of the propositions made by the different parties, parties aimed at assessing if and how the real-world impacts of their proposed action strategies fitted the commonly agreed-upon minimum set of sustainability values.

Norton's approach to social learning places the accent on the pragmatist revision of societal values based on the deliberation over the consequences of proposed action strategies. However, to understand the diversity of social learning needs in transdisciplinary research, this approach must be broadened for at least two reasons.

First, the type of convergence, or "balancing" in the terms of Norton, on a set of core sustainability values envisioned by Norton is not always possible or needed in practice. A less ambitious objective, such as social learning for building an agreement on process values might also be a desirable outcome of the social learning process. In the example of the Platte River habitat, the Fish and Wildlife service created a framework for negotiation among the parties. The parties implicitly used and accepted the process values embedded in this framework. Without such an external institutional actor, learning might be required to set up the key process values, such as social inclusiveness or representation of citizens that can act as spokespersons for the non-human living world in the process.

Second, the main criterion proposed for evaluating the impact of the value-based management decisions is its practical impact on problem-solving. It is an important criterion that is grounded in well-recognized approaches to validity in philosophical pragmatism based on classical authors, such as John Dewey and William James. In this perspective of philosophical pragmatism, societal values are considered valid in a given community of inquiry if they stand the test of practical experimentation with these values in concrete problem-solving at a given point in time and if there is a willingness to further submit them to this process of testing and possible revision.

Nevertheless, without entering a deep philosophical debate, the concept of revision used by Norton, where the values are evaluated in terms of their instrumental impact on problem-solving, is too restrictive to cover all situations of social learning that contribute to convergence over sustainable values or process values in transdisciplinary research. In addition to the impact on problem-solving, debates over legitimacy and relevancy among project partners also play a role in the process of revision. This broader approach can be captured through the concept of "comprehensive consequences" (Sen, 2009, p. 215). From a comprehensive outcome perspective, societal actors assess societal values regarding their impact on problem-solving, their legitimacy as part of a broader value framework, and the fairness of the process that led to the acceptance of these values.

4.2 Amartya Sen's deliberative approach to social choice with incommensurable societal values

One of the merits of the work of Amartya Sen—who was awarded the 1998 Nobel Prize in economics for his work on social choice—is that it broadens our understanding of the role of deliberation over societal values in complex social choice situations characterized by heterogeneous and sometimes antagonistic societal values. In particular, the approach of Sen helps further broaden the trial-and-error approach to partial convergence over societal values discussed in the context of Bryan Norton's environmental philosophy to other types of social learning needs and mechanisms.

A key foundation of the work of Amartya Sen is the realization that so-called *incommensurability** among societal values in a broad sense—the impossibility to establish a comparison between the values that specify what societal value choice is better or worse than another (Chang, 1997)—is not a problem for everyday decision-making. Indeed, incommensurability over societal values is everywhere, despite which human actors can reach common decisions on action strategies and broad societal orientations over many collective issues.

The shift in perspective proposed by Sen to overcome many of the paradoxes of social choice under diverse and incommensurable values is to abandon the idea of the need for an absolute ranking of the values to reach decisions considered reasonably valid by all. To paraphrase Sen (2009, p. 102), when two mountains are within reach, one can use various clues to validly affirm that one has climbed the highest mountain of these two without requiring further investigation into the height of the absolute highest mountain on Earth or even without agreeing on all the clues used to arrive at this conclusion. Similarly, in everyday decision-making, human actors can take common decisions based on partially overlapping agreements or consider decisions that are provisionally valid and open for revision given the availability of more information.

In his major works on social choice, *Rationality and Freedom* (Sen, 2002) and *The Idea of Justice* (Sen, 2009), Sen further develops this idea of decision-making with partial ordering and incomplete information. These works allow for distinguishing between three major ideal types of convergence over values between actors with different or incomplete value rankings.

The first ideal type concern situations where each of the individuals can rank the societal values in a reasonably consistent manner, though the ranking between these individuals is not congruent. Sen considers two ideal types of agreement that actors use to solve a situation of incompatible value rankings. The first ideal type is based on a partial agreement on the ranking. The most advanced form of agreement exists if the individuals have a shared belief regarding the validity of some part of the ranking, which Sen calls a "fair agreement on particular pairwise rankings" (ibid, p. 105). For instance, if two individuals rank five values respectively in the order V1 > V2 > V3 > V4 > V5 (for the first individual) and V5 > V4 > V1 > V2 > V3 (for the second), they share at least an agreement over the ranking V1 > V2 > V3. As stated by Sen, in such cases, they can use this partial agreement to make common judgments on how to "enhance justice" or "reduce injustice" in specific problem situations.

The second ideal type is based on a minimum agreement on some core values. Indeed, even if there is no advanced agreement on pairwise rankings, some common judgments remain possible when rankings are incongruent among individuals. Indeed, there may be one salient value that is so important that it is sufficient to motivate a common judgment of justice or injustice in a situation, even if ambiguity remains over the other value rankings (ibid, p. 397). For instance, in the example of five values, V4 might represent acting against famine or exclusion from access to healthcare. These values might be recognized by all parties involved as a key value to defend, even if there is no straightforward manner to compare the other values of the overall value set in a mutually consistent way.

The third ideal type described by Sen concerns the situation where each of the individuals expresses doubts or hesitation about his value ranking, as they lack key information or clues on how to manage the available information to decide upon the ranking. In these situations, any value statement would be provisional and should be accompanied by a shared understanding of how and under what circumstances the value statements can be adjusted, completed, re-examined, or extended to include new problem features. This type is labeled by Sen as "tentative incompleteness" (ibid, p. 107). As argued, this tentative incompleteness requires agreements on "process values," such as acceptable means for assessing the credibility of new information or guarantees for inclusiveness in the deliberation over the revision process.

In practice, these three ideal types must be combined to enhance overall justice in society. However, depending on the situation, the actors might consider that the most urgent social learning must occur first within one of the types. Based on the level of value incongruence or incompleteness, they might consider that the priority lies in the identification of a set of minimum substantial value agreements, a more advanced pairwise ranking of several substantial values, or agreements on the process to gather and deliberate over new information on a tentatively accepted common value framework.

To illustrate these various types, Sen discusses the hypothetical dilemma of three individuals claiming a flute (ibid, p. 12; pp. 396–397). Although it is an extreme case of incommensurability rarely encountered in real life, the case shows how the various types of social learning might be mobilized to attenuate the incommensurability and converge on some common value judgments. Similarly, the case is also a reminder of the gradual nature of the convergence process through social learning, as per many contextual factors and prior levels of collaboration and trust.

In the hypothetical dilemma constructed by Sen, three children "Anne, Bob, and Carla" quarrel about a flute. Each refers to a different social justice value to substantiate their demand for the flute. The first, Anne, is the only one who can play the flute, and she claims the flute on the basis that it would be unjust to deny the flute to the only one who can play it. The second, Bob, defends his case by pointing out that he is so poor that he has no toys of his own, and the other two concede that they are richer and already well-off. The third, Carla, is the person who made the flute, and one might be inclined to give the flute to her in recognition of her understandable claim to something she has made.

Indeed, there is no real good solution to the dilemma, as one can mobilize arguments from various ethical traditions to justify each of these positions. However, Sen highlights that there remains some room for further learning, which shows some possible ways out of the dilemma.

First, a possibility regards the minimum level of congruence. It could be the case that Bob is extremely poor such that the arguments based on economic fairness prompt one to opt for ranking the inequality considerations highest to judge the situation. A second possibility suggested by Sen regards some fuzzy boundaries between the societal values perspectives. For instance, the difference between the three children might be not as strict as in the theoretical dilemma, and not only Bob but also Carla is poor. If the deliberation would lead to ranking both economic inequality and the right to the fruits of one's labor above utilitarian arguments, then this would lend some support to give the flute to Carla.

Finally, a third possibility (not explicitly mentioned by Sen) could use the incompleteness argument and organize processes of further information gathering and testing of provisional solutions. Indeed, to decide upon the allocation of the flute, one might temporarily give it to Anne but also ask for further information regarding the arguments over the other societal values. For instance, it might be unclear how challenging it is for the others to learn to play the flute, and Anne could help in this regard, including any other means available to overcome the poverty gap between Bob and the two other children. Further information on these issues might lead to a different appreciation of what societal values has the highest relevance in the given problem situation.

The interesting point in the example of the three children given by Sen is that the difference between the children's arguments does not represent divergences about what constitutes individual advantage (getting the flute is considered advantageous by each of the children) but about the societal values that can generally justify decisions (here, about the allocation of goods). As underlined by Sen, the arguments are about "how social arrangements should be made and what social institutions should be chosen, and through that, about what social realizations would come about." According to Sen, "it is not simply that the vested interests of the three children differ (though, of course, they do), but that the three arguments each point to a different type of impartial and non-arbitrary reason" (ibid, p. 15).

The strength of Sen's analysis, in line with many other scholars of public deliberation, is how it shows the working of a framework for social learning over societal values that do not need an absolute viewpoint but still aim at a strong level of the objective validity of the structuring of the diversity of value perspectives. Indeed, the societal values under discussion are not the subjective values of individual participants but publicly shared values that can withstand critical scrutiny by a community of discussants. The end goal is to reach a level playing field for communication on an intersubjective basis such that the various statements about partial rankings or process values are not inescapably confined to a subjective appraisal that others may not understand.

4.3 Illustrating the various types of social learning in transdisciplinary research practices

The analysis of some key insights of the literature on the deliberative approach to social choice shows the diversity of possible outcomes of social learning processes over issues of common concern in situations of heterogeneous societal values. At first glance, sustainability transformations with highly heterogeneous values leave few opportunities for consensus around the basic values or organizing the process for building new common values perspectives. However, when abandoning the viewpoint of reaching a consensus over complete value rankings and adopting a bounded rational perspective on the real-world situations of collaboration with incomplete and partial agreements, societal actors have at their disposal a much wider set of opportunities for social learning.

From a general perspective, based on the analysis by Sen, one can expect various types of social learning with varying degrees of demanding targets. The more demanding targets can strive for pairwise agreements on several value rankings adopted by societal actors. The less demanding targets may focus on one clear case of a societal value to which all parties adhere. Further, beyond these two contrasted outcomes, one might expect situations where the rankings of societal actors are so incomplete that no agreement on the ranking is possible. In such situations, societal actors may aim to adopt provisional common action strategies that can support further learning and completion of the value framework.

Moving from the analysis of the literature on social choice to the context of building transdisciplinary research commons requires more information from real-world practices of transdisciplinary research deliberation. Therefore, this section proceeds along two steps to analyze the mechanisms of social learning. First, the various types discussed by Sen will be confronted with the mechanisms of social learning processes documented in the case study sample of transdisciplinary research projects presented in Chapter 3. Through a cluster analysis of the sub-sample of cases with strong investment in social learning, the cases from this sub-sample will be grouped around the most similar social learning mechanisms. Second, for each identified type, one example of a transdisciplinary research process will be discussed in depth.

The selection of cases is based on more and less successful research projects. Both cases with a high and low direct impact on usable knowledge production will be used. Indeed, for the analysis of social learning, both are potentially useful. In cases with high direct impact, specific efforts for deliberation may not be vital to overcoming situations of divergence over key sustainability values. However, in the cases with low impact, partners may have implemented social learning processes for fostering convergence that successfully laid the groundwork for further collaboration in follow-up research.

Overall, the screening of the 44 cases in the overall sample led to identifying 12 transdisciplinary research projects that actively implemented deliberative mechanisms for social learning and where these mechanisms are documented in research publications (see the detailed list in Annex 2, column "SL"). For each of the 12 cases, the key variables used by Sen in his analysis of the types of social learning processes were coded based on the information available in the research publications and accompanying project documents. These key variables include (1) the level of agreement targeted by the social learning process, from minimal agreements to partial overlapping rankings; (2) the definition of some or various common action strategies that satisfy the societal value perspectives of the partners; and (3) the use of specific tools for conflict resolution.

The clustering of the most similar cases based on these variables induces a modification of the key types identified by Sen. The modification can be accommodated by including a fourth type of convergence process. The cluster analysis confirms the relevancy of the two paradigmatic cases of agreement in pairwise rankings and minimal agreement over salient societal value categories. Even so, the analysis of the situation of absence of agreement over the ranking or absence of individual consistent rankings yields two sub-types. The first sub-type concerns situations where actors, despite divergence, adopt common action strategies that support further learning. A second sub-type concerns situations where no such common action strategy is identified through the research, but social learning still allows for agreeing on a set of process values to organize collaboration for trust building and improving mutual understanding.

Hence, the cluster analysis of the social learning cases in the overall sample leads to identifying the following four types:

1 Agreement on process values for common inquiry into the problem identification

- Cases where social learning yields an agreement over the process values that should lead the interaction among the partners (no common action, no agreement on ranking)

2 Common action strategies accommodating divergent perspectives

- Cases where social learning yields a common strategy that satisfies the key societal values of the partners (only specific common action, no agreement on ranking)

3 Identifying converging and diverging perspectives

- Cases where social learning leads to identifying some area of convergence around one or some salient societal values (one or some specific common actions, based on the convergence around one or some salient societal values and divergence on the ranking of the other societal values)

4) Common action programs with a substantial overlap in value rankings

- Cases where social learning leads to identifying substantial overlaps in value rankings—so-called partial ordering—and a set of specific common action strategies that satisfy the overlapping societal values

An important caveat applies to this presentation of key features of social learning. As noted, in practice, many projects combine different social learning types, whether by implementing one type after another or by combining features of various types. Nevertheless, the analysis of specific types can provide important insights. Each of the ideal types addresses specific social learning challenges and mobilizes different deliberative mechanisms. Furthermore, knowledge of these types can fulfill a heuristic role in shaping and adjusting expectations among the research partners. Indeed, the identification of these types by the research partners allows them to clarify the social learning needs and the level of social learning appropriate for the given project resources, the history of collaboration among the partners, and the problem situation at hand.

The remainder of this section illustrates each of the four types through an example from the case study sample. Each of these cases mainly addresses one of the social learning types and explicitly discusses this type in the project publications.

4.3.1 Agreement on process values for common inquiry

The first example illustrates the absence of congruent value rankings on the core sustainability values in a situation of persistent distrust among the project partners. Social learning corresponds to the needs identified in the first social learning type, which is the creation of a community of inquiry that respects agreed-upon process values to improve mutual understanding.

The research partnership of the multistakeholder "working group for waders" that emerged from a research project on ground-nesting birds in Scottish Moorlands is a good illustration of the use of various capacity-building tools to foster the building of a community of inquiry (Ainsworth et al., 2020). The case mainly relies on insights from the conflict transformation literature, particularly regarding the role of a protected or informal environment in trust building among the parties (Redpath et al., 2013; Van Breda and Swilling, 2019).

The Moorlands are well known for high conservation value habitats for several ground-nesting birds. All stakeholders and scientists agree that bird populations are declining in Scotland at an alarming rate but disagree about the solutions and the evidence behind different proposed solutions (Hodgson et al., 2018, 2019). However, in the Moorlands, there is a lack of data on the causes of the near extinction of a bird of prey, the hen harrier. This decline may stem from the change in habitat management or the illegal shooting of the hen harrier. The latter occurs to increase the presence of one of its preys, the red grouse, which is a ground-nesting bird specifically managed for recreational hunting. Further, for other ground-nesting birds, such as the curlew, the nesting habits are not well known, and their protection requires close collaboration between farmers, hunters, and nature protection organizations.

In response to this dispute over the available knowledge on the causes of bird decline, the Scottish Government provided funding support to a stakeholder group—the Moorland Forum—to organize and supervise the "Understanding Predation" project, whose objective was to initiate a conflict transformation process. The Forum decided to organize a transdisciplinary research project, involving hunters, recreationists, farmers, and members of environmental associations.

According to Ainsworth et al. (2020), two major shifts in the framing of the conflict played an important role in successfully overcoming the lack of collaboration. First, the focus on gathering evidence on predator-prey dynamics of ground-nesting birds more generally allowed the research team to take a step back from the more acute conflict around hen harrier conservation and red grouse management. As stated by the team: "we aimed to build a publicly accessible evidence base . . . from science and stakeholders' local knowledge . . . highlighting where these forms of knowledge agreed or disagreed and analyzing the reasons for any differences" (ibid, p. 47). Accordingly, the stakeholders and scientists realized that conservation management of ground-nesting birds was a priority objective for almost all participants. Moreover, the definition of healthy populations of predator and prey species was crucial, despite different ideas on the appropriate management methods to reach this objective among scientists and conservationists and recreational users and hunters.

Second, based on insights from the conflict transformation literature, the research team used small-group and plenary meetings to build trust among stakeholder groups. For instance, before gathering all the stakeholders and scientists in a formal plenary workshop, the research team organized a set of nine small-scale group meetings in a more confidential environment. At the start of each meeting, the participants agreed on a confidentiality statement and could approve the workshop report before the analysis or dissemination by the research team. Further, as the conflict was too acute in the earlier stages of the project, the research team only invited stakeholders from like-minded organizations to the small-group meeting by using the results of an online survey that allowed for a prior mapping of the main stakeholder values and areas of conflict. The research team asked the participants in the small peer groups to compare their sources of data with the data from literature reviews to understand the potential disagreements between the two sources of knowledge. This approach enabled participants to engage in meaningful deliberations while maintaining overall consistency by covering the same topics in all the groups and referring to the common literature review and prior survey.

The combination of small-group "safe space" and regular plenary co-production workshops did not aim to reach a consensus on all the issues but to create the conditions for trust and mutual understanding. In the first plenary meeting, participants with different interests were voluntarily seated next to each other to encourage informal confidence building. In the final seminar, stakeholders mutually prioritized a list of future collaboration actions in the Moorlands. The continuing collaboration for knowledge gathering in the "Working for Waders" program around a set of shared goals for conservation management is also a clear indication of the success of the research project.

4.3.2 Common action strategies accommodating divergent perspectives

The second example regards the emergence of common action strategies around a core objective in a situation with highly divergent social-actor perspectives. The case aims to identify income generation activities from coastal ecosystems in a sustainable manner in Southern Kenya.

In the coastal ecosystems in Southern Kenya, the local communities experience major security issues regarding illegal fishing techniques and cross-border robbery and trafficking along the Kenya-Tanzania border. In response to these challenges, the SPACES project consortium set up a group-based qualitative research in four villages each in Southern Kenya and Mozambique to better understand the opportunities for men and women to improve their well-being through the sustainable use of the coastal ecosystem services (Galafassi et al., 2018).

From the beginning of the project, it was clear that the community members diverged on two possible implementation paths for poverty alleviation in the coastal ecosystem (Galafassi et al., 2018). Some members saw the lack of economic opportunities and the lack of security as issues related to individual capacities. Therefore, they asserted the need to access education and capacity building as promoted by external actors. Other members highlighted historical social inequalities in the community as a major barrier, especially regarding gendered access rules to ecosystem resources that induce different access to capital, education, and mobility for men and women (Fortnam et al., 2019).

The proposed protocol for social learning in this situation was based on a combination of concept mapping and storytelling. The concept mapping aimed to identify the main factors affecting the well-being of the community members and the strengths and direction of causal relations between these factors. A team of professional facilitators accompanied the process, organizing some of the prior knowledge through participants' surveys and engaging the community members in assessing the main findings. However, as shown in an in-depth analysis of the workshop recordings and transcripts, the major learning in the workshops occurred through the sharing of lived stories and narratives. The latter provided insights into the diverse meanings given by the community members to key concepts such as insecurity and well-being (Galafassi et al., 2018).

Despite a lack of convergence among participants around the main pathways to poverty alleviation in the coastal ecosystems, the "shared conceptual repertoire" (ibid) that emerged from the research process allowed for identifying some common action strategies that are relevant from the perspective of different societal values. These common areas of action include the organization of the sustainable use of products from the fragile mangrove forests and coral reefs (Directorate, E.S.P.A., 2018) and the empowering of women who are currently excluded in this area from developing key income generation activities regarding ecosystem services from the mangrove ecosystem (Galafassi et al., 2018).

For instance, in the case of one of the project villages in Southern Kenya, situated along the Tsunza Mangrove, the increased mutual understanding among community members and associations resulting from the research process induced a set of new initiatives. Among these initiatives are the formation of joint saving groups by women, the submission of funding applications for community forest conservation programs, and training for women entrepreneurship activities related to identified small-scale business opportunities such as oyster trading and traditional poultry farming (Daw, 2018).

4.3.3 Identifying converging and diverging perspectives

The third example corresponds to a situation of high initial trust among the project partners and a willingness to build collaboration around common values identified through a set of multistakeholder deliberative workshops. The case is a research project to understand the options for sustainable mobility in the large metropolitan area of Stockholm, Sweden.

Initially, this project had an important focus on technical solutions for so-called smart mobility, which can lower car use and improve multi-modality. Indeed, digitalization and electrification of mobility are likely to be key components of any energy-efficient mobility future. Digitalization enables more efficient transport logistics, the development of integrated booking systems among different modes of transport, better known as mobility-as-a-service (MAAS), and social networking. Electrification, if based on renewable energy provision, can lower the carbon footprint of cars and trucks and lower air pollution.

As noted in the previous chapters, the transformation toward more sustainable mobility will require more than just proposing an array of technical solutions. Nevertheless, existing research and development remain biased toward technical dimensions for reaching possible sustainability outcomes, while user perspectives and institutional dimensions are seldom explored in depth. Thus, to overcome this research gap, the Mistra SAMS research center in Stockholm has set up two living labs that combine the development of digital innovations with behavioral, environmental, and economic analysis of sustainability choices (Bieser et al., 2021; Sjöman et al., 2020; Vaddadi et al., 2022). One living lab organizes a space for telework from a co-working space in Tullinge, located 20 km south of Stockholm, in a neighborhood center where this type of service did not yet exist. This so-called telecommuting center offers 14 workplaces plus conferencing facilities. The second living lab explores the use of smartphone applications to improve mobility choices.

As mentioned on its project website, Mistra SAMS used a deep transdisciplinary approach, which involves interdisciplinary analysis and close collaboration with users and practitioners. Specifically, as explained by the project coordinator Anna Kramers (personal interview, October 3, 2019), the choices of the technology to be tested and the specific research questions to be addressed in the living lab research were not all specified in advance at the start of the project. In a workshop with the 16 partners from academia, industry, and the public sector, the project participants tried to understand what the living lab research would contribute to solving the problems of Stockholm city. As observed by the stakeholders, there were many co-working places; so, how could this project affect the ongoing transformation of work and workplace organization in a positive way? An important question raised by the city of Stockholm was the inclusive nature of the proposed digitalization of mobility and work solutions. The partners converged on investigating the sustainability impacts of the co-working space from the perspective of a more diversified public, including both the workers from the company and the freelance workers in the neighborhood, and the broader relation with the revitalization of the neighborhood (personal interview, September 19, 2019).

Overall, the social learning among the scientific researchers and societal actors was important to further deepen the research question beyond the technological innovations. This situation led Mistra SAMS to address research questions around the societal values of the two main social-actor partners, which were the Ericsson Company and the city. In particular, the living labs allowed for mapping a set of strategies for more effective energy saving through teleworking at a hub: providing energy-efficient transport options at the hub, such as bike sharing services; creating local destinations, such as local groceries or lunch places; and energy savings at the hub (Vaddadi et al., 2022). Nevertheless, despite the convergence around the issues of behavioral change for sustainable mobility, the project did not dig deeper into the broader social equity questions around mobility, as the living lab was situated in a well-off neighborhood. The project not only achieved behavioral change of both neighborhood inhabitants and participants of the Erickson company but also called for further research to analyze the type of impact telecommuting hubs might have for instance in a poorer neighborhood.

Thus, the project laid the groundwork for further learning beyond the issue of smart mobility solutions and multi-modality. A follow-up project awarded to Mistra SAMS (2021–2024) further explored these questions, in particular through setting up a third Living Lab at a remote location, in the municipality of Botkyrka. In the case of Mistra SAMS, the secret of the successful gradual learning process seems to lie in the strong partnerships with some key societal partners, the systematic consultation of the partners before moving to the next step, and the agile adaptation of the research tasks based on new inputs and insights from the research (Kramers and Akerman, 2019).

4.3.4 Common action program with a substantial overlap in the value rankings

The fourth example illustrates a complete social learning process that can structure the diversity of value perspectives of different societal actors from the public sector, local communities, and associations and from different cultural backgrounds. Based on this social learning, the partners could open up new opportunities for collaboration within a strong mutual understanding of each other's value perspectives and an identification of areas of overlap between the respective value rankings.

The case concerns a long-term and well-documented research project on healthcare delivery to nomadic pastoralists in Chad (the health intervention project) with different phases running from 1996 to 2006 (Bergmann et al., 2012, ch. III.F; Hirsch Hadorn et al., 2008, ch. 17). This project was set up in Chad after the observation in the early 1990s that nomadic pastoralists did not visit the local health centers. It revealed a social justice problem: healthcare services were organized by the State in a form that the nomads did not use; thus, in practice, they were virtually excluded from primary social services. According to a report by the Swiss Tropical Institute, polio vaccination coverage was 11.6% among mobile pastoralists communities, against 80% among settled communities (Lechthaler and Abakar, 2015). Notably, among mobile pastoralist communities, vaccination coverage among livestock was significantly higher than vaccination coverage for children (Abakar et al., 2018). As shown in a qualitative focus group study, major barriers to vaccination uptake by the nomadic population were mistrust and access to health system challenges (ibid).

Therefore, the research tasks were defined as follows. The first aim was to get an overall picture of the traditional forms of healthcare practiced by the nomads. Second, the team wanted to understand the barriers to the use of medical services offered by the State and develop healthcare services nomads would effectively use. Hence, the project combined anthropological fieldwork into the traditional health system of the pastoralists with clinic surveys to map the main needs for interventions and socio-geographical surveys to understand their daily livelihood concerns.

The health intervention project illustrates a successful knowledge integration process based on an iterative research design. In this project, similar to the New York asthma study, after each phase of field research and surveying, the researchers organized a workshop with the main societal actors to discuss the results and set the priorities for the next phase of research. The main difference with the New York study is that, in addition, at the start of the research project, the research team organized an explicit social learning process among the project members to foster a mutual understanding of the different value-oriented perspectives on healthcare delivery.

Indeed, the first rounds of research diagnosed many health problems within the population and revealed the importance of animal health for nomadic pastoralists. Livestock is the basis of the pastoralists' economic wealth and social respect. Moreover, relative to Western medicinal practice, in the nomads' traditional healthcare approach, the same health practitioners treat animals and humans. Thus, to address these different value frameworks, the project organized social learning among the partners to implement a so-called one-health approach to the delivery of health services, which considers the animal-human health improvement synergies and promotes the collaboration between human health and veterinary services (Schwabe, 1984).

The involved researchers mention three main reasons for the success of the research program. First, the research team took the perspectives of the traditional community on the organization of the health system seriously, which created trust and provided an entry point for the development of the new healthcare services. Second, the research was based on a solid institutional partnership between the Swiss Tropical Institute, the Chadian Veterinary Laboratory, and the Chadian Ministry of Health, which secured a long-term commitment of all partners. This commitment allowed for a highly flexible and adaptive research design. Third, effective knowledge sharing among all partners facilitated knowledge integration between livestock owners, traditional healers, and scientists. For instance, the detailed monitoring by the traditional livestock owners of animal health resulted in doubts about the efficacy of one of the livestock vaccines. This knowledge was taken up by the research team and later confirmed by laboratory analysis. The latter led to the replacement of the vaccine with a new one and an increase in trust in the usefulness of vaccination.

Overall, the knowledge co-production process was highly structured, with a clear division of work and well-identified moments of sharing of results and joint planning, especially during the five national workshops held during the entire project. The formulation of the problem was gradually broadened from problems of capacity building for health care delivery infrastructure to a broader concern for livelihood problems of the pastoralists, such as access to safe migration routes for the livestock and access to grazing lands allowing for improved management of animal health and milk production. In subsequent rounds of research and intervention, the program was further extended and eventually embedded in government health schemes for the entire pastoralist community, which represents around 10% of the total population in Chad.

4.4   Fostering critical engagement across differences

As the examples in this chapter show, without appropriate procedures for social learning among the partners, transdisciplinary research processes can fail to organize effective collaboration among project partners. Examples of failures in generating effective collaboration are the lack of common purpose when co-constructing the initial research design or misunderstandings that emerge later in the project when discussing the intermediary research results. In such cases of effective or potential failure, research partners might decide to invest in different social learning processes among the partners.

The four types of social learning analyzed in this chapter aim to illustrate various mechanisms for structuring the diversity of value perspectives. Project partners can decide to invest in one or several of the mechanisms as a condition for successful knowledge co-production. The choice of the appropriate type of social learning process depends on the perceived complexity of the coordination needs among the partners and the initial levels of trust. Indeed, not all situations of divergence are conducive to collaboration failure in all fields of sustainability research or for all research purposes. In some projects, minimal convergence over some process values may be sufficient. In other cases, more encompassing substantial agreements over key sustainability values may be required, such as when the scale of common actions to be undertaken is especially broad. In the latter case, where enhanced coordination is required, what seems essential is not to reach a convergence over all social values but to structure the diversity of societal values such that participants can explore the opportunities for workable compromises on common action strategies.

Furthermore, as shown in some of the case studies in our sample, the history of collaboration among partners or the experience of the individual partners with social learning has a strong impact on the degree to which partners are willing to invest in fostering social learning. Partners with divergent views but with positive experiences from social learning processes in other projects are more likely to adopt a collaborative attitude at the onset than other participants who may need more time to build trust and embark on a collaborative research endeavor (Innes and Booher, 2010). Therefore, social learning in some cases can be a gradual process, where the progress in one research project, even if quite modest, can lay the ground for further social learning and more ambitious collaborative undertakings in subsequent research efforts.

A common thread from this analysis of social learning in transdisciplinary research is the importance of a critical engagement of research partners to reflect on their own societal value backgrounds. Indeed, to engage in social learning, partners must adopt a critical approach to their value-related positions.

In this context, scholars highlight a set of process standards to embed the critical role of social learning in heterogeneous actor networks (Sørensen and Torfing, 2007; Dryzek, 2007). In his work on network governance in highly pluralistic and multi-scale problem settings, John Dryzek proposes an adaptation of the Habermasian principles of authentic deliberation to the organization of fair and inclusive communication within heterogeneous actor networks. Specifically, Dryzek highlights three important process standards that apply to the governance of heterogeneous actor networks (Dryzek, 2002, 2007, p. 268): impartiality, non-coercive dialogue, and generality (see Figure 4.1). Satisfying these process standards contributes to fostering effective engagement of all participants in discussing the multiplicity of points raised by different concerned actors.

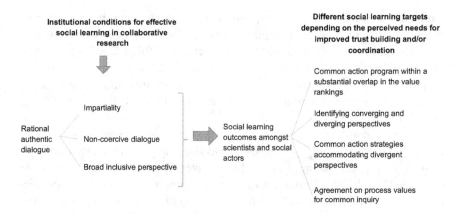

Institutional conditions for effective
social learning in collaborative
research

Different social learning targets
depending on the perceived needs for
improved trust building and/or
coordination

Common action program within a
substantial overlap in the value
rankings

Impartiality

Rational
authentic
dialogue

Non-coercive dialogue

Broad inclusive perspective

Social learning
outcomes amongst
scientists and social
actors

Identifying converging and
diverging perspectives

Common action strategies
accommodating divergent
perspectives

Agreement on process values
for common inquiry

FIGURE 4.1   Process standards for authentic deliberation in heterogeneous actor
networks

The first standard concerns the organization of impartial reflection on one's value position and the value-related positions of each of the participants. This attitude has been described in various terms in the literature, such as "open impartiality" (Sen, 2009, p. 123), "neutrality" (Misak, 2000, p. 109), or "cooperative effort to reach intersubjective validity" (Habermas, 1986, pp. 88–89) among others. What is common between these different notions is the idea that each participant must be capable of being reasonable in taking note of other people's perspectives. Indeed, to effectively create engagement with a multiplicity of discourses, each participant must articulate their perspective in the debate and welcome information and arguments from the perspective of others.

The second standard goes beyond the condition of impartiality and addresses power-related issues more explicitly. This standard requires a critical attitude to guarantee the non-coercive character of the dialogue, requiring equality in the capacity to raise and challenge points. This second standard aims to overcome the potential undue exercise of power and rent-seeking strategies of participants in public deliberation. For instance, in situations of strong conflict or power differentials between partners, social learning is not necessarily geared toward overcoming the antagonism between societal actors. Instead, when deep differences are entrenched, at least during the research period, establishing respectful engagement requires a critical attitude to the undue exercise of power or rent-seeking.

Further, guaranteeing the non-coercive character of the dialogue is more important in situations with less direct power differentials. This perspective is, for instance, reflected in critical theory perspectives on social learning, which aim to unearth relationships involving distorted communication processes, in particular by understanding how manipulation of information contributes to resistance to mutually beneficial change (Willis, 2007, pp. 81–87). In general, in this critical role of social learning, partners aim to deconstruct unquestioned societal value perspectives that perpetuate dominating relationships and flow from unequal capacities to participate in the debate (Fraser and Honneth, 2003).

The third standard—the generality of the common perspectives—requires that the participants are capable of connecting the particular experiences to some general point that applies to a broad diversity of stakeholder groups. As stated by Dryzek, "if communications cannot connect the particular to the general, they may reinforce and harden the position of an enclave or a subculture but not reach those with different viewpoints" (Dryzek, 2007, p. 268).

The relevance of these process standards for organizing procedures for critical analysis of the various value perspectives depends on the available capacities for social learning and how these capacities are perceived by participants. Overall, as in the discussion of co-management and research co-design in Chapter 3, the choice among various ways for organizing the procedures for social learning will be highly context-specific and might change during the course of the project. Indeed, divergence in societal values is not a problem per se for successful collaboration. On the contrary, as mentioned in the introduction to this chapter, diversity can be a source of innovation and may broaden the possibilities for finding workable compromises around common value perspectives on sustainability orientations that satisfy the mutual interests of the participants.

However, given the absence of an external benchmark on the desired level of divergence and convergence, the project partners must adjust their expectations for social learning based on their appreciation of social learning needs. As argued in this chapter, research partners can use various indications for evaluating the required intensity of social learning. These indications do not only include the complexity of the coordination needs in the problem field. Other factors play a role as well, such as the previous experience of the research partners with boundary-crossing research collaborations, which may lead to high or low levels of initial trust among the partners. Moreover, as highlighted in the more general literature on public deliberation, social learning may be motivated by the aspiration to strengthen the general process standards of authentic deliberation in heterogeneous actor networks.

References

Abakar, M. F., Seli, D., Lechthaler, F., Schelling, E., Tran, N., Zinsstag, J. and Muñoz, D. C. (2018). Vaccine hesitancy among mobile pastoralists in Chad: A qualitative study. *International Journal for Equity in Health*, 17(1), 1–10.

Ainsworth, G. B., Redpath, S. M., Wilson, M., Wernham, C. and Young, J. C. (2020). Integrating scientific and local knowledge to address conservation conflicts: Towards a practical framework based on lessons learned from a Scottish case study. *Environmental Science and Policy*, 107, 46–55.

Barnaud, C., Trebuil, G., Dumrongrojwatthana, P. and Marie, J. (2008). Area study prior to companion modelling to integrate multiple interests in upper watershed management of northern Thailand. *Journal of Southeast Asian Studies*, 45(4), 559–585.

Barnaud, C., van Paassen, A., Trébuil, G., Promburom, T. and Bousquet, F. (2010). Dealing with power games in a companion modelling process: Lessons from community water management in Thailand highlands. *The Journal of Agricultural Education and Extension*, 16(1), 55–74.

Bergmann, M., Jahn, T., Knobloch, T., Krohn, W., Pohl, C. and Schramm, E. (2012). *Methods for transdisciplinary research: A primer for practice*. Frankfurt: Campus Verlag.

Bieser, J. C., Vaddadi, B., Kramers, A., Höjer, M. and Hilty, L. M. (2021). Impacts of telecommuting on time use and travel: A case study of a neighborhood telecommuting center in Stockholm. *Travel Behaviour and Society*, 23, 157–165.

Chang, R. (Ed.). (1997). *Incommensurability, incomparability, and practical reason*. Cambridge, MA: Harvard University Press.

Daw, T. (2018). *Uncovering the amazing behind the scenes achievements by Tzunza community to build on SPACES knowledge and dialogues*. www.espa-spaces.org/uncovering-the-amazing-behind-the-scenes-achievements-by-tzunza-community-to-build-on-spaces-knowledge-and-dialogues/. Accessed 26 February 2023.

Directorate, E.S.P.A. (2018). *Mangrove conservation is protecting both livelihoods and carbon stores*. Report on Impact Stories. Research into Results, Edingburgh.

Dryzek, J. S. (2002). *Deliberative democracy and beyond: Liberals, critics, contestations*. Oxford: Oxford University Press.

Dryzek, J. S. (2007). Networks and democratic ideals: Equality, freedom, and communication. In E. Sørensen and J. Torfing (Eds.), *Theories of democratic network governance* (pp. 262–273). London: Palgrave Macmillan.

Fortnam, M., Brown, K., Chaigneau, T., Crona, B., Daw, T. M., Gonçalves, D., . . . and Schulte-Herbruggen, B. (2019). The gendered nature of ecosystem services. *Ecological Economics*, 159, 312–325.

Fraser, N. and Honneth, A. (2003). *Redistribution or recognition?: A political-philosophical exchange*. New York: Verso Books.

Galafassi, D., Daw, T. M., Thyresson, M., Rosendo, S., Chaigneau, T., Bandeira, S., . . . and Brown, K. (2018). Stories in social-ecological knowledge cocreation. *Ecology and Society*, 23(1), 23.

Habermas, J. (1986). *Morale et communication* (translated by Christian Bouchindhomme). Paris: Les Editions du Cerf.

Herrero, P., Dedeurwaerdere, T. and Osinski, A. (2019). Design features for social learning in transformative transdisciplinary research. *Sustainability Science*, 14(3), 751–769.

Hirsch Hadorn, G., Hoffmann-Riem, H., Biber-Klemm, S., Grossenbacher-Mansuy, W., Joye, D., Pohl, C., . . . and Zemp, E. (Eds.). (2008). *Handbook of transdisciplinary research*. Dordrecht: Springer.

Hodgson, I. D., Redpath, S. M., Fischer, A. and Young, J. (2018). Fighting talk: Organisational discourses of the conflict over raptors and grouse moor management in Scotland. *Land Use Policy*, 77, 332–343.

Hodgson, I. D., Redpath, S. M., Fischer, A. and Young, J. (2019). Who knows best? Understanding the use of research-based knowledge in conservation conflicts. *Journal of Environmental Management, 231,* 1065–1075.

Innes, J. E. and Booher, D. E. (2010). *Planning with complexity: An introduction to collaborative rationality for public policy.* Abingdon: Routledge.

Kramers, A. and Akerman, J. (2019). *Mistra Sams annual report 2018.* KTH Royal Institute of Technology, Stockholm.

Lechthaler, F. and Abakar, M. F. (2015). *Étude de base sur l'utilisation des services de santé maternelle et infantile au Tchad : une enquête en milieu rural auprès des populations sédentaires et nomades à Yao et à Danamadji* [Unpublished report]. Swiss Tropical and Public Health Institute, Basel.

Misak, Ch. (2000). *Truth, politics, morality.* London: Routledge.

Norton, B. (2015). *Sustainable values, sustainable change.* Chicago: The University of Chicago Press.

Norton, B. G. (2005). *Sustainability.* Chicago, IL: The University of Chicago Press.

Pohl, C. and Hirsch Hadorn, G. (2007). *Principles for designing transdisciplinary research.* Munich: Oekom Verlag.

Redpath, S. M., Young, J., Evely, A., Adams, W. M., Sutherland, W. J., Whitehouse, A., . . . and Gutierrez, R. J. (2013). Understanding and managing conservation conflicts. *Trends in Ecology and Evolution, 28*(2), 100–109.

Reed, M. S., Evely, A. C., Cundill, G., Fazey, I., Glass, J., Laing, A., . . . and Stringer, L. C. (2010). What is social learning? *Ecology and Society, 15*(4).

Schneider, F., Giger, M., Harari, N., Moser, S., Oberlack, C., Providoli, I., . . . and Zimmermann, A. (2019). Transdisciplinary co-production of knowledge and sustainability transformations: Three generic mechanisms of impact generation. *Environmental Science and Policy, 102,* 26–35.

Schwabe, C. W. (1984). *Veterinary medicine and human health.* Philadelphia: Williams and Wilkins.

Sen, A. (2002). *Rationality and freedom.* Cambridge, MA: Harvard University Press.

Sen, A. (2009). *The idea of justice.* Cambridge, MA: Harvard University Press.

Sjöman, M., Ringenson, T. and Kramers, A. (2020). Exploring everyday mobility in a living lab based on economic interventions. *European Transport Research Review, 12*(1), 5.

Sørensen, E. and Torfing, J. (Eds.). (2007). *Theories of democratic network governance.* Heidelberg: Springer.

Vaddadi, B., Ringenson, T., Sjöman, M., Hesselgren, M. and Kramers, A. (2022). Do they work? Exploring possible potentials of neighbourhood telecommuting centres in supporting sustainable travel. *Travel Behaviour and Society, 29,* 34–41.

Van Breda, J. and Swilling, M. (2019). The guiding logics and principles for designing emergent transdisciplinary research processes: Learning experiences and reflections from a transdisciplinary urban case study in Enkanini informal settlement, South Africa. *Sustainability Science, 14*(3), 823–841.

Willis, J. W. (2007). *Foundations of qualitative research: Interpretive and critical approaches.* Thousand Oaks, CA: Sage Publishing.

5

DEVELOPING INTEGRATED BOUNDARY-CROSSING ORGANIZATIONAL NETWORKS

As argued throughout the book, to successfully produce usable knowledge on interdependent social and ecological system dynamics within basic and applied transdisciplinary research, research partners must engage actively in various knowledge co-production and social learning activities. Important aspects of these activities are the co-construction of research design, the co-management of the knowledge co-production process, and social learning on sustainability values by researchers and societal actors. To consolidate transdisciplinary research in more diverse and comprehensive research networks, researchers and science policy officials must, however, look beyond the level of these collaborations within research projects and develop a set of higher-level institutional mechanisms for building transdisciplinary research competences and research networks in larger communities.

This chapter aims to take a fresh look at this question of the institutionalization of transdisciplinary research partnerships into larger organizational structures for research capacity building. The key hypothesis of this chapter is that the capacity building can be organized by involving researchers and societal actors in larger polycentric organizational networks. The acquisition of competences in these larger networks can be organized through a diversity of exploratory research activities, which are part of the regular repertoire of activities at institutions of higher education. For instance, teachers can organize initiations in co-constructed research in the context of courses on sustainability issues, or researchers can gather in open-ended workshops to identify new transdisciplinary research strands. Furthermore, capacity building for research can rely on well-known mechanisms such as organizing discussion platforms in larger clusters of thematic research or organizing meta-analyses of general process principles for transdisciplinary research.

DOI: 10.4324/9781032624297-6

What is key in the implementation of these well-known mechanisms in the context of transdisciplinary sustainability research is the need to consider the requirements of knowledge co-production and social learning at the level of larger organizational networks. Hence, the institutional mechanisms for building the larger networks should also foster the acquisition of competences that are not always part of the regular academic curricula, such as broad interdisciplinary competences spanning the social and ecological dimensions and competences for research co-design and research co-management with societal actors.

Building upon contemporary research in organizational theory, this chapter first discusses the general institutional logic behind the design of flexible, polycentric networks. As highlighted, this organizational approach is only a first step to understand the specific needs for the institutionalization of transdisciplinary research. In a second step, the institutional analysis of the networks will be broadened to consider knowledge co-production and transformational and critical social learning within the piloting, clustering, and networking of transdisciplinary project work.

5.1 From disciplinary divisions and departments to flexible network organizations

The work of Oliver Williamson on governance networks (for which he was awarded the 2009 Nobel Laureate in Economics jointly with Elinor Ostrom) provides a good starting point for the institutional analysis of building flexible network organizations. Indeed, the now classical synthesis by Oliver Williamson of the key economic aspects of large-scale organizational architectures allows for understanding why networks can provide a third alternative to the classical forms of organizational hierarchies and case-by-case market-like interactions (Williamson, 1996). First, Oliver Williamson shows how, under certain conditions, actors go beyond case-by-case interactions by integrating a set of tasks in an organization with a common purpose, instead of solving all problems by case-by-case contracting over such tasks between individual agents, such as in freelance labor or decentralized bargaining between competing groups. Second, Williamson shows that the alternative to case-by-case contracting is not only large-scale centralized organizations (so-called functional hierarchies) but that this organization can take a more decentralized form with the building of autonomous teams or flexible networks (see Figure 5.1).

Williamson's economic analysis hints neither at one best organizational form to overcome the insufficiencies of market-like cases-by-case transactions nor at a pure form. In practice, actors build hybrids between the abstract categories of hierarchies and networks. The key insight of Williamsons' synthesis is that there is no unified theory of organization

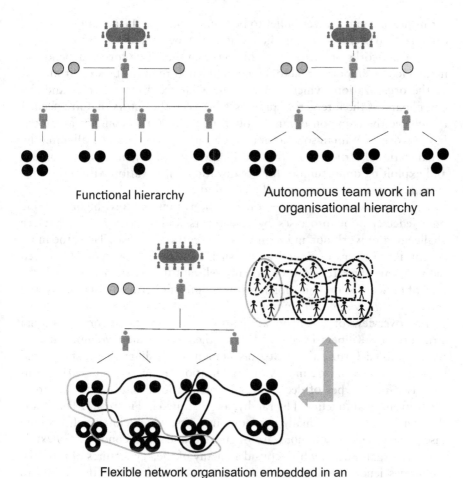

Functional hierarchy

Autonomous team work in an organisational hierarchy

Flexible network organisation embedded in an organisational hierarchy

Legend

General direction and generic staff support

Operational units and teams

Research groups

Societal actor groups

Division heads and middle management

Enabling of boundary crossing network collaborations

FIGURE 5.1 Ideal types of organizational forms for dealing with different types of task environments

forms nor is there a silver bullet to be found. Instead, the advantage of one organizational type over another, whether it be different types of hierarchies or networks or various hybrids between these two forms, depends on many factors. Important factors include the nature of the task environment of the organization, which can be somewhat fixed or evolving, and the complexity of the interaction processes between the actors that are needed to achieve the common organizational purpose. In this context, as shown in the work of Williamson, actors search for improvements by aligning the organizational structure to the specificities of the organizational context and exploiting opportunities for organizational innovation within the constraints of past organizational choices (ibid).

Regarding science commons, organizations must address highly specific knowledge-creation processes by researchers and societal actors that are challenging to work out and monitor on a centralized basis. Thus, the more decentralized forms of organizations such as networks or hybrids between networks and hierarchies are especially relevant in this context, though the type of networked organizational forms is different between disciplinary and transdisciplinary science commons.

The overview of the main alternatives to conventional organizational structures by Kuipers et al. (2018), in their companion volume on new organizational forms, allows for disentangling the different organizational choices in decentralized modes of organization. Kuipers et al. (2018) contrast two main types of decentralized organizations that are distinct from the conventional functional hierarchy, as illustrated in Figure 5.1. The first is the division into functionally autonomous units, which closely reflects how disciplinary science commons are organized, and the second is the flexible network organization, which considers many of the key features of transdisciplinary science commons. According to Kuipers et al. (2018), the benefits to choose one of these organizational forms depend on the degree of variation of the tasks of the organization at various points in time and the complexity to monitor their execution.

A short snapshot of the key features of functional hierarchies allows for understanding why the science commons radically departs from this centralized mode of organization. As specified by Kuipers et al. (ibid), in its pure form, a conventional functional hierarchy is characterized by centralized management and specialization of tasks in a set of separate operational divisions whose execution is planned and monitored by the general managers (ibid, p. 164, see also upper left part of Figure 5.1). Such an organization is especially appropriate and effective in the context of a well-specified and only moderately evolving task environment. Paradigmatic examples of such task environments are the mass production of basic consumption goods by a firm or the delivery of standard administrative services to citizens by a municipality.

A key feature of functional hierarchies is the layered nature of the organization, typically comprising a minimum of three layers (Miller, 2005, p. 357). Indeed, monitoring the contribution of all individuals to a common purpose in a large organization is not a trivial task, and there is no special reason to believe the central manager is the best person to supply all the monitoring services. Someone else, a specialist, typically the division head in an organization with several divisions, is often better placed to provide the monitoring more expertly than the principal herself. The result is a three-level (at least) hierarchy, in which the managers attempt to guide the division heads to act in the organizations' interest, while the latter regards monitoring the agents within the organizational divisions.

The second type of large-scale organization, the so-called functional specialization in autonomous teams, departs from this conventional model (Kuipers et al., 2018, p. 136). In the organization through autonomous teams, the managers delegate part of the supervision of tasks and definition of strategy directly to the teams themselves. The resulting organizational architecture is different. Instead of a top-down organization in organizational divisions that execute tasks defined by the central managers, in this second type, each team has a large autonomy in setting its goals and monitoring the execution of tasks. Obviously, the decentralized definition of tasks and strategies is much more appropriate for the complex and highly evolving knowledge environments researchers face in their respective areas of expertise.

In the structure of decentralized autonomous teams, for those functions that are delegated to the teams, the role of the manager shifts from a command-and-control role to a role of enabler of decentralized coordination and cooperation processes (ibid). Therefore, in practice, the functional specialization in autonomous teams is a hybrid between pure networks, as the researchers have a large autonomy in goal setting and execution, and hierarchies. Indeed, how the units are divided and resources are allocated in a research organization remains structured in an identifiable functional hierarchy by the central management. The latter is typically the case in the conventional disciplinary organization of universities and public research institutions for instance.

The third organization type, the flexible network organization, is closer to a pure network organization. Indeed, in this case, the organizational hierarchy does not specify the boundaries of the decentralized networks of researchers involved in autonomous teamwork (ibid, p. 138). The topics addressed by the teams are much more open-ended and teams can compose and re-compose constantly to adapt to a highly changing and diverse task environment. In this context, as in the second type, the manager also has an enabling role in decentralized collaboration dynamics. However, additional management tasks need to be fulfilled regarding the constant formation of new teams with different combinations of competences to address case-specific issues and the building of boundary-crossing competences such that actors can flexibly operate in several teams.

In general, the organization of publicly funded scientific research fits most of the features of the decentralized modes of organization (the second and the third organizational type). Indeed, the standard economic analysis of publicly funded research shows that research organizations must satisfy a set of constraints that imply a decentralized organizational architecture.

As shown in the seminal contributions of Kenneth Arrow and Richard Nelson in the economics of knowledge, knowledge produced in basic and applied research share important public good characteristics, such as non-rivalry in use and non-divisibility (Antonelli, 2005). Hence, the case for undersupply through markets or voluntary action alone arises. This potential undersupply is a major argument for public intervention in scientific research, such as through public endowments to universities and other public research institutes. Therefore, public authorities and (by delegation) authorities at universities have a key role to play in the centralized funding of research and monitor the overall productivity of researchers in the use of these funds.

However, public research funders who distribute the funding to the researchers (directly or indirectly) through the research organizations are not best placed to judge the allocation of the funds. Indeed, the information about promising avenues of research and the best available scientific knowledge is not centralized but dispersed among scientific researchers and professionals in their specific fields of investigation (Dasgupta, 1988). Hence, research-funding bodies delegate a large part of the project assessment and research evaluation to peer review panels of scientists (Li and Agha, 2015). Thus, a major part of the quality management of publicly funded scientific research is organized at the level of the autonomous disciplinary units and communities. Moreover, the disciplinary communities are organized on a decentralized basis to conduct the peer review of the research outputs, mainly through peer-reviewed scholarly journals, to organize knowledge exchange on further theory development within the respective disciplines.

The transdisciplinary research commons inherit many of the basic organizational features of this public sector science. However, instead of a fairly stable set of autonomous teams organized along disciplinary and sub-disciplinary boundaries, it is based on a flexible network structure along the lines of the third type identified in the overview by Kuipers et al. (2018). Indeed, the research topics are not merely clustered according to similar specialized expertise within given disciplines. Instead, for each specific transformation pathway, understanding the key social and ecological system interdependencies and identifying the legitimate and relevant societal values perspectives results from a co-production process among researchers and societal actors' partners of the project.

Further, concerning disciplinary research, the task environment of the researchers is defined relative to a set of evolving research questions that emerge from the advancement in scientific understanding within the discipline. In this context, team formation can be organized by looking for researchers interested in such closely related research questions and who have the right competences per the standards of the discipline. In transdisciplinary research, as the research tasks are co-produced in interdisciplinary networks of researchers and societal actors, the task environment is much more open when forming new research teams. The match with the required competences of potential research partners is also less defined, as the evolving nature of the research tasks might require the mobilization of knowledge types or process competences not foreseen at the start of the co-production process. Further, transdisciplinary research requires also a set of new competences, such as competences for research co-design and research co-management with societal actors.

5.2 Embedding knowledge co-production and social learning in the institutional enabling of transdisciplinary research

The literature on flexible networks, reviewed by Kuipers et al. (ibid), identifies three core enabling functions of decentralized flexible networks that directly apply to the creation of an institutional environment for transdisciplinary research at universities and institutions of higher education. They include the generic functions of training, knowledge exchange, and building social networks. This section briefly presents the challenge of embedding the knowledge co-production features of transdisciplinary research in these three research-enabling functions. The next section will zoom in on the implementation and present some illustrative examples.

First, for the training functions, innovative teaching formats will be required to foster the building of co-production and social learning competences. Moreover, the teaching must propose methods and approaches for the learning of interdisciplinary knowledge integration across social and ecological system aspects. Typically, it will involve teaching programs that mobilize multi-disciplinary expertise in specific fields of sustainability transformations but involve students in the transdisciplinary research design of common integrated frameworks for socio-ecological systems analysis. Per the arguments developed in Chapter 3 on knowledge co-production on sustainability challenges in integrated socio-ecological systems, these frameworks cannot be defined in advance, as they cannot be specified independently from the choice of feasible and desirable sustainability transformation pathways. Thus, part of the innovative teaching on transdisciplinary sustainability research involves real-world analysis of specific transformation pathways by co-constructing common frameworks among

Enabling platform level
➤ co-production of enabling initiatives for
boundary crossing research collaborations

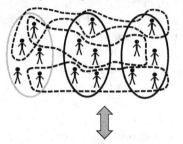

- Building competences for co-produced socio-ecological analysis in teaching curricula and research training

- Organizing boundary crossing knowledge exchange in thematic or generic clusters/networks/workshops

- Exploring opportunities for knowledge co-production/social learning among potential project partners

Research projects Level

- Usable knowledge co-production on sustainability transformations

- Social learning on sustainability values in transdisciplinary research

FIGURE 5.2   Co-produced transdisciplinary research-enabling functions.

Legend: project boundaries—full line; boundary-crossing interactions—dotted line; black circles designate research groups, and white circles, social-actor groups.

disciplinary perspectives, along with deliberation over societal values with concerned societal actors.

The second enabling function addresses the organization of the exchange of knowledge on the transdisciplinary processes and methods in the flexible organizational networks. Given the diverse nature of the research activities involving different combinations of disciplines and types of social-actor partnerships, it is unlikely to find a reasonably uniform approach to the main process features of transdisciplinary research across these activities. Nevertheless, knowledge exchange can be organized in a multitude of network clusters. This clustering across various networks allows researchers and societal actors to gather around topics of common interest for transdisciplinary research, while still acknowledging the broad heterogeneity of knowledge types that are mobilized. Therefore, the goal of the knowledge exchange in these clusters is to strengthen the capacity of the potential research partners to address knowledge co-production and social learning challenges in a wide range of partnership types and possible combinations of disciplinary knowledge.

Given the central role of knowledge co-production and social learning with societal actors, these network clusters for knowledge exchange should strive to actively include societal actors' perspectives on sustainability transformations. Indeed, even though processes for improving social legitimacy and social relevancy likely differ from one project to another, researchers and societal actors involved in various projects can learn from each other and broaden the possible perspectives on likely causes of success and failure. Moreover, the knowledge exchange clusters may offer new opportunities for pursuing discussions on the validation of results from various social-actor viewpoints and contribute to more effective knowledge transfer.

Finally, a key enabling function for transdisciplinary research concerns social networking among potential research partners. Indeed, in capacity building for transdisciplinary sustainability research, the research topics can only partially be defined independently of the constitution of the research team and the choices made by the members of the team on the framing of the plurality of possible interdependent social and ecological system dynamics. Therefore, the programming of new research topics also partially depends on their co-production in a gradual learning process among disciplinary researchers and societal actors on possible avenues for collaborative research.

One interesting tool that integrates such elements of enabling knowledge co-production at the stage of exploring team formation is documented in management studies on flexible network organizations. They are the so-called search conferences (Weisbord and Janoff, 1995; Kuipers, 2018, pp. 347, 411, 431). In such meetings, diverse members of an organization gather to imagine common projects across boundaries of organizational tasks and areas of expertise. Similarly, in the so-called open space conferences (Owen, 2008), cooperative arrangements are sought around a specified topic among all the relevant persons in an organization without a pre-defined agenda or group composition. These tools have been developed mainly in the context of business and non-profit organizations. As described later, some research organizations have designed their version of these tools to enable social networking for research programming in transdisciplinary research.

5.3 Implementing integrated boundary-crossing networks for teaching, knowledge exchange, and team formation

This section discusses examples of implementing the three institutional enabling mechanisms discussed in the literature on flexible network organizations (i.e., building competences, knowledge exchange, and strategic programming of future research). As noted, in the case of transdisciplinary sustainability research, the implementation of these mechanisms cannot be disconnected from knowledge co-production and social learning with societal actors on feasible and desirable sustainability transformations in the various thematic areas of concern.

5.3.1 Building transdisciplinary teaching and training curricula

The first important task is building transdisciplinary collaboration and research competencies in the teaching curricula at universities and institutions of higher education (Fam et al., 2018; Herweg et al., 2021; Ahrend and Podann, 2021; Schmohl and Philipp, 2021; Griffin et al., 2022; Vienni Baptista and Klein, 2022). Accordingly, various organizations have set up transdisciplinary teaching programs. Such programs often build upon former pedagogical innovations developed since the 1970s that included training for research approaches that involve social-actor partnerships, such as urban studies or development cooperation (Nicolaides et al., 2022). Nevertheless, not all innovative teaching programs are automatically transdisciplinary. In many cases, they remain purely multi-disciplinary or do not explicitly organize deliberation around heterogeneous sustainability values to co-construct specific socially legitimate and relevant transformation pathways.

Two prominent educational initiatives can illustrate the organization of transdisciplinary education at the university that meets some of the challenges. The first is organized by the transdisciplinary research and teaching group, TdLab, at ETH Zürich, and the second is piloted by Gothenburg University in Sweden in the context of the Mistra Urban Futures research consortium.

The TdLab at the polytechnical institute ETH in Zürich comprises a group of professors, lecturers, researchers, and graduate students collectively in charge of teaching and research activities across disciplinary and sectoral boundaries. The TdLab organizes a series of teaching activities on issues of sustainable development with societal stakeholders. As specified in two articles on building transdisciplinary competences through the TdLab curriculum, these courses actively address transdisciplinary research co-design and social learning on sustainability values (Krütli et al., 2018; Pearce et al., 2018; Pohl et al., 2018).

First, the proposed teaching activities actively organize a discussion with societal actors on the problem co-construction and the co-validation of the research results. As stated in the presentation of the curriculum, "the students frame the problem, along with non-academic actors who have an interest in the problem" (Pearce et al., 2018, p. 168). The authors directly link this approach to the concept of transformational learning based on real-world problems developed by Meeth (1978, p. 173): "Whereas interdisciplinary programs start with the discipline, transdisciplinary programs start with the issue or problem and, through the processes of problem-solving, bring to bear the knowledge of these disciplines that contribute to a solution or resolution." Such transformative learning assumes not only that learning is based on personal experience but that learning often requires to be challenged by the experiences and perceptions of others (König, 2015).

Second, the teaching activities directly address value-related learning by combining interdisciplinary system analysis with discussing the sustainability targets and the social possibilities of change in the specific thematic context with the students. The various objectives are designated more theoretically by referring to the three objectives of usable knowledge production introduced in Chapter 2, which are the production of systems knowledge, target knowledge, and transformational knowledge. In the context of usable knowledge production on sustainability transformations, systems knowledge covers the interdisciplinary analysis of the socio-ecological system interdependencies. The second, so-called target knowledge, addresses the legitimate goals that society "should set in order to create an improved or transformed system" (Pearce et al., 2018, p. 168). The third, transformation knowledge, deals with the strategy to adopt "to get where we want to go" (ibid), which implies engaging with the perspectives of the change agents and identifying the socially most relevant value-related orientations in the given field of sustainability transformations. As stated by the authors, this focus on value-related discussion in the courses represents a paradigm shift "from relying on science to describe and to explain phenomena in the world to expanding its use for also clarifying societal goals (target knowledge) and how to get to those goals (transformation knowledge)" (ibid, p. 169; see also König et al., 2021).

Two courses provide a good illustration of this approach to transdisciplinary learning. The first course is called "Transdisciplinary Case Study" and can be selected by all the students of ETH. Within this program, the students co-construct a research item with stakeholders around solutions to a society-wide sustainability challenge. During the course, the students must collaborate with stakeholders to define the relevant research questions, work in an interdisciplinary team, and frame the case and its content from a variety of perspectives.

The second course was an eight-day extracurricular course designed for Ph.D. and post-doc students, the so-called TdLab Winter School "Science meets practice," organized nearly every year from 2011 to 2020 (Stauffacher et al., 2012; Pearce et al., 2018, 2022). In these Winter Schools, Ph.D. and post-doc students engaged during a full week with the residents of a small town in Switzerland to collaboratively frame problems encountered by these residents and learn from each other, using stakeholder workshops and other transdisciplinary knowledge co-production tools and methods. Coached by experienced transdisciplinary researchers, the goal was to provide an opportunity for the students to learn how to make a meaningful connection between their own research and the concerns of the wider public.

The teaching program in Gothenburg, Sweden, connected to both Gothenburg University and Chalmers University of Technology, shows a second set of prominent initiatives on transdisciplinary teaching at the university in the context of the Mistra Urban Futures research consortium (Hemström et al., 2021, ch3). The course for doctoral students organized from 2017 to 2019 is a good illustration of initiation into knowledge co-production processes. The practice-based core of the course was formed by the case studies conducted in Gothenburg on just and sustainable city development as part of the larger research program at the center. Each component of the course addressed one case study, developed through different themes including holistic thinking, collaborative methods, border management, and transdisciplinary theory. Knowledge co-production was fostered by combining perspectives, literature, and lectures, from researchers and practitioners in all of the themes. Joint deliberation over legitimate and relevant sustainability challenges was structured via group work and in a collaborative writing process. In the collaborative writing process, researcher and practitioner pairs focused on sustainability challenges in their current work and an evaluation of the transdisciplinary research process (ibid, p. 85).

A third example of active knowledge co-production for enabling transdisciplinary training is situated at the master's thesis level. Since 2019, UCLouvain University, Belgium, through the initiative of a university vice-president specifically in charge of sustainability transformations, has adopted an ambitious sustainability transition plan for the University (UCLouvain, 2023a). One core activity for promoting transdisciplinary research in the sustainability transition plan is the transdisciplinary "Oikos" master thesis program, launched at UCLouvain in 2021 by the Louvain Learning Lab and the research platform for transdisciplinary research (LPTransition) (UCLouvain, 2023b).

The Oikos master theses are conducted by pools of students from different disciplines on topics co-constructed with research directors from various disciplines and societal actors. In the context of this program, potential research directors interested in the initiative are invited to participate in a major "search conference" that takes place every year to form pools around topics that cross the boundaries between the social and natural sciences and provide a clear added value for understanding socio-ecological interdependencies. Following the discussions in the search conference, the research directors of a given pool meet in the next academic year to fine-tune the proposed research questions and propose these to the students in master 1. In master 2 and the second part of master 1, the students who have chosen the proposed topic form a group that regularly meets to foster synergies and mutual enrichment of the work in their respective master theses. The originality of these group-based thesis projects is to give a large place to knowledge co-production and social learning in the formation of groups that work on a common research topic.

5.3.2 Fostering knowledge exchange on transdisciplinary process features

The second important task for the building of a truly integrated flexible network organization of transdisciplinary research is the organization of the network clusters for knowledge exchange on transdisciplinary process features and project outcomes.

As stated earlier, these network clusters for knowledge exchange can be quite specific. However, they may address issues that are relevant to all kinds of transdisciplinary research. For instance, researchers and societal actors can work in thematic clusters that address specific sustainability transformation areas. In other cases, research partners may gather without specified thematic concern but organize knowledge exchange for a sub-group of the community such as doctoral students. They may build knowledge exchange platforms around cross-cutting meta-issues, such as evaluating protocols or certain features.

For instance, the Leuphana University in Lüneburg, Germany, actively invested in such knowledge exchange platforms in the context of strengthening its ecosystem of transdisciplinary research projects (Ahrend and Podann, 2021). Since 2006, the university reorganized its faculties and departments in an interdisciplinary and transdisciplinary way around grand societal challenges directly related to societal actors' demands in the area around the university.

According to scholars of transdisciplinarity, the success of this case especially regards establishing an inter-faculty center for transdisciplinary research methods, which can raise transdisciplinary research at the heart of the universities' activities. In particular, the key strength of the inter-faculty center is related to the building of a high-level joint understanding of transdisciplinary process values in Leuphana university, while fostering an increase in the degree of formal institutionalization of the center (Vienni Baptista and Rojas-Castro, 2020). Indeed, instead of centralizing the sustainability issues in a new overarching institute, which is challenging to integrate with the co-constructed nature of each transdisciplinary research perspective on specific sustainability transformations, the center established a research-enabling relationship with the existing disciplinary departments by organizing knowledge exchange and capitalization around ongoing transdisciplinary research projects.

The example of Leuphana University is not a standalone initiative, even though it is remarkable in the scope of the involvement of the university's central management. Many research organizations established, on a more decentralized basis, so-called communities of practice to exchange knowledge on key process features of transdisciplinary research. As stated by Schneider et al. (2019, p. 31), such communities of practice "want to improve their competences and practices through sharing experiences, reflecting on own practices and values, and engaging in or learning from research." Through its link with practice, knowledge co-production with societal actors is a key aspect of the communities of practice. For instance, as suggested by Schneider et al. (2019), these communities can "create reflective spaces by connecting interested actors, enhance reflexivity by mirroring their practices, and presenting alternative perspectives or help actors to better understand the context they are working in or causal relations they are not aware of" (ibid).

Many network-enabling initiatives explicitly refer to this concept. One example is the Community of Practice on change-oriented approaches in Partnership Research in Agronomy, established in February 2021 at the International Cooperation Center in Agronomic Research for Development (CIRAD) (Louafi et al., 2023). This Community of Practice is directly related to a CIRAD cross-sectoral initiative on impact evaluation, which also addresses issues regarding transdisciplinary research. In this context, the Community of Practice organizes knowledge exchange on the ex-ante design of impact trajectories and their follow-up (Barret et al., 2018; Blundo Canto et al., 2020; and personal communication, coordinator of the Community Practice, 13th June 2022, Agropolis International, Montpellier, France). A key feature, in line with the general discussion on communities of practice, is the active inclusion of practice partners in this initiative, such as the member organizations of the network of development cooperation organizations F3E (2023).

A third initiative regards the "Louvain4" research clusters organized at UCLouvain, Belgium. They are quite similar to the communities of practice (UCLouvain, 2023c). The Louvain4 clusters stem from a bottom-up team formation around flagship themes for organizing integrated interdisciplinary and practice-related research on topics such as water governance, energy, or food. Through this clustering in smaller well-identifiable thematic communities, the idea is to develop knowledge transfer on transversal issues and build specific competences for transversal work. Telling examples of the success of this process of building network clusters around integrated interdisciplinary research are the follow-up collaborations on the impact of extreme weather events at the level of municipalities. Indeed, after the extreme weather of 2021, various municipalities contacted the university to update the maps for the prediction of flooding, which are not adapted to the most recent data on the likely impacts of climate change. The success in setting set up these new collaborations in such a short time is a direct result of the preliminary work on team identification and building synergies among various disciplinary competences dealing with water governance issues at the university.

Further, to complete this overview of enabling knowledge exchange in boundary-crossing networks, it is important to mention the role of inter-university initiatives. Indeed, the illustrations in this section mainly focused on internal organizational innovations at each university, as these are likely to provide the best long-term guarantee for the institutionalization of transdisciplinary research. Nevertheless, inter-university initiatives also play a key role in contributing to the consolidation of knowledge on transdisciplinary processes. In Europe, the long-standing involvement of the Swiss Academy of Sciences in various enabling activities around the team of the "Network for Transdisciplinary Research" (Swiss Academies of Arts and Sciences, 2023) is a prominent example of such highly effective inter-university initiatives for promoting transdisciplinary research.

5.3.3 Knowledge co-production and social learning in social networking among potential project partners

The third enabling function—social networking among potential project partners—has a cross-cutting nature, as it has an impact on the identification of potential partners in the various teaching and knowledge clustering initiatives and the programming of new research avenues in project work.

The initiatives organized at the Technical University of Berlin (TU Berlin) provide a good example of the organization of open-ended meetings for prospective team formation and strategic research programming. Since 2014, TU Berlin promotes transdisciplinary research through a combination of centralized management initiatives and enabling bottom-up team formation and knowledge exchange (Ahrend and Podann, 2021). As a first step, the centralized management of the university organized university-wide discussion arenas to define flagship themes for transdisciplinary research. In the second step, the researchers were invited to network their respective research projects around these transdisciplinary research themes. Finally, in the third step, the university launched a series of pilot projects on some of these themes. In each of these pilots, societal actors play an active role as research partners to co-design the research frameworks and co-validate the results through collaborative knowledge transfer.

Along with the role of these open-ended meetings in the gradual institutionalization of research clusters and transdisciplinary pilot projects, the TU Berlin team has contributed to the transdisciplinary research program of the Berlin University Alliance, comprising TU Berlin, Humboldt University, Freie Universität, and Charité-Universitätsmedizin Berlin. A highly original activity of the University Alliance in this context is the so-called research fora on grand challenges. These research fora, not unlike the "search conferences," gather researchers from partner universities to co-construct socially relevant and legitimate research perspectives with societal actors around selected topics of sustainability (University Alliance, 2022a). According to the organizers, each forum contributes to more permanent structures for transdisciplinarity in the Alliance by implementing "innovative formats, new collaborations and networks" (University Alliance, 2022b).

5.4 New management functions for boundary-crossing network integration

Studies on the governance of flexible networks and overcoming possible network failures provide key insights into the main ingredients for realizing an organization-wide institutionalization process of transdisciplinary research. From the review in this chapter, a combination of a set of new horizontal network-enabling functions, along with the adjustment of conventional centralized management functions to the needs of transdisciplinary research, is a promising way to successfully support the institutionalization process. Distilling some of the key lessons of this literature (Kuipers et al., 2018, pp. 272–304) and the examples reviewed, it is possible to highlight the following governance features contributing to the effective institutionalization of transdisciplinary research:

At the level of the adjustment of centralized management functions:

- Promote the hiring of professors with transdisciplinary research competences in various specific disciplinary fields of expertise
- Earmark funding streams for so-called strategic research on grand societal challenges, which require transdisciplinary competences
- Develop specialized generic services for supporting transdisciplinary methodologies, such as training in specific workshop formats with societal actors on co-constructing research designs
- Embed the promotion of transdisciplinary research within the more general procedures for democratic decision-making and strategy formulation within the organization

At the level of the enabling functions for fostering the integration of boundary-crossing networks:

- Promote the building of transdisciplinary competences in the courses at the Bachelor's, Master's, and Ph.D. levels by integrating
  - active discussion with societal actors on problem co-construction
  - learning on value-related issues that impact the design of the research framework (for instance, on sustainability orientations in a specific field of investigation)
- Organize knowledge exchange clusters on transdisciplinary process features by
  - involving existing transdisciplinary researchers and teams that wish to initiate transdisciplinary research

- involving academic research and societal actors in clusters on thematic areas of concern in various specific fields of sustainability transformations

- Enable social networking for transdisciplinary team formation, in particular through open-ended workshop formats leading to the co-design of socially relevant and legitimate questions among emerging teams for transdisciplinary teaching or research

Even though each of the three decentralized enabling functions of collaboration in a flexible network organization (focused on organizing training, knowledge exchange, and social networking) results in different organizational tasks, it is important to underline the many synergies that exist between them. These synergies create various opportunities for students and researchers to become involved in transdisciplinary research at various stages of their curriculum. For instance, an early experience with transdisciplinary research to address a given sustainability issue at a master's student level can be a stepping stone for participating in a more in-depth transdisciplinary research project in the same field at a later stage. Another pathway for involvement runs from interdisciplinary to transdisciplinary research. For example, a researcher who participates in a specific task of interdisciplinary mixed methods research in a transdisciplinary research project may become interested in understanding the process of the research co-design in transdisciplinary collaborations better. In a workshop that gathers research partners from several projects, they might subsequently get involved in knowledge exchange on various process features of transdisciplinary knowledge co-production.

Further, to strengthen the possible synergies between the research-enabling functions, scholars underline the importance of the social-interactive and emotional features of collaboration across heterogeneous actors. Creating a feeling of belonging to a group within a flexible network with very heterogeneous members and diverse ongoing projects might be quite challenging (Kuipers et al., 2018, pp. 428–429). Indeed, scholars of transdisciplinary research underline the importance of emotional and social-interactional dimensions for building effective knowledge commons. Such features include collaborative culture, a climate of conviviality, and promoting positive feelings about network members, including respect, admiration, and recognition (Lux et al., 2019, p. 188; Pohl et al., 2017, p. 23). The emotional and social-interactional features can be especially challenging to promote in the distributed network of heterogeneous and distributed boundary-crossing transdisciplinary research commons. Therefore, it is important to invest in various mechanisms to improve these social-interactional and emotional dimensions of teamwork, such as the strengthening of "a climate of conviviality, social-interactive qualities of the participants, effective leadership, meaningful personal relations, group identity, complementary team roles and socializing outside meetings" (Boix-Mansilla et al., 2016, p. 589).

Finally, as also highlighted by Kuipers et al. (2018), introducing new tools for flexible networking while staying under the general umbrella of a conventional functional hierarchy is unlikely to be sufficient to generate an effective uptake of the flexible network architecture. On the contrary, members can perceive new measures as just another constraint imposed by the central managers who remain in their role of task supervision from a hierarchical management perspective. This situation, in turn, might induce frustration or loss of time among the members who invested their efforts in new horizontal and flexible organizational practices.

Regarding transdisciplinary sustainability research, implementing the various tools for transdisciplinary collaborations while under the general umbrella of disciplinary research divisions and centralized monitoring may induce similar frustrations regarding inconsistent institutional incentives. Therefore, without actively integrating the envisioned measures for supporting flexible boundary-crossing networks in a comprehensive institutional strategy, the practices of transdisciplinary co-production and partnership-based social learning may remain limited to a few institutional niches. In such cases, the investment in sustainability research may fail to reach a sufficiently large critical mass of opportunities for learning by motivated researchers from various disciplines or stakeholders with specific thematic knowledge interests.

Moreover, without a general institutional strategy, the niches for transdisciplinary research may only survive in areas where they are promoted by external incentives, such as business-oriented partnerships or specific advocacy coalitions, instead of organizing support for different groups of transdisciplinary research partners on various topics of concern. Obviously, for a broader involvement of various types of research partners and topics, special attention should be given to empowering research and societal actors with fewer resources and initial capacities to step into transdisciplinary research.

The possible failures of institutionalization of organizational networks for transdisciplinary research hint at an important cross-cutting challenge of building flexible network-based organizations. This challenge is the embedding of the networks in more general procedures for democratic decisions within the organization by discussing the purposes of these networks within the established collective decision-making procedures of the organization.

There is extensive scholarship on the various approaches to this question of organizing democratic governance of organizational networks (see for instance Dryzek, 2002; Sørensen and Torfing, 2007). Some common principles highlighted in this literature are the expansion of the concerned actors to be involved in the collective decision-making; that is, involving spokespersons of the transdisciplinary research communities, extending the scope of the issues addressed in the deliberations, and promoting the effective participation by all (Dryzek, 2007).

A more in-depth analysis of the application of these democratic standards to the institutionalization of flexible network architectures falls outside the scope of the analysis of institutional design of transdisciplinary knowledge co-production in this book. However, a vital lesson of this scholarship for our purposes is the need to accompany the implementation of the various centralized and enabling functions for transdisciplinary research by an inclusive and organization-wide deliberation process on its goals, scope, and allocation of means for fostering effective participation by all.

References

Ahrend, Ch. and Podann, A. (2021). Institutionalisierung. In T. Schmohl and Th. Philipp (Hg.). *Handbuch Transdisziplinäre Didaktik* (pp. 141–150). Bielefeld: Transcript Verlag.

Antonelli, C. (2005). Models of knowledge and systems of governance. *Journal of Institutional Economics*, 1(1), 51–73.

Barret, D., Blundo-Canto, G., Dabat, M.-H., Devaux-Spatarakis, A., Faure, G., Hainzelin, E., Mathé, S., Temple, L., Toillier, A., Triomphe, B. and Vall, E. (Illus.). (2018). *ImpresS ex post. Methodological guide to ex post impact evaluation of agricultural research in developing countries*. Montpellier: CIRAD.

Blundo Canto, G., de Romémont, A., Hainzelin, E., Faure, G., Monier, C., Triomphe, B., Barret, D. and Vall, E. (Illus.). (2020). *ImpresS ex ante methodological guide to ex ante co-construction of development-oriented research impact pathways (second version)*. Montpellier: CIRAD.

Boix-Mansilla, V., Lamont, M. and Sato, K. (2016). Shared cognitive—emotional—interactional platforms: Markers and conditions for successful interdisciplinary collaborations. *Science, Technology and Human Values*, 41(4), 571–612.

Dasgupta, P. (1988). The welfare economics of knowledge production. *Oxford Review of Economic Policy*, 4(4), 1–12.

Dryzek, J. S. (2002). *Deliberative democracy and beyond: Liberals, critics, contestations*. Oxford: Oxford University Press.

Dryzek, J. S. (2007). Networks and democratic ideals: Equality, freedom, and communication. In E. Sørensen and J. Torfing (Eds.), *Theories of democratic network governance* (pp. 262–273). London: Palgrave Macmillan.

F3E. (2023). *Des ressources pour l'évaluation. Des repères pour l'action*. https://f3e. asso.fr/. Accessed 11 January 2023.

Fam, D., Neuhauser, L. and Gibbs, P. (Eds.). (2018). *Transdisciplinary theory, practice and education: The art of collaborative research and collective learning*. Basel: Springer.

Griffin, D., Gallagher, S., Vigano, V., Mousa, D., Van Vugt, S., Lodder, A. and Byrne, J. R. (2022). Best practices for sustainable inter-institutional hybrid learning at CHARM European University. *Education Sciences*, 12(11), 797.

Hemström, K., Simon, D., Palmer, H., Perry, B. and Polk, M. (2021). *Transdisciplinary knowledge co-production: A guide for sustainable cities*. Rugby: Practical Action Publishing.

Herweg, K., Tribelhorn, Th., Lena Lewis, A., Providoli, I., Trechsel, L. J. and Stein-böck, C. (2021). *Transdisciplinary learning for sustainable development*. Bern: Bern Open Publishing.

König, A. (2015). Towards systemic change: On the co-creation and evaluation of a study programme in transformative sustainability science with stakeholders in Luxembourg. *Current Opinion in Environmental Sustainability, 16*, 89–98.

König, A., Ravetz, J., Raber, B., Stankiewicz, J., Rojas-Aedo, R., Hondrila, K. and Pickar, K. (2021). Taking the complex dynamics of human—environment—technology systems seriously: A case study in doctoral education at the University of Luxembourg. *Frontiers in Sustainability, 2*, 673033.

Krütli, P., Pohl, C. and Stauffacher, M. (2018). Sustainability learning labs in small island developing states: A case study of the Seychelles. *GAIA-Ecological Perspectives for Science and Society, 27*(1), 46–51.

Kuipers, H., van Amelsvoort, P. and Kramer, E.-H. (2018). *Het Nieuwe Organiseren (derde, volledig herziene druk)*. Leuven and Den Haag: Acco (translated: 2020, *New Ways of Organizing*, Leuven and Den Haag: Acco).

Li, D. and Agha, L. (2015). Big names or big ideas: Do peer-review panels select the best science proposals? *Science, 348*(6233), 434–438.

Louafi, S., Thomas, M., Kankowski, F., Leclerc, Ch., Barnaud, A., Baufumé, S., . . . and Temple, L. (2023). Communities of practice in crop diversity management: From data to collaborative governance. In H. F. Williamson and S. Leonelli (Eds.), *Towards responsible plant data linkage: Data challenges for agricultural research and development* (pp. 273–288). Heidelberg: Springer.

Lux, A., Schäfer, M., Bergmann, M., Jahn, T., Marg, O., Nagy, E., Ransiek, A. C. and Theiler, L. (2019). Societal effects of transdisciplinary sustainability research—How can they be strengthened during the research process? *Environmental Science and Policy, 101*, 183–191.

Meeth, L. R. (1978). Interdisciplinary studies: A matter of definition. *Change: The Magazine of Higher Learning, 10*, 10.

Miller, G. J. (2005). Solutions to principal-agent problems in firms. In Cl. Ménard and M. M. Shirely (Eds.), *Handbook of new institutional economics* (pp. 349–370). Heidelberg: Springer.

Nicolaides, A., Eschenbacher, S., Buergelt, P. T., Gilpin-Jackson, Y., Welch, M. and Misawa, M. (Eds.). (2022). *The Palgrave handbook of learning for transformation*. London: Palgrave Macmillan.

Owen, H. (2008). *Open space technology: A user's guide*. Oakland, CA: Berrett-Koehler Publishers.

Pearce, B. J., Adler, C., Senn, L., Krütli, P., Stauffacher, M. and Pohl, C. (2018). Making the link between transdisciplinary learning and research. In *Transdisciplinary theory, practice and education* (pp. 167–183). Cham: Springer.

Pearce, B. J., Deutsch, L., Fry, P., Marafatto, F. F. and Lieu, J. (2022). Going beyond the AHA! moment: Insight discovery for transdisciplinary research and learning. *Humanities and Social Sciences Communications, 9*(1), 1–10.

Pohl, C., Krütli, P. and Stauffacher, M. (2017). Ten reflective steps for rendering research societally relevant. *GAIA-Ecological Perspectives for Science and Society, 26*(1), 43–51.

Pohl, C., Krütli, P. and Stauffacher, M. (2018). Teaching transdisciplinarity appropriately for students' education level. *GAIA-Ecological Perspectives for Science and Society*, 27(2), 250–252.

Schmohl, T. and Philipp, Th. (2021). *Handbuch Transdisziplinäre Didaktik*. Berlin: Transcript Verlag.

Schneider, F., Giger, M., Harari, N., Moser, S., Oberlack, C., Providoli, I., . . . and Zimmermann, A. (2019). Transdisciplinary co-production of knowledge and sustainability transformations: Three generic mechanisms of impact generation. *Environmental Science and Policy*, 102, 26–35.

Sørensen, E. and Torfing, J. (Eds.). (2007). *Theories of democratic network governance*. Heidelberg: Springer.

Stauffacher, M., Zingerli, C., Fry, P., Pohl, C. and Krütli, P. (2012). Science meets practice: A winter school offers new perspectives. *GAIA-Ecological Perspectives for Science and Society*, 21(2), 145–147.

Swiss Academies of Arts and Sciences. (2023). *Network for transdisciplinary research*. https://transdisciplinarity.ch/en/about-td-net/. Accessed 4 January 2023.

UCLouvain. (2023a). *Sustainability transition plan*. https://uclouvain.be/en/discover/university-transition/plan-transition.html. Accessed 4 January 2023.

UCLouvain. (2023b). *Yearly workshop on the co-construction of interdisciplinary and transdisciplinary master theses on sustainable development*. www.lptransition.be/research. Accessed 4 January 2023.

UCLouvain. (2023c). *Louvain4: UCLouvain interdisciplinary research initiative*. https://uclouvain.be/en/research/louvain4.html. Accessed 11 January 2023.

University Alliance. (2022a). *Doing transdisciplinary research on the topic of global health*. www.berlin-university-alliance.de/en/news/items/2021/210427-global-health-call.html. Accessed 17 October 2022.

University Alliance. (2022b). *Research forums*. www.berlin-university-alliance.de/en/commitments/knowledge-exchange/research-forums/index.html. Accessed 17 October 2022.

Vienni Baptista, B. and Klein, J. T. (Eds.). (2022). *Institutionalizing interdisciplinarity and transdisciplinarity: Collaboration across cultures and communities*. Abingdon: Routledge.

Vienni Baptista, B. and Rojas-Castro, S. (2020). Transdisciplinary institutionalization in higher education: A two-level analysis. *Studies in Higher Education*, 45(6), 1075–1092.

Weisbord, M. R. and Janoff, S. (1995). *Future search*. New York: Berret Koehler.

Williamson, O. E. (1996). *The mechanisms of governance*. Oxford: Oxford University Press.

6
IMPLEMENTING KNOWLEDGE CO-PRODUCTION ON SUSTAINABILITY TRANSFORMATIONS IN ACADEMIA AND BEYOND

The analysis in this book of over three decades of transdisciplinary sustainability research shows the urgent need for new modes of organizing scientific research. The reform of the science fabric is particularly urgent, given the multiple social and ecological crises humanity is facing today. As aptly summarized by Christian Pohl et al. (2021, p. 19), these new modes of transdisciplinary research can be characterized by (1) specific process features based on knowledge co-production among partners who actively explore boundaries as learning opportunities and (2) specific research outputs regarding the production of transformative and critical knowledge on sustainability challenges.

The first characteristic highlighted by Pohl et al. (2021) requires the organization of knowledge co-production processes that transcend the conventional separation between various knowledge types, such as between practitioners' and researchers' knowledge and between descriptive and normative perspectives on societal transformation. Indeed, transdisciplinary sustainability research aims to grasp the complex coupled dynamics of social and ecological systems at multiple scales with heterogeneous societal actors. Thus, transdisciplinary research partners mobilize both case-specific knowledge, which is often non-codified, and more generic interdisciplinary scientific knowledge frameworks to analyze feasible real-world transformation pathways.

The organization of these boundary-crossing knowledge generation processes is neither an attempt to produce an illusionary unity among heterogeneous perspectives nor a means to highlight irreducible differences that stifle all possibilities of collaboration. On the contrary, in transdisciplinary research, boundaries are actively explored as opportunities for learning from different perspectives. As underlined by Akkerman and Bakker (2011), based on this mutual learning, participants in boundary-crossing practices can

DOI: 10.4324/9781032624297-7

develop various socially negotiated modes of interaction, ranging from the simple recognition of a shared problem space to coordinated action, continuous joint work, or the co-construction of new common action strategies.

The second characteristic, the production of transformative and critical knowledge, regards the open-ended and pluralistic nature of sustainability challenges. Indeed, the coupled dynamics between social and ecological systems can induce a plurality of feasible and desirable sustainability transformation pathways. Therefore, researchers and societal actors must understand the socially legitimate and relevant values that orient the context-specific choices among this diversity of possible pathways. This understanding has a transformative dimension for both societal actors and researchers. First, understanding specific sustainability transformations requires the identification of the most relevant sustainability challenges from the perspective of the societal change agents that drive the societal transformations in the specific context. Second, addressing specific sustainability transformations also involves a critical stance from the researchers. Indeed, some of the necessary changes may challenge the dominant value-based frameworks that inform socio-ecological modeling practices. By disregarding social learning on these value-based frameworks, the research outcomes might perpetuate unsustainable practices or maintain unbalanced power relationships to the benefit of the incumbent actors.

However, for the individual researchers, societal actors, and research managers, given the long history of the specialized disciplinary organization of research, a main challenge regards the implementation of such boundary-crossing and transformative knowledge generation processes in practice. For sure, there is no single best way forward, and each research organization must consider the local constraints in developing these tools and mechanisms. Further research is therefore needed to document the various options to do so and to build so-called toolbox environments providing inspiration and advice (see, e.g., https://itd-alliance.org/ and https://transdisciplinarity.ch/en). Nevertheless, the literature review and case study analysis in this book give some indications of research questions on the measures that are needed to further build a larger organizational network of transdisciplinary research commons.

In the first place, the analysis shows that regarding transdisciplinary knowledge co-production, research funders, policy officials, and research managers should strive to multiply the opportunities for knowledge co-production by researchers and societal actors in research projects on sustainability transformations. These opportunities can be quite modest, such as through the inclusion of a transdisciplinary case study chapter in a Ph.D. project or a transdisciplinary analysis of a sub-topic by a researcher within a conventional multi-disciplinary consortium. Alternatively, they can include more comprehensive transdisciplinary initiatives, such as the funding of research projects or consortia that orchestrate the co-construction of research design and co-validation of results throughout the entire research cycle. Multiplying such opportunities for the emergence and implementation of transdisciplinary initiatives is especially important, as no centralized approach to the consolidation of transdisciplinary research is likely to cover the diversity of societal actors and knowledge types mobilized in each case-specific transdisciplinary knowledge co-production process.

Further, to meet the social learning needs on sustainability values, each transdisciplinary research project should foresee the possibility of investing time and resources in structuring the space of the different value perspectives of societal actors and researchers. Indeed, as in the various case studies, the growing scope and impact of the interdependencies between social and ecological systems imply the development of new environmental, social, and civic value orientations that forsake the modern myth of continuous growth with unlimited resources. Most of these values, such as the orientation toward environmental justice or reconciliation of human prosperity with planetary boundaries, are intensely debated. Depending on the specific field of sustainability transformations and the involved societal actors, the disruptive learning of sustainability values can be somewhat consensual among the partners, inducing various degrees of convergence. In other cases, the learning will be more critical, such as when powerful interests attempt to perpetuate unsustainable development paths.

Moreover, a set of measures at the level of research organizations can contribute to consolidating the transdisciplinary knowledge commons. As discussed, important mechanisms for the integration of the boundary-crossing networks built around the transdisciplinary research projects are the overall building of transdisciplinary competences, social networking for partner identification, and systematization of knowledge exchange on modes of organization of knowledge co-production and social learning. Hence, to support these cross-cutting mechanisms, research organizations can create new professional profiles and promote transdisciplinary research skills.

For instance, research organizations can organize a supporting service to accompany teachers who implement transdisciplinary competence building in teaching curricula. Such a service could train a dedicated staff person to assist organizational units and departments to promote teaching practices based on knowledge co-production with societal actors on specific sustainability transformation topics. As discussed in Chapter 5, such teaching curricula reform might include full-fledged transdisciplinary partnerships with real-world actors, such as in the collaborative visioning exercises organized with partners in the city of Gothenburg in the context of the course for doctoral students organized at the University of Gothenburg. In other cases, it may focus on specific transdisciplinary competences, such as the analysis of real-world case studies in the courses on sustainable development at the TdLab of the Swiss Federal Institute of Technology (ETH).

Likewise, research organizations might organize supporting services for social networking among potential project partners of transdisciplinary research projects and teaching initiatives. These social network-building activities could take the form of so-called search conferences discussed in Chapter 5. The search conferences are open-ended meetings to identify and define possible topics for knowledge co-production among societal actors and various disciplinary researchers. Examples of such meetings include the sandpit workshops funded by the UK Research and Innovation Council (Bridle et al., 2013; UKRI, 2021) or the transdisciplinary research fora on grand challenges organized by the Berlin University Alliance (see Chapter 5), to cite just a few. Other initiatives for transdisciplinary network-building may be organized at the master's student level, such as the interdisciplinary and transdisciplinary master thesis project on sustainability development at UCLouvain (see Chapter 5) or the master theses of the citizen academy organized by the University of Ghent (Block et al., 2022). The distinguishing feature of these various transdisciplinary network-building activities is the fact that the teams are constituted based on discussions to explore a common research design on interdependent social and ecological system dynamics. Given the partnership dimension of transdisciplinary research, network-building activities cannot be dissociated from the identification of potentially productive areas of knowledge co-production on sustainability transformations.

A third area of organizational support for consolidating transdisciplinary research commons concerns the systematization of knowledge exchange on transdisciplinary process features. By organizing knowledge exchange on process features, research organizations can strengthen the capacities of researchers and societal actors to conduct transdisciplinary research on a broad variety of topics of concern. Moreover, by organizing various opportunities for knowledge exchange in thematic clusters and in more generic organization-wide initiatives, research organizations can create additional support for researchers and societal actors with less access to learning platforms on process features. An example of such a platform is the "Liaison and Transfer Organisations on Social Innovation," established at various universities in Québec. These platforms connect societal actors and researchers to create a discussion on the co-validation of transdisciplinary project results and transdisciplinary approaches in various thematic areas of socio-ecological research (Dagenais et al., 2008). As discussed in Chapter 5, the cross-cutting activities of knowledge exchange on process features allow researchers and societal actors to identify further needs for co-validation or explore opportunities for using certain tools and mechanisms for knowledge co-production and social learning in new thematic areas of inquiry.

To wrap up this journey through these different organizational and institutional measures, it is important to indicate some limits of our analysis and highlight perspectives for future research. The analysis in this book focused on transdisciplinary knowledge commons for sustainability research. Though important, the analysis did not dig deeper into the contributions of the purely disciplinary, multi-disciplinary, and interdisciplinary research projects that address sustainability issues. In many cases, these more conventional approaches are mobilized to furnish more insight into well-identified sub-system components or operate within relatively well-defined value orientations, such as in calls for proposals on the implementation of policy measures for sustainability transformations, as defined ex-ante by research funders.

However, in practice, the boundary between purely transdisciplinary research, where co-constructing research design with societal actors plays a central role throughout the research, and conventional research practices is not always clear-cut (Klein, 2010). Conventional research practices often include consultation and feedback from societal actors, though without including them as full-fledged partners in the knowledge co-production process. When researchers and societal actors intensify the consultation and feedback activities, the research process may be gradually adjusted to include transdisciplinary process features.

The case of so-called broad interdisciplinarity can illustrate this point. According to the analysis of Klein (ibid), broad interdisciplinarity is characterized by research that bridges disparate approaches—for instance ecology and history—and develops comprehensive general views or synthetic frameworks (cf. also Pohl et al., 2021). In broad interdisciplinary research, research partners face heterogeneous methodologies, distinct approaches to problem identification, and a diversity of different conceptual frameworks. Hence, even when societal actors are not directly involved in building a common research design, the collective action challenges them to bridge the different knowledge types that are often similar to the case of transdisciplinary research. For instance, interdisciplinary knowledge co-production can also be hampered by the instrumentalization of the research process by one of the partners who mainly focus on their disciplinary knowledge interests or by unstructured diversity of conceptual approaches.

Given this proximity of the collective action problems, transdisciplinary research can benefit from the lessons learned from knowledge co-production in such broad interdisciplinary research projects. Moreover, from the case study analysis, broad interdisciplinarity is often a key ingredient of transdisciplinary sustainability research. In such cases, learning about knowledge co-production in broad interdisciplinarity may directly contribute to the successful implementation of transdisciplinary research processes.

Another illustration of the gray zone between transdisciplinarity and some more conventional modes of research organization is the case of so-called mission-oriented research. As discussed in a widely disseminated discussion paper by Mariana Mazzucato (2018), mission-oriented research is a key problem-solving-centered research approach to innovation that is often embedded in calls for proposals on grand societal challenges, such as cybersecurity, mental health, or sustainability issues. Often these calls for proposals do not formally require transdisciplinary knowledge co-production with societal actors. Moreover, these calls are often defined regarding measurable and time-bound targets or require project consortia to provide such targets regarding so-called key performance indicators.

However, as highlighted throughout the book, research funders can neither always specify ex-ante the full scope of relevant problems to address nor identify the list of societal actors to include to discuss the value-related issues. It may be related to the value-laden nature of the desirable societal solutions to some of the grand societal challenges or path-dependent constraints on real-world social possibilities for implementing these solutions. Therefore, in practice, research funders often favor projects that also propose some level of knowledge co-production with societal actors throughout the research process. In such cases (as in the case of broad interdisciplinarity), the overlap between collective action problems encountered in mission-driven research and transdisciplinary research can create fruitful opportunities for cross-fertilization between successful research practices.

A second limit of the analysis in the book is related to the collaboration with other transdisciplinary researchers beyond the field of sustainability research. Indeed, the book focuses on transdisciplinary sustainability research and does not explore the many overlaps with other transdisciplinary areas of investigation that do not have a specific focus on sustainability (Hirsch Hadorn et al., 2008). Although such exploration is beyond the scope of this book, the general definition of transdisciplinarity that is used for the analysis hints at such a further dialogue.

Indeed, as specified in the introduction, the book uses a general definition of transdisciplinarity as an approach that is broadly interdisciplinary and based on a research partnership with societal actors. Moreover, as developed in-depth above, this partnership is characterized by a set of process features (regarding knowledge co-production for integrating different knowledge types) and the production of transformative and critical knowledge outputs. This general definition is highly relevant to the broad field of research on sustainability. As articulated through the various examples analyzed in the book, the combination of broad interdisciplinarity and knowledge co-production with societal actors can effectively tackle socio-ecological system interdependencies with heterogeneous value perspectives on the overall orientation of the system dynamics.

However, as amply illustrated by the systematic review of transdisciplinary scholarship by the Swiss Academies of Arts and Sciences (2023), this general approach is also highly relevant and widely used in other fields of advanced research on society-wide challenges. Some of the theoretical discussions in the book already referred to some of these fields, such as collaborative planning research in urban studies (see Section 3.1.1) or the socio-technical approach to living labs (see Section 3.2.1). The illustrations in this book focused on cases in these fields of research that deal with sustainability issues in socio-ecological systems. Nevertheless, many of these cases also covered research fields that address other issues, such as social welfare concerns in urban neighborhoods (see Section 3.2.4) or research on socioeconomic distributional consequences of technological choice (see Section 4.3.3).

Other prominent fields of research illustrate the use of this general approach for transdisciplinarity based on combining broad interdisciplinarity and partnership research. One case in point is the field of research in the social economy in Québec, which develop a broad set of transdisciplinary research practices through over two decades of research funding for so-called community research alliances (Hall and MacPherson, 2011). Other examples, in a different field, are partnerships between scientific researchers and societal actors for translation research in criminology, focusing on the process through which criminological research is generated and used by practitioners and policymakers (Pesta et al., 2019).

Obviously, even though these research fields all develop transdisciplinary modes of organization, the organization of the knowledge co-production and social learning process will be based on choices that are specific to each area of investigation. Nevertheless, the use of broad interdisciplinarity and partnership approaches in different fields creates cross-fertilization opportunities. These opportunities cover knowledge exchange on transdisciplinary process features and their usefulness to tackle various collective action challenges in building transdisciplinary knowledge commons. Furthermore, at the institutional level, the experience acquired from successful transdisciplinary research in these different fields may also contribute to the broad recognition of transdisciplinarity as a promising mode of organizing scientific research on complex societal challenges. Therefore, this recognition may be promoted by identifying, within a given research organization, the similarities between various fields of transdisciplinary research and jointly exploring and supporting the design features for successful transdisciplinary knowledge co-production.

Finally, the analysis in the book mainly focused on transdisciplinary research at universities, high schools, and national research organizations as the key players for organizing transdisciplinary research of a more basic and applied nature. However, along with the development of transdisciplinary research in the academic environment, a wealth of associations, entrepreneurs, and managers in public administrations are using tools from transdisciplinary research in applied settings (OECD, 2020).

The strength of the academic transdisciplinary research approaches is to combine the production of transdisciplinary knowledge with an interest in generic methodological and theoretical development and contribute to knowledge transmission, education, and competence building. On the other hand, the strength of the applied and directly policy-related approaches is the strong motivation of societal actors to reach a broad critical mass of transdisciplinary research practices. Even though such approaches do not systematically strive at peer review validation of the research outputs, as is the case in academic research, policy-related transdisciplinary research practices offer invaluable opportunities for further mutual learning on boundary-crossing research practices.

Overall, the entry point in this book on transdisciplinary sustainability research in academic research therefore hints at a much broader field of work, which includes broad interdisciplinary approaches with extensive social-actor interaction, related fields of transdisciplinary research on grand societal challenges, and directly policy-related transdisciplinary research practices. Given the many complementarities between the approaches, the best way forward to foster the urgently needed sustainability transformations is to explore the many synergies between the different approaches to support various collective learning processes on feasible and desirable interdependent sustainability transformations of social and ecological systems.

References

Akkerman, S. F. and Bakker, A. (2011). Boundary crossing and boundary objects. *Review of Educational Research*, *81*(2), 132–169.

Block, T., Prové, C., Dehaene, M., Abeele, P. V. and Beeckmans, L. (2022). Understanding urban sustainability from mode 2 science and transdisciplinary education: How Master Thesis Ateliers of the Ghent Stadsacademie tackle wicked issues. *Environment, Development and Sustainability*, 1–26.

Bridle, H., Vrieling, A., Cardillo, M., Araya, Y. and Hinojosa, L. (2013). Preparing for an interdisciplinary future: A perspective from early-career researchers. *Futures*, *53*, 22–32.

Dagenais, C., Janosz, M. and Dutil, J. (2008). *Étude des besoins des chercheurs de l'Université de Montréal en matière de transfert des connaissances issues de la recherche*. Bureau de la Recherche-Développement-Valorisation. Université de Montréal, Montréal, Canada.

Hall, P. V. and MacPherson, I. (2011). *Community-university research partnerships: Reflections on the Canadian social economy experience*. Victoria, Canada: University of Victoria.

Hirsch Hadorn, G., Hoffmann-Riem, H., Biber-Klemm, S., Grossenbacher-Mansuy, W., Joye, D., Pohl, C., . . . and Zemp, E. (Eds.). (2008). *Handbook of transdisciplinary research*. Dordrecht: Springer.

Klein, J. T. (2010). A taxonomy of interdisciplinarity. In R. Frodeman, J. Thompson Klein and C. Mitcham (Eds.), *The Oxford handbook of interdisciplinarity* (pp. 15–30). Oxford: Oxford University Press.

Mazzucato, M. (2018). *Mission-oriented research and innovation in the European Union*. Final Report. Publications Office of the European Commission, Luxembourg.

OECD. (2020). *Addressing societal challenges using transdisciplinary research*. OECD Science, Technology and Industry Policy Papers 88, OECD Publishing, Paris.

Pesta, G. B., Blomberg, T. G., Ramos, J. and Ranson, J. W. (2019). Translational criminology: Toward best practice. *American Journal of Criminal Justice*, 44(3), 499–518.

Pohl, C., Klein, J. T., Hoffmann, S., Mitchell, C. and Fam, D. (2021). Conceptualising transdisciplinary integration as a multidimensional interactive process. *Environmental Science and Policy*, *118*, 18–26.

Swiss Academies of Arts and Sciences. (2023). *Network for transdisciplinary research*. https://transdisciplinarity.ch/en/about-td-net/. Accessed 4 January 2023.

UKRI. (2021). *Sandpits*. www.ukri.org/councils/epsrc/guidance-for-applicants/types-of-funding-we-offer/transformative-research/sandpits/. Accessed 1 February 2023.

CONCLUSION

Contemporary sustainability challenges, characterized by socio-ecological interdependencies of unprecedented scale, require new modes of knowledge generation to identify feasible and desirable transformation pathways. In this context, conventional disciplinary and expert-led-only modes of research organization seem ill-suited for managing the wicked problem features of many sustainability issues, such as strongly coupled social and ecological system dynamics, value controversies over sustainability orientations, and the involvement of societal actors in cross-sectoral and multi-scale actor networks.

Different types of transdisciplinary research have emerged over many years in response to these challenges, labeled partnership research (Hoekstra et al., 2020), community science (Khandor and Mason, 2011; Charles et al., 2020), participatory action research (Wittmayer et al., 2014; Chevalier and Buckles, 2013), mode 2 science (Nowotny et al., 2001), and team science (Killion et al., 2018), among others. This book builds upon the experience gained with these transdisciplinary research processes over the last three decades, with the objective of strengthening the effectiveness of transdisciplinary research methods that are mobilized to improve our understanding of society-wide sustainability transformations.

The core hypothesis of this book is that researchers and societal actors must overcome a series of collective action problems to meet the need for knowledge integration from science and practice in transdisciplinary sustainability research. This book examined the institutional design of transdisciplinary research processes from the perspective of the theory of knowledge commons to disentangle the basic components of collective action challenges.

DOI: 10.4324/9781032624297-8

In fact, the collective action problems in transdisciplinary research, such as the instrumentalization of the collaborative process by one of the partners or the lack of coordination among heterogeneous value perspectives, show a great deal of similarity to the problems examined in the theory of decentralized collective goods production through non-state collective action, or the so-called theory of commons-based production. While the theory of the commons initially focused on the community-based management of natural resources, it has gradually broadened its scope to other commons-based production domains, including immaterial goods, such as knowledge commons.

As discussed in Chapter 2, scholars of the commons highlight the importance of three general design features that contribute to successfully overcoming collective action challenges, which also play a vital role in the case of transdisciplinary knowledge commons. First, to effectively manage the provision of common goods in decentralized settings—whether in the community management of natural resources or in scientific research commons—societal actors need entitlements to develop and implement self-organized strategies for decision-making and control over collective good provision. Second, as elaborated in the so-called second generation collective action theory by Elinor Ostrom (1998), such self-organized management is facilitated by the development of common value orientations. The latter contributes to building mutual trust and reduces the effort required to coordinate the production of common action strategies. Finally, decentralized solutions to collective-action problems require an appropriate supportive institutional environment. Such an environment plays a significant role in building the generic competencies of actors who wish to engage in decentralized collective action and social learning.

The transdisciplinary research practices reviewed in the different book chapters highlight how each of these design features is relevant to transdisciplinary sustainability research. Specifically, the qualitative comparative analysis of cases of transdisciplinary sustainability research identified the following general design features that play an important role in enhancing the likelihood of successful co-production of usable knowledge on sustainability transformations.

1) First, regarding collective action for collaborating on a common transdisciplinary research purpose, the analysis of the various components of knowledge co-production in Chapter 3 indicates

    i. the importance of effectively integrating societal actors' knowledge (along with the knowledge from scientific researchers) in the analysis of sustainability transformations of interdependent social and ecological systems

  ii. the importance of the co-construction of the research design with societal actors, particularly in building a common framework of analysis between heterogeneous disciplinary perspectives and different types of knowledge from science and practice

  iii. the need to involve societal actors and scientific researchers in co-management processes of various degrees of strength

2 Second, regarding the common understanding of diverse value orientations, the analysis of social learning processes in Chapter 4 shows

  i. the need to identify demands of societal actors and scientific researchers for social learning, including learning for reaching improved mutual understanding of sustainability values and structuring of the various perspectives on societal values

  ii. the contribution of social learning processes on societal values to fostering processes of convergence over core values and critical deconstruction of value perspectives that perpetuate rent-seeking and the undue exercise of power

3 Third, regarding the supportive institutional environment, the analysis of the building of larger organizational networks for transdisciplinary research in Chapter 5 shows

  i. the importance of building flexible boundary-crossing networks among different disciplines, researchers, and societal actors

  ii. the contribution of the organization of cross-cutting activities for

    i. the development of transdisciplinary competences in the teaching curricula

    ii. the organization of knowledge exchange on transdisciplinary process features

    iii. the networking of researchers and societal actors around coproduced research frameworks on specific sustainability transformation topics.

The case studies of transdisciplinary research examined in this book and the analysis of scholarly literature aim to improve our understanding of these design principles. Nevertheless, additional comparative case study research, further fieldwork, and systematic surveying is needed to further develop this analysis of the most salient governance mechanism for collective action in transdisciplinary research.

    Further work might also deepen the epistemological framework of pragmatist constructivism discussed in Chapter 4, which summarizes the core guiding principles of transdisciplinary research as an innovative mode of knowledge generation. This epistemological framework combines the key strengths of constructivism, reflected in design features such as the co-construction of research among researchers and societal actors, and philosophical pragmatism, reflected in design features such as the practical building of communities of collaborative inquiry through co-management and social learning. From a pragmatist constructivist perspective, both scientific knowledge and knowledge from societal actors contribute to knowledge generation about wicked sustainability problems. Pragmatist constructivism allows searching for a middle ground in transdisciplinary research between the risks of technocratic excesses and scientific dogmatism, on the one hand, and losing any idea of robust and validated scientific research outcomes as a common good, on the other, through the risk of the reduction of the validity to the outcome of power relationships and social conflicts.

Finally, the organization of institutional support for transdisciplinary research will involve the development of a new type of research-enabling environment, based on interactions within polycentric networks. In particular, the enabling of transdisciplinary research places emphasis on crossing disciplinary boundaries and building process competences for *boundary-crossing learning** in hybrid networks of societal actors and researchers. The latter competences are essential assets for dealing with different stakeholder contexts and transitioning from projects with relatively consensual sustainability values to those that necessitate carefully managing value conflicts.

The focus placed in this book on involving researchers and societal actors in integrated polycentric networks as an important governance feature of transdisciplinary research reflects similar developments in the more general analysis of polycentric approaches to deliberation in environmental governance. As emphasized by scholars of deliberation, such as John Dryzek, Simon Niemeyer, and David Schlosberg, the institutionalization of deliberative processes on a larger scale needs to integrate deliberation at local sites with a larger polycentric approach (Schlosberg et al., 2019; Niemeyer, 2020; Dryzek, 2022). This polycentric approach organizes capacity building in a system of nested governance, already called for by Elinor Ostrom in her work on polycentric network governance. However, as underscored by scholars of deliberation, for the wider activation of deliberative capacities, such a polycentric system also needs to implement different governance mechanisms for guaranteeing authentic deliberation in each of the problem-solving and social learning processes in local sustainability transformations (Owen and Smith, 2015; Niemeyer, 2020; Niemeyer et al., 2023).

Although the above arguments on local deliberative capacities are developed in a more general framework—analyzing the general conditions for authentic deliberation—they nicely summarize the key message on capacity-building for transdisciplinary research in this book. Indeed, the more general discussions on the conditions for effective deliberation hint at the danger of dissociating the building of larger institutional systems of transdisciplinary capacity-building from the context-specific activities of research co-design, co-management, and social learning. More specifically, it allows us to pin down, in a more general manner, the point made in Chapter 5 on combining the institutional enabling of transdisciplinary research with activities of knowledge co-production and social learning. In short, building larger nested polycentric institutional architectures relies on designing, testing and evaluating new modes of organization also through co-produced activities and processes by societal actors and researchers.

The articulation of knowledge co-production activities and institutional mechanisms for capacity building implies that a considerable upscaling of transdisciplinary co-production will only be possible by involving both academic researchers and a broad array of different societal actors in this endeavor. What is the role of citizens or professionals in contributing to transdisciplinary research on society-wide transformations in specific sectors? What kind of policy mix do we need to promote these collaborative processes that require intense social learning between the involved societal actors around new values and modes of coordination? How can universities support promising trends in transdisciplinary research and produce evidence-based knowledge to move from trial-and-error processes to robust and long-lasting societal transformations?

These questions are at the heart of initiatives by societal actors, scientists, and policymakers worldwide, who are building new networks and research partnerships to contribute to sustainable human development. Regarding transdisciplinary sustainability research, citizens, members of social movements, and members of mission-driven organizations are partners that contribute knowledge and information to scientific endeavors. At the same time, they operate as societal actors fully engaged in collective action in their communities and social networks. Through their privileged position as change agents, societal actors acquire knowledge of possible solutions, first-hand knowledge of social drivers, and motivations for implementing feasible and desirable solutions for sustainability challenges. Hence, through knowledge co-production between scientific researchers and societal actors, new solution pathways actively promoted by societal actors can co-evolve with innovative scientific perspectives and accelerate sustainability transformation processes.

Effective policies must support transdisciplinary research partnerships. Public sector officials are directly involved in the design, planning, implementation, and evaluation of the support measures for public research funding. Moreover, through their expertise and access to various policies and social networks, public-sector officials provide and use many forms of expertise that can promote sustainability transformations. Policymakers, governments, and public administrators can play primary roles in supporting transdisciplinary research. This role can include both the direct participation of public sector officials in transdisciplinary partnership research and, more broadly, the organization of institutional recognition and support for scientific researchers' and societal actors' knowledge co-production through transdisciplinary research.

Finally, universities play a pivotal role in the emergence and consolidation of relatively recent transdisciplinary research traditions. First, through the university's basic research mission, academic researchers add value to transdisciplinary research projects by offering innovative perspectives and critical reflections on transdisciplinary research methodologies. Second, and even more importantly, by actively engaging in transdisciplinary partnership research, universities can provide training and capacity building for a new generation of young scholars and students, who are not yet acquainted with the new set of tools and methods for scientifically credible and socially robust knowledge co-production processes through transdisciplinary research. Thus, universities can actively contribute to the integration of the various approaches developed in transdisciplinary partnership science into the overall science fabric.

However, the steps required to achieve these goals are challenging. Indeed, to address multiple social and ecological crises, we need new knowledge to understand the nature of large-scale regenerative societal systems, such as sustainable cities, rural territories, and production systems. Moreover, the systemic, multi-dimensional, and highly pluralistic nature of collaborative efforts is required to resist the traditional disciplinary and ivory-tower modes of conducting scientific research. Fortunately, as many examples in this book show, researchers at universities and research organizations actively experiment and innovate with integrated and collaborative modes of transdisciplinary research to address these challenges. This book aimed to take stock of these inspiring and crucial developments in the context of institutional challenges to further consolidate transdisciplinary research in the organization of contemporary scientific research.

References

Charles, A., Loucks, L., Berkes, F. and Armitage, D. (2020). Community science: A typology and its implications for governance of social-ecological systems. *Environmental Science and Policy*, 106, 77–86.

Chevalier, J. M. and Buckles, D. J. (2013). *Handbook for participatory action research, planning and evaluation*. Ottawa: SAS2 Dialogue.

Dryzek, J. S. (2022). *The politics of the earth: Environmental discourses*. Oxford: Oxford University Press.

Hoekstra, F., Mrklas, K. J., Khan, M., McKay, R. C., Vis-Dunbar, M., Sibley, K. M., . . . and Gainforth, H. L. (2020). A review of reviews on principles, strategies, outcomes and impacts of research partnerships approaches: A first step in synthesizing the research partnership literature. *Health Research Policy and Systems*, 18, 1–23.

Khandor, E. and Mason, K. (2011). The street health report 2007: Community-based research for social change. In M. Kirst, N. Schaefer-Mc Daniel, S. Hwang and P. O'Campo (Eds.), *Converging disciplines. A transdisciplinary research agenda to urban health problems* (pp. 57–68). New York: Springer.

Killion, A. K., Sterle, K., Bondank, E. N., Drabik, J. R., Bera, A., Alian, S., . . . and Thayer, A. W. (2018). Preparing the next generation of sustainability scientists. *Ecology and Society, 23*(4).

Niemeyer, S. (2020). Deliberation and ecological democracy: From citizen to global system. *Journal of Environmental Policy and Planning, 22*(1), 16–29.

Niemeyer, S., Veri, F., Dryzek, J. S. and Bächtiger, A. (2023). How deliberation happens: Enabling and activating deliberative reasoning. *American Political Science Review*, 1–18.

Nowotny, H., Scott, P. B. and Gibbons, M. T. (2001). *Re-thinking science: Knowledge and the public in an age of uncertainty.* Cambridge: Polity Press.

Ostrom, E. (1998). A behavioral approach to the rational choice theory of collective action: Presidential address, American Political Science Association, 1997. *American Political Science Review, 92*(1), 1–22.

Owen, D. and Smith, G. (2015). Survey article: Deliberation, democracy, and the systemic turn. *Journal of Political Philosophy, 23*(2), 213–234.

Schlosberg, D., Bäckstrand, K. and Pickering, J. (2019). Reconciling ecological and democratic values: Recent perspectives on ecological democracy. *Environmental Values, 28*(1), 1–8.

Wittmayer, J. M., Schäpke, N., van Steenbergen, F. and Omann, I. (2014). Making sense of sustainability transitions locally: How action research contributes to addressing societal challenges. *Critical Policy Studies, 8*(4), 465–485.

ANNEX 1

Glossary of key conceptual terms

Terms defined in the glossary are marked in italic and with an asterisk upon their first appearance in the text.

Boundary-crossing learning

The literature on boundary-crossing learning defines a boundary as socio-cultural differences leading to discontinuities in interaction and action (Akkerman and Bakker, 2011). Defining boundaries as discontinuities rather than differences without mutual interactions, it becomes clear how boundaries are real in their consequences while being malleable and dynamic constructs. Different forms of dialogue between multiple perspectives can be organized at the boundaries, which can induce boundary-crossing learning. Overall, people and objects that cross or stand between boundaries articulate meanings and perspectives of various intersecting worlds while negotiating meanings beyond the boundary from which something new may emerge (ibid).

Incommensurability of societal values

In this book, we follow many authors who define the incommensurability of societal values in a broad sense. In this broad sense, it designates the impossibility to establish a comparison between the set of societal values at hand that allows for specifying what societal value choice is better or worse for each of the societal values (Chang, 1997). Thus, the term "measure" does not strictly refer to quantitative measures but to all kinds of justified choices based on a ranking of the values according to a better-worse scale. As argued in Chapter 5 and the literature, incommensurability does not lead to the impossibility of choice, as various other criteria can be used to make a justified choice. One example among such justifications is choosing the option that is not overall better but improves the situation per one consideration of importance to all actors (Levi, 2004). Another justification is to choose the set of options that satisfies a partial ranking among the values, for which there is a reasonable consensus among societal actors (Sen, 2009).

Institutional rules

The term "institutional rules" is used in this book according to the convention in institutional analyses in the social sciences to denote rules governing the behavior of actors (Pahl-Wostl, 2009). Formal institutional rules are linked to the official channels of governmental bureaucracies. They are codified in regulatory frameworks or any kind of legally binding document. Correspondingly, they can be enforced by legal procedures. Informal institutional rules refer to socially shared rules such as social or cultural norms. In most cases, they are not codified or written down. They are enforced outside of legally sanctioned channels.

In this broad context, institutions can be defined as a structural feature of social systems that provides a certain degree of order and stability to social interaction by regulating and affecting the beliefs and behavior of the actors (Sørensen and Torfing, 2007). This definition covers various approaches in institutional analysis. For instance, in so-called rational choice institutionalism, institutions are analyzed according to the rules of the game to which individual actors respond based on their individual preferences (Ostrom, 1990; North, 1999). Sociological institutionalism refers to the set of rules, norms, and cognitive paradigms that shape the identities, capacities, and aspirations of societal actors (Hall and Taylor, 1996).

Integrated socio-ecological systems research

Socio-ecological system research differs in the degree to which the social and ecological are viewed as merely interacting sub-systems or part of a single, integrated system (Binder et al., 2013). The interactive approach considers the social and ecological as relatively independent sub-systems, with a one-way interaction between them, such as the impact of human behavior on ecological outcomes. The integrated systems approach focuses on the emergent system patterns that result from the strong social-ecological system interdependencies (Schlüter et al., 2019). The interdependencies can result from different types of feedback between the social and ecological systems, such as the relation between the impacts of human actions on the ecological systems, the adaptation of the decision-making process to the ecological impacts, and the link back to new types of behavior and impacts (Binder et al., 2013). In other approaches, interdependencies result in higher-level system properties, such as adaptive capacity building in the overall system by enhancing a diversity of solutions to deal with external perturbations (Pahl-Wostl, 2009).

Knowledge co-production in transdisciplinary research

It designates a mode of research based on collaboration between researchers and societal actors to generate scientifically sound, socially relevant, and legitimate knowledge (Polk, 2015; Pohl et al., 2021). Hence, the collaboration includes knowledge integration between researchers and societal actors, co-designing various components of the research framework (Schneider et al., 2019), and clarifying the societal background values of the research participants (Hirsch Hadorn et al., 2008; Herrero et al., 2019).

Research styles

The notion of research style is an analytical tool that allows for identifying the emergence of specific enduring approaches to scientific inquiry (Hacking, 2012). Historical examples are the research styles of Greek geometry, controlled experimentation, and statistical analysis (Crombie, 1995). Each research style introduces new types of objects and evidence related to these objects and involves specific standards of validity of the scientific statements about these objects (Sciortino, 2017). Moreover, each research style (an epistemological notion) can further be differentiated into so-called community-related thought styles. The latter is characterized by the emergence within specific research styles of communities with a common knowledge base, style of communicative behavior and literary expression, and approach to the problem of interest (Fleck, 1979).

Scientific research commons

In the general commons-based production framework, covering community-managed natural resources, urban commons, and knowledge commons, commons refer to collective goods that are jointly shared, used, and managed by groups of varying sizes and interests (Hess and Ostrom, 2007, p. 5). Especially since the mid-1990s, an increasing number of scholars started to analyze the conditions for commons-based knowledge production to counter the increased production of knowledge behind digital fences or privately owned knowledge providers with the rise of distributed, digital information (Kranich, 2007). Regarding scientific research, "scientific research commons" refers to the many collective aspects of scientific research that are jointly used and produced by research communities, networks, and umbrella organization researchers (Benkler, 2008). These collective aspects include the quality management of the research results, such as research community-managed peer review, the organization of the dissemination of research results, the organization of sharing of pre-publication and post-publication research data and information in research consortia and beyond, and agenda-setting of promising research topics to advance research (Frischmann et al., 2014).

Social and ecological sustainability

This book defines the sustainability of socio-ecological systems from within the framework of mere sustainability, which is the pursuit of environmental sustainability while integrating environmental sustainability challenges with wider issues of justice, equity, and governance (Agyeman and Evans, 2004; Coleman and Gould, 2019). The issue of environmental sustainability can be defined along the lines of the definition of sustainable development by the 1987 United Nations Brundtland Commission as the goal of meeting the needs of the present without compromising the ability of future generations to meet their own needs. The latter implies, as an important sustainability component, considering the planetary resource limits in human development to maintain the functioning of basic life-supporting systems and processes on the planet Earth for present and future generations (Rockström et al., 2009). However, reaching these goals requires addressing the root causes of unsustainability, regarding the wider issues of justice, equity, and governance. As shown in the literature on environmental justice and environmental citizenship, socioeconomic and power-related distributive concerns, fair collective decision-making processes, recognition of the contribution of all sociocultural groups, and building capacities for meaningful participation of all parties beyond merely formal process guarantees for inclusive governance of all parties in societal transformations (Dobson, 2007; Schlosberg, 2013).

Social learning

Studies on governing socio-ecological systems conceptualize social learning as a process of change of understanding in the individuals involved that becomes situated in wider social units given the exchange of ideas, arguments, and information in social networks and communities of practice (Reed et al., 2010). This definition provides a criterion for evaluating whether social learning occurred in certain groups and networks without conflating the social learning notion with broader expected results, such as generating improved participation or governance outcomes that depend on contributions from other factors (ibid).

Socio-ecological systems

Socio-ecological systems are complex adaptive systems characterized by feedback across multiple social and ecological dynamics scales (Fischer et al., 2015). In the literature on socio-ecological systems, the term "social" is used in a broad sense to include various behaviors of individual human beings in social contexts, the social relationships between human beings, and the evolution of cultural-cognitive meanings among human beings (Levin et al., 2013; Hicks et al., 2016). Thus, the term "socio-ecological systems" is used as a synonym for coupled human-environment systems (Scholz, 2011) or coupled human and natural systems (Liu et al., 2007).

Transdisciplinary sustainability research

Transdisciplinary research is an integrative mode of organizing scientific research to solve or transition societal and related scientific problems by differentiating and integrating knowledge from various scientific and societal bodies of knowledge (Lang et al., 2012). Transdisciplinary sustainability research designates basic and applied research to solve sustainability issues practices based on knowledge co-production among researchers from various scientific disciplines from the natural science and social science (humanities) for the interdisciplinary analysis of integrated socio-ecological systems (Klein, 2010) and (among scientific researchers and societal actors) the improved understanding of the socially legitimate and relevant perspectives on the solution pathways (Lux et al., 2019).

References

Agyeman, J. and Evans, B. (2004). "Just sustainability": The emerging discourse of environmental justice in Britain? *The Geographical Journal*, 170(2), 155–164.

Akkerman, S. F. and Bakker, A. (2011). Boundary crossing and boundary objects. *Review of Educational Research*, 81(2), 132–169.

Benkler, Y. (2008). *The wealth of networks*. New Haven, CT: Yale University Press.

Binder, C. R., Hinkel, J., Bots, P. W. and Pahl-Wostl, C. (2013). Comparison of frameworks for analyzing social-ecological systems. *Ecology and Society*, 18(4), 26.

Chang, R. (Ed.). (1997). *Incommensurability, incomparability, and practical reason*. Cambridge, MA: Harvard University Press.

Coleman, K. and Gould, R. (2019). Exploring just sustainability across the disciplines at one university. *The Journal of Environmental Education*, 50(3), 223–237.

Crombie, A. C. (1995). Commitments and styles of European scientific thinking. *History of Science*, 33(2), 225–238.

Dobson, A. (2007). Environmental citizenship: Towards sustainable development. *Sustainable Development*, 15(5), 276–285.

Fischer, J., Gardner, T. A., Bennett, E. M., Balvanera, P., Biggs, R., Carpenter, S., . . . and Luthe, T. (2015). Advancing sustainability through mainstreaming a social—ecological systems perspective. *Current Opinion in Environmental Sustainability*, 14, 144–149.

Fleck, L. (1979 [1935]). *Genesis and development of a scientific fact*. Chicago: The University of Chicago Press.

Frischmann, B. M., Madison, M. and Strandburg, C. (2014). *Governing knowledge commons*. Oxford: Oxford University Press.

Hacking, I. (2012). Language, truth and reason' 30 years later. *Studies in History and Philosophy of Science*, 43(4), 599–609.

Hall, P. A. and Taylor, R. C. R. (1996). Political science and the three new institutionalisms. *Political Studies*, 44(4), 936–957.

Herrero, P., Dedeurwaerdere, T. and Osinski, A. (2019). Design features for social learning in transformative transdisciplinary research. *Sustainability Science*, 14(3), 751–769.

Hess, C. and Ostrom, E. (Eds.). (2007). *Understanding knowledge as a commons: From theory to practice*. Cambridge, MA: MIT Press.

Hicks, C. C., Levine, A., Agrawal, A., Basurto, X., Breslow, S. J., Carothers, C., . . . Levin, P. S. (2016). Engage key social concepts for sustainability. *Science*, 352(6281), 38–40.

Hirsch Hadorn, G., Hoffmann-Riem, H., Biber-Klemm, S., Grossenbacher-Mansuy, W., Joye, D., Pohl, C., . . . and Zemp, E. (Eds.). (2008). *Handbook of transdisciplinary research*. Dordrecht: Springer.

Klein, J. T. (2010). A taxonomy of interdisciplinarity. In R. Frodeman, J. Thompson Klein and C. Mitcham (Eds.), *The Oxford handbook of interdisciplinarity* (pp. 15–30). Oxford: Oxford University Press.

Kranich, N. (2007). Countering enclosure: Reclaiming the knowledge commons. In Ch. Hess and E. Ostrom (Eds.), *Understanding knowledge as a commons: From theory to practice* (pp. 85–122). Cambridge, MA: MIT Press.

Lang, D. J., Wiek, A., Bergmann, M., Stauffacher, M., Martens, P., Moll, P., . . . and Thomas, C. J. (2012). Transdisciplinary research in sustainability science: Practice, principles, and challenges. *Sustainability Science*, 7(1), 25–43.

Levi, I. (2004). The second worst in practical conflict. In P. Baumann and M. Betzler (Eds.), *Practical conflicts*. Cambridge: Cambridge University Press.

Levin, S., Xepapadeas, T., Crépin, A. S., Norberg, J., De Zeeuw, A., Folke, C., . . . and Walker, B. (2013). Social-ecological systems as complex adaptive systems: Modeling and policy implications. *Environment and Development Economics*, 18(2), 111–132.

Liu, J., Dietz, T., Carpenter, S. R., Alberti, M., Folke, C., Moran, E., . . . and Ostrom, E. (2007). Complexity of coupled human and natural systems. *Science*, 317, 1513–1516.

Lux, A., Schäfer, M., Bergmann, M., Jahn, T., Marg, O., Nagy, E., Ransiek, A. C. and Theiler, L. (2019). Societal effects of transdisciplinary sustainability research—How can they be strengthened during the research process? *Environmental Science and Policy*, 101, 183–191.

North, D. (1999). *Understanding the process of institutional change*. Princeton, NJ: Princeton University Press.

Ostrom, E. (1990). *Governing the commons: The evolution of institutions for collective action*. Cambridge: Cambridge University Press.

Pahl-Wostl, C. (2009). A conceptual framework for analysing adaptive capacity and multi-level learning processes in resource governance regimes. *Global Environmental Change*, 19(3), 354–365.

Pohl, C., Klein, J. T., Hoffmann, S., Mitchell, C. and Fam, D. (2021). Conceptualising transdisciplinary integration as a multidimensional interactive process. *Environmental Science and Policy*, 118, 18–26.

Polk, M. (2015). Transdisciplinary co-production: Designing and testing a transdisciplinary research framework for societal problem solving. *Futures*, *65*, 110–122.

Reed, M. S., Evely, A. C., Cundill, G., Fazey, I., Glass, J., Laing, A., . . . and Stringer, L. C. (2010). What is social learning? *Ecology and Society*, *15*(4).

Rockström, J., Steffen, W., Noone, K., Persson, Å., Chapin, F. S., Lambin, E. F., . . . and Foley, J. A. (2009). A safe operating space for humanity. *Nature*, *461*(7263), 472–475.

Schlosberg, D. (2013). Theorising environmental justice: The expanding sphere of a discourse. *Environmental Politics*, *22*(1), 37–55.

Schlüter, M., Haider, L. J., Lade, S. J., Lindkvist, E., Martin, R., Orach, K., . . . and Folke, C. (2019). Capturing emergent phenomena in social-ecological systems. *Ecology and Society*, *24*(3), 11.

Schneider, F., Giger, M., Harari, N., Moser, S., Oberlack, C., Providoli, I., . . . and Zimmermann, A. (2019). Transdisciplinary co-production of knowledge and sustainability transformations: Three generic mechanisms of impact generation. *Environmental Science and Policy*, *102*, 26–35.

Scholz, R. W. (2011). *Environmental literacy in science and society. From knowledge to decisions*. Cambridge: Cambridge University Press.

Sciortino, L. (2017). On Ian Hacking's notion of style of reasoning. *Erkenntnis*, *82*(2), 243–264.

Sen, A. (2009). *The idea of justice*. Cambridge, MA: Harvard University Press.

Sørensen, E. and Torfing, J. (Eds.). (2007). *Theories of democratic network governance*. Heidelberg: Springer.

ANNEX 2

Case study list

Case studies from the "most different" case study sampling of well-documented transdisciplinary research projects within the five levers of change. Initial sampling from a keyword search in four journals between 2005 and 2020 (*Ecological Economics, Ecology and Society, Environmental Science and Policy, Sustainability Science*) and the case study volume by Bergmann et al. (2012). In a second step, the sample was completed to reach a minimum of five papers for each lever of change through a general search in Google Scholar on "transdisciplinary sustainability research" or "participatory sustainability research" and keywords representative of that lever of change (cf. the detailed discussion of the sampling strategy in Section 3.1.2).

Projects with marked with "(*video*)" are documented with a short video interview and background materials on www.lptransition.be/td

	co-M	co-D	SL	C4	C5	C6
None or very few usable knowledge outputs						
Green infrastructure in Eindhoven to combat the summer heat, the Netherlands				L1		Bodilis (2018)
Intensive grazing in mountain landscapes, France				L2		Lamarque et al. (2013)
Sustainable land use in the Upper Valais mountain area, Switzerland				L2		Brand et al. (2013)

(Continued)

(Continued)

	co-M	co-D	SL	C4	C5	C6
Housing insulation for the energy transition in Bottrop, Germany (*video*)				L2		Bierwirth et al. (2017)
Loss of peatland through reforestation, Finland				L3		Saarikoski et al. (2019)
Scenarios for biofuel use in Europe				L3		Baudry et al. (2018a, 2018b)
Sustainable energy options, (electricity, heating) in Ebhausen, Germany				L3		McKenna et al. (2018)
Sustainable energy options (electricity, heating) in Urnach, Switzerland				L3		Trutnevyte et al. (2011, 2012)
Nature conservation and agricultural production in the Elbe valley, Germany				L4		Bergmann et al. (2012, ch. III.K)
Understanding values and impacts of bicycle infrastructure, Auckland, New Zeeland				L5		Macmillan and Woodcock (2017)
A framework for housing refurbishment, United Kingdom				L5		Macmillan et al. (2016)
Water management in an urban context, Switzerland				L5		Pahl-Wostl and Hare (2004)
Sustainable mobility and urban densification in Las Vegas, Nevada, US				L2		Stave (2002, 2010)
Assessing the social and environmental value of urban green in Gothenburg, Sweden				L3		Klingberg et al. (2017), Andersson-Sköld et al. (2018)
Partnerships with housing renovation companies in the Rhine-Main area, Germany				L4		Bergmann et al. (2012, ch. III.G)
Moderate to significant usable knowledge outcomes, for a limited part of the intended users/beneficiaries						
Citizen science in Manchester neighborhoods with industrial pollution, United Kingdom				L1		Newman et al. (2020)

	co-M	co-D	SL	C4	C5	C6
Scenario building and empowerment in rural development, India, Philippines, and Indonesia				L5		Bourgeois et al. (2017)
Farming activities in biodiversity-rich mountain areas in the Piedmont, Italy				L4		Höchtl et al. (2006)
Sustainable agriculture and small-scale tourism in a mountain area, France (*video*)				L4		Lavorel et al. (2019)
Income generation activities from mangrove ecosystems, Kenya			SL	L5	78	Galafassi et al. (2018), Fortnam et al. (2019)
ATD Food assistance project with the urban poor in Brussels, Belgium (*video*)			SL	L5	64	Joos-Malfait et al. (2019), Osinski (2020)
Mitigation in Urban Context, Rotterdam, the Netherlands (*video*)				L5	65	Roorda et al. (2014), Tillie et al. (2012)
Renewable energy options through local/regional energy sources, Austria				L2		Binder et al. (2014)

	co-M	co-D	SL	C4	C5	C6
Moderate to significant project outcomes, for a large part of the intended users/ beneficiaries						
Nuclear radiation around mines, Niger and Namibia				L1		Conde (2014)
Renovation of historic houses in the inner city of Cahors, France				L1	47	Claude et al. (2017)
Digital services for sustainable mobility solutions in Stockholm, Sweden (*video*)			SL	L1	79	Bieser et al. (2021), Sjöman et al. (2020)
Public transport in park-and-ride facilities for urban mobility in Potsdam, Germany				L3	55	Schmale et al. (2015, 2016)

(Continued)

(Continued)

	co-M	co-D	SL	C4	C5	C6
Changing a rural diet with high saturated fat, Finland				L4		Puska et al. (2009)
Mobility style analysis in various cities, Germany				L4		Bergmann et al. (2012, ch. III.B), HirschHadorn et al. (2008, ch. 6)
Indigenous knowledge of basket weaving in the Brazilian Amazon				L4		Athayde et al. (2017)
Energy poverty in the informal urban settlements of Enkanini, South Africa			SL	L5	62	Van Breda and Swilling (2019)
Protection of lobster fisheries and sensitive coastal habitats, Belize				L2	53	Verutes et al. (2017), Arkema et al. (2019)
Community mapping of land use and ecosystem-based plan, Xáxli'p community, Canada			SL	L4		Diver (2017)
Urban traffic slowing and cultural identity, Australia				L2	51	Macmillan et al. (2014), Macmillan and Mackie (2016), Mackie et al. (2018)
Very comprehensive usable knowledge outcomes, for a large part of the intended users/beneficiaries						
Seed selection for forage autonomy, France			SL	L1	49	Goutiers et al. (2016), Lacombe et al. (2017)
Adding value to the food value chain in small-holder dairy farming, Kenya				L1		Restrepo et al. (2020)
Creation of a Nature Park designation in the Black Forest, Germany				L4		Rhodius et al. (2020, ch. 6)
Small-scale sustainable forestry in Larzac, France			SL	L2	53	Simon and Etienne (2010)

	co-M	co-D	SL	C4	C5	C6
Conservation management in Scottish Moorlands, United Kingdom			SL	L4	77	Ainsworth et al. (2020)
Management and re-use of organic waste in Brussels, Belgium (*video*)			SL	L2		Bortolotti et al. (2019)
Community health surveying of asthma prevalence from pollution in New York, USA			SL	L4	58	Corburn (2005)
Urban homeless communities field surveys in Toronto, Canada				L4		Khandor and Mason (2011)
Improved access to health services for nomadic pastoralists, Chad			SL	L4	80	Bergmann et al. (2012, ch. III.F); Hirsch Hadorn et al. (2008, ch. 17)
River pollution and recreational fishing, Switzerland			SL	L2		Burkhardt and Zehnder (2018)

Legend

- List of case studies represented in 4 clusters of increasingly strong co-production of usable knowledge outputs (cf. Annex 3 for the coding scale that was used)
- Co-M (co-management), Co-D (co-design), SL (social learning): average values of the Likert scale, for the cases listed in each of the 4 clusters (cf. Annex 3 for the coding scale that was used)

	very strong and comprehensive
	very strong
	strong
	moderate
	weak

- SL: in the column on social learning, cases with extensive documentation of the social learning process (independently of the level of social learning) are indicated with SL; these cases served as the basis for the cluster analysis in chapter 4.
- C4: Thematic field according to one of the five levers of change, as defined in section 3.1.2: (L1) Socio-technical levers of change, (L2) Biophysical

levers of change in socio-ecological systems, (L3) Socioeconomic levers of change, (L4) Multistakeholder governance for policy implementation, and (L5) Including the diversity of sociocultural perspectives
- C5: Page number of discussion of the case in the main text
- C6: References of the project publications

References

Ainsworth, G. B., Redpath, S. M., Wilson, M., Wernham, C. and Young, J. C. (2020). Integrating scientific and local knowledge to address conservation conflicts: Towards a practical framework based on lessons learned from a Scottish case study. *Environmental Science and Policy, 107*, 46–55.

Andersson-Sköld, Y., Klingberg, J., Gunnarsson, B., Cullinane, K., Gustafsson, I., Hedblom, M., . . . and Thorsson, P. (2018). A framework for assessing urban greenery's effects and valuing its ecosystem services. *Journal of Environmental Management, 205*, 274–285.

Arkema, K. K., Rogers, L. A., Toft, J., Mesher, A., Wyatt, K. H., Albury-Smith, S., . . . and Samhouri, J. (2019). Integrating fisheries management into sustainable development planning. *Ecology and Society, 24*(2), 1.

Athayde, S., Silva-Lugo, J., Schmink, M., Kaiabi, A. and Heckenberger, M. (2017). Reconnecting art and science for sustainability: Learning from indigenous knowledge through participatory action-research in the Amazon. *Ecology and Society, 22*(2), 36.

Baudry, G., Macharis, C. and Vallee, T. (2018a). Range-based multi-actor multi-criteria analysis: A combined method of multi-actor multi-criteria analysis and Monte Carlo simulation to support participatory decision making under uncertainty. *European Journal of Operational Research, 264*(1), 257–269.

Baudry, G., Macharis, C. and Vallée, T. (2018b). Can microalgae biodiesel contribute to achieve the sustainability objectives in the transport sector in France by 2030? A comparison between first, second and third generation biofuels though a range-based multi-actor multi-criteria analysis. *Energy, 155*, 1032–1046.

Bergmann, M., Jahn, T., Knobloch, T., Krohn, W., Pohl, C. and Schramm, E. (2012). *Methods for transdisciplinary research: A primer for practice.* Frankfurt: Campus Verlag.

Bierwirth, A., Augenstein, K., Baur, S., Bettin, J., Buhl, J., Friege, J., . . . and Vondung, F. (2017). *Knowledge as transformative energy: On linking models and experiments in the energy transition in buildings.* Wuppertal: Wuppertal Institute for Climate, Energy and the Environment.

Bieser, J. C., Vaddadi, B., Kramers, A., Höjer, M. and Hilty, L. M. (2021). Impacts of telecommuting on time use and travel: A case study of a neighborhood telecommuting center in Stockholm. *Travel Behaviour and Society, 23*, 157–165.

Binder, C. R., Absenger-Helmli, I., Bedenik, K., Chappin, E., Dijkema, G., Goetz, A., . . . and Vilsmaier, U. (2014). TERIM—transition dynamics in energy regions: An integrated model for sustainable policies. *Tagungsband 15. Klimatag: 2–4 April 2014* (pp. 78–79). Innsbruck: Universität Innsbruck.

Bodilis, C. (2018). *Integration and visualisation of urban sprawl and urban heating indicators from complex data in a context of nature-based solutions* [Master thesis]. Aveiro: Universidade de Aveiro.

Bortolotti, A., Kampelmann, S., De Muynck, S., Papangelou, A. and Zeller, V. (2019). Conditions and concepts for interdisciplinary urban metabolism research—the case of an inter-project collaboration on biowaste. *Flux*, *2*, 112–127.

Bourgeois, R., Penunia, E., Bisht, S. and Boruk, D. (2017). Foresight for all: Co-elaborative scenario building and empowerment. *Technological Forecasting and Social Change*, *124*, 178–188.

Brand, F. S., Seidl, R., Le, Q. B., Brändle, J. M. and Scholz, R. W. (2013). Constructing consistent multiscale scenarios by transdisciplinary processes: The case of mountain regions facing global change. *Ecology and Society*, *18*(2), 43.

Burkhardt-Holm, P. and Zehnder, A. J. (2018). Fischnetz: Assessing outcomes and impacts of a project at the interface of science and public policy. *Environmental Science and Policy*, *82*, 52–59.

Claude, S., Ginestet, S., Bonhomme, M., Moulène, N. and Escadeillas, G. (2017). The Living Lab methodology for complex environments: Insights from the thermal refurbishment of a historical district in the city of Cahors, France. *Energy Research and Social Science*, *32*, 121–130.

Conde, M. (2014). Activism mobilising science. *Ecological Economics*, *105*, 67–77.

Corburn, J. (2005). *Street science: Community knowledge and environmental health justice*. Cambridge, MA: MIT Press.

Diver, S. (2017). Negotiating Indigenous knowledge at the science-policy interface: Insights from the Xáxli'p Community Forest. *Environmental Science and Policy*, *73*, 1–11.

Fortnam, M., Brown, K., Chaigneau, T., Crona, B., Daw, T. M., Gonçalves, D., . . . and Schulte-Herbruggen, B. (2019). The gendered nature of ecosystem services. *Ecological Economics*, *159*, 312–325.

Galafassi, D., Daw, T. M., Thyresson, M., Rosendo, S., Chaigneau, T., Bandeira, S., . . . and Brown, K. (2018). Stories in social-ecological knowledge cocreation. *Ecology and Society*, *23*(1), 23.

Goutiers, V., Charron, M. H., Deo, M. and Hazard, L. (2016). Capflor®: un outil pour concevoir des mélanges de prairies à flore variée. *Fourrages*, *228*, 243–252.

Hirsch Hadorn, G., Hoffmann-Riem, H., Biber-Klemm, S., Grossenbacher-Mansuy, W., Joye, D., Pohl, C., . . . and Zemp, E. (Eds.). (2008). *Handbook of transdisciplinary research*. Dordrecht: Springer.

Höchtl, F., Lehringer, S. and Konold, W. (2006). Pure theory or useful tool? Experiences with transdisciplinarity in the Piedmont Alps. *Environmental Science and Policy*, *9*(4), 322–329.

Joos-Malfait, V., Myaux, D. and Osinski, A. (coord.). (2019). *L'expérience de l'aide alimentaire. Quelles alternatives. Rapport d'une recherche en croisement des savoirs*. Bruxelles: Fédération des Services Sociaux (FdSS).

Khandor, E. and Mason, K. (2011). The street health report 2007: Community-based research for social change. In M. Kirst, N. Schaefer-Mc Daniel, S. Hwang and P. O'Campo (Eds.), *Converging disciplines. A transdisciplinary research agenda to urban health problems* (pp. 57–68). New York: Springer.

Klingberg, J., Broberg, M., Strandberg, B., Thorsson, P. and Pleijel, H. (2017). Influence of urban vegetation on air pollution and noise exposure—a case study in Gothenburg, Sweden. *Science of the Total Environment*, *599*, 1728–1739.

Lacombe, C., Couix, N. and Hazard, L. (2017). *Envisager l'accompagnement du changement des systèmes agricoles vers l'agroécologie comme un processus co-conçu. Cas de la co-conception locale d'un outil de diagnostic agroécologique des fermes ovin-lait dans le Sud-Aveyron* [Conference presentation]. 7ième Colloque du réseau OPDE, Des Outils pour Décider Ensemble, 26–27 October, Montpelier, France. HAL - Archive ouverte de l'Institut national de recherche pour l'agriculture, l'alimentation et l'environnement (INRAE), Paris.

Lamarque, P., Artaux, A., Nettier, B., Dobremez, L., Barnaud, C. and Lavorel, S. (2013). Taking into account farmers' decision making to map fine-scale land management adaptation to climate and socioeconomic scenarios. *Landscape Urban Plann, 119*, 147–157.

Lavorel, S., Colloff, M. J., Locatelli, B., Gorddard, R., Prober, S. M., Gabillet, M., . . . and Peyrache-Gadeau, V. (2019). Mustering the power of ecosystems for adaptation to climate change. *Environmental Science and Policy, 92*, 87–97.

Mackie, H., Macmillan, A., Witten, K., Baas, P., Field, A., Smith, M., . . . and Woodward, A. (2018). Te Ara Mua—Future Streets suburban street retrofit: A researcher-community-government co-design process and intervention outcomes. *Journal of Transport and Health, 11*, 209–220.

Macmillan, A., Connor, J., Witten, K., Kearns, R., Rees, D. and Woodward, A. (2014). The societal costs and benefits of commuter bicycling: Simulating the effects of specific policies using system dynamics modeling. *Environmental Health Perspectives, 122*(4), 335–344.

Macmillan, A., Davies, M., Shrubsole, C., Luxford, N., May, N., Chiu, L. F., . . . and Chalabi, Z. (2016). Integrated decision-making about housing, energy and wellbeing: A qualitative system dynamics model. *Environmental Health, 15*(1), 23–34.

Macmillan, A. and Mackie, H. (2016). Optimising low carbon mobility for health and equity. In D. Hopkins and J. Higham (Eds.), *Low carbon mobility transition*. Oxford: GoodFellow Publishers.

Macmillan, A. and Woodcock, J. (2017). Understanding bicycling in cities using system dynamics modelling. *Journal of Transport and Health, 7*, 269–279.

McKenna, R., Bertsch, V., Mainzer, K. and Fichtner, W. (2018). Combining local preferences with multi-criteria decision analysis and linear optimization to develop feasible energy concepts in small communities. *European Journal of Operational Research, 268*(3), 1092–1110.

Newman, G., Shi, T., Yao, Z., Li, D., Sansom, G., Kirsch, K., . . . and Horney, J. (2020). Citizen science-informed community master planning: Land use and built environment changes to increase flood resilience and decrease contaminant exposure. *International Journal of Environmental Research and Public Health, 17*(2), 486.

Osinski, A. (2020). Evaluating transition pathways beyond basic needs: A transdisciplinary approach to assessing food assistance. *Food Ethics, 5*(1), 1–34.

Pahl-Wostl, C. and Hare, M. (2004). Processes of social learning in integrated resources management. *Journal of Community and Applied Social Psychology, 14*(3), 193–206.

Puska, P., Vartiainen, E., Laatikainen, T., Jousilahti, P. and Paavola, M. (2009). *The North Karelia project: From North Karelia to national action*. Helsinki: National Institute for Health and Welfare.

Restrepo, M. J., Lelea, M. A. and Kaufmann, B. A. (2020). Assessing the quality of collaboration in transdisciplinary sustainability research: Farmers' enthusiasm to work together for the reduction of post-harvest dairy losses in Kenya. *Environmental Science and Policy*, *105*, 1–10.

Rhodius, R., Bachinger, M. and Koch, B. (Eds.). (2020). *Wildnis, Wald, Mensch. Forschungsbeiträge sur Entwicklung einer Nationalparkregion am Beispiel des Schwarzwalds*. Munich: Oekom Verlag.

Roorda, C., Wittmayer, J., Henneman, P., Van Steenbergen, F., Frantzeskaki, N. and Loorbach, D. (2014). *Transition management in the urban context: Guidance manual*. Rotterdam: Dutch Research Institute for Transition (DRIFT), Erasmus University Rotterdam.

Saarikoski, H., Mustajoki, J., Hjerppe, T. and Aapala, K. (2019). Participatory multi-criteria decision analysis in valuing peatland ecosystem services—Trade-offs related to peat extraction vs. pristine peatlands in Southern Finland. *Ecological Economics*, *162*, 17–28.

Schmale, J., Von Schneidemesser, E., Chabay, I., Maas, A. and Lawrence, M. G. (2016). Building interfaces that work: A multi-stakeholder approach to air pollution and climate change mitigation. In J. L. Drake, Y. Y. Kontar, J. C. Eichelberger, S. T. Rupp and K. M. Taylor (Eds.), *Communicating climate-change and natural hazard risk and cultivating resilience* (pp. 65–76). Heidelberg: Springer.

Schmale, J., Von Schneidemesser, E. and Dörrie, A. (2015). An integrated assessment method for sustainable transport system planning in a middle-sized German city. *Sustainability*, *7*(2), 1329–1354.

Simon, C. and Etienne, M. (2010). A companion modelling approach applied to forest management planning. *Environmental Modelling and Software*, *25*(11), 1371–1384.

Sjöman, M., Ringenson, T. and Kramers, A. (2020). Exploring everyday mobility in a living lab based on economic interventions. *European Transport Research Review*, *12*(1), 5.

Stave, K. (2002). Using system dynamics to improve public participation in environmental decisions. *System Dynamics Review: The Journal of the System Dynamics Society*, *18*(2), 139–167.

Stave, K. (2010). Participatory system dynamics modeling for sustainable environmental management: Observations from four cases. *Sustainability*, *2*(9), 2762–2784.

Tillie, N., Aarts, M., Marijnissen, M., Stenhujs, L., Borsboom, J., Rietveld, E., . . . and Lap, S. (2012). *Rotterdam. People make the inner city*. Rotterdam: Gemeente.

Trutnevyte, E., Stauffacher, M., Schlegel, M. and Scholz, R. W. (2012). Context-specific energy strategies: Coupling energy system visions with feasible implementation scenarios. *Environmental Science and Technology*, *46*(17), 9240–9248.

Trutnevyte, E., Stauffacher, M. and Scholz, R. W. (2011). Supporting energy initiatives in small communities by linking visions with energy scenarios and multi-criteria assessment. *Energy Policy*, *39*(12), 7884–7895.

Van Breda, J. and Swilling, M. (2019). The guiding logics and principles for designing emergent transdisciplinary research processes: Learning experiences and reflections from a transdisciplinary urban case study in Enkanini informal settlement, South Africa. *Sustainability Science*, *14*(3), 823–841.

Verutes, G. M., Arkema, K. K., Clarke-Samuels, C., Wood, S. A., Rosenthal, A., Rosado, S., . . . and Ruckelshaus, M. (2017). Integrated planning that safeguards ecosystems and balances multiple objectives in coastal Belize. *International Journal of Biodiversity Science, Ecosystem Services and Management*, *13*(3), 1–17.

ANNEX 3

Coding scales

Coding scales used to code the cases from the case study list for the core explanatory variables (research co-design, co-management, social learning, information gathering and communication) and the outcome variable (co-production of usable knowledge outputs). Similar scales were used to code the control variables (types of involved societal actors, disciplines and thematic fields); however, they did not lead to significant correlations with the usable knowledge outcomes.

Explanatory variables

Research co-design

Did the project publication explicitly mention the co-construction of research questions or research frame as a core component of the research process?

Likert scale

1) not at all
2) on very little aspects of the produced knowledge
3) on a few key aspects
4) covering a substantial number of the aspects
5) covering nearly all aspects

Process co-management

Did societal actors participate in governing the research process at least through one of the following types?

- co-research (societal actors jointly organizing the data gathering with the researchers)
- co-intervention (joint organization of real-world interventions as part of the research protocol)
- co-decision (joint supervision of doctoral or post-doctoral research or joint decision-making in the consortium board, if applicable).

Likert scale

1) **not at all**
2) **on very little aspects of the produced knowledge**
3) **on a few key aspects**
4) **covering a substantial number of the aspects**
5) **covering nearly all aspects**

Organized processes of social learning

Was there an explicit workshop for social learning among the project members, situated within one of the four social learning categories of the main text, defined in Section 4.3:

- Agreement on process values for common inquiry into the problem identification
- Common action strategies accommodating divergent perspectives
- Identifying converging and diverging perspectives
- Common action program with a substantial overlap in the value rankings

Likert scale

1) **not at all**
2) **on very little aspects of the produced knowledge**
3) **on a few key aspects**
4) **covering a substantial number of the aspects**
5) **covering nearly all aspects**

Consultation of societal actors for information gathering in the research process

Was there science-practitioners interaction through one of the following modes?

- Information gathering on context-specific (local or global) features of the problem situation or the variables of the research framework
- Informing on the project and on outcomes and collect comments, for soliciting feedback from societal actors

Likert scale

1) not at all
2) on very little aspects of the produced knowledge
3) on a few key aspects
4) covering a substantial number of the aspects
5) covering nearly all aspects

Outcome variable

Usable knowledge outputs

Did the project produce one of the following project outputs (if several outputs, then code the sum of the evaluation on the Likert scale of each of the output categories)?

- New solutions (technical solutions, but also diagnosis and evaluation tools) used by societal actors during the project or within the two years that follow the project, beyond the interventions that were already planned in the research protocol at the beginning of the project
- Common action plans (for societal actors, government) with clear implementation plans accepted by the intended users and beneficiaries of the project
- New organizational mechanisms established (hierarchies/networks) during the project or within the two years that follow the project, beyond the interventions that were already planned in the research protocol at the beginning of the project

Likert scale

1 Not at all
2 A small project outcome, for a limited part of the intended users/beneficiaries
3 Moderate to significant project outcome, for a limited part of the intended users/beneficiaries
4 Moderate to significant project outcome, for a large part of the intended users/beneficiaries

INDEX

future visioning workshops 88; merging of knowledge 86; participatory qualitative research 84–86; qualitative systems dynamics mapping 85; storytelling 113

random controlled trials 77
Reed, Mark 101
research styles 42, 162
risk assessment 28, 29
role-playing games 100

Sen, Amartya 104–106
social choice: accommodation of divergent perspectives 112, 113; agreement over process value 110–112; pairwise agreement over values 105; salient societal values 106, 110
social learning 162; in adaptive management 102; identifying needs 120; typology of social learning outputs 119
socio-ecological systems 164; historical interdependencies 5, 6; and integrated research 161; socio-ecological interdependency 9

sustainability: environmental citizenship 7, 8; environmental justice 7; planetary boundaries 6, 7; social and ecological 162
sustainability transformations 6; levers of change 57, 58

thought styles 26, 162
transdisciplinarity: transdisciplinarity beyond academia 149–151; transdisciplinary sustainability research 164
transdisciplinary teaching: doctoral training 134; master courses 131–133; master theses 134

usable knowledge production: actionable knowledge 2; first-order effects 56; second-order effects 56; usable knowledge outputs 54, 55

values: convergence amongst 110; heterogeneity of societal values 14, 15, 17; see also incommensurability; social choice

wicked problems 1
Williamson, Oliver 124, 126

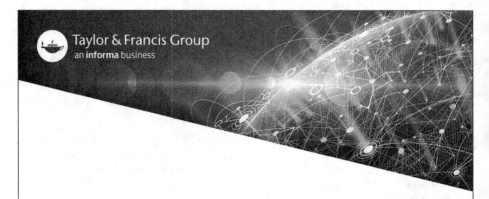

Printed in the United States
by Baker & Taylor Publisher Services